The Future of the Sociological Classics

For Mel Williams

The Future of the Sociological Classics

Edited by

BUFORD RHEA

Professor of Sociology, East Carolina University

London
GEORGE ALLEN & UNWIN
Boston   Sydney

© George Allen & Unwin (Publishers) Ltd, 1981.
This book is copyright under the Berne Convention. No
reproduction without permission. All rights reserved.

George Allen & Unwin (Publishers) Ltd,
40 Museum Street, London WC1A 1LU, UK

George Allen & Unwin (Publishers) Ltd,
Park Lane, Hemel Hempstead, Herts HP2 4TE, UK

Allen & Unwin Inc.,
9 Winchester Terrace, Winchester, Mass 01890, USA

George Allen & Unwin Australia Pty Ltd,
8 Napier Street, North Sydney, NSW 2060, Australia

First published in 1981

British Library Cataloguing in Publication Data

Rhea, Buford
  The Future of the sociological classics.
1. Sociology
I. Rhea, Buford
301   HM51
ISBN 0-04-301136-5
ISBN 0-04-301137-3 Pbk

Library of Congress Cataloging in Publication Data

Rhea, Buford
  The Future of the sociological classics.
Bibliography: p.
Includes index.
Contents: Karl Max / Irving M. Zeitlin – Hobbes, Toennies,
Vico / Werner J. Cahnman – Max Weber and contemporary
sociology / Dennis H. Wrong – [etc.]
1. Sociology – Addresses, essays, lectures. 2. Sociologists – History.
I. Rhea, Buford.
HM51.F9   301   81-10879
ISBN 0-04-301136-5   AACR2
ISBN 0-04-301137-3 (pbk.)

Set in 10 on 11 point Times by Grove Graphics, Tring
and printed in Great Britain
by Biddles Ltd, Guildford, Surrey

Contents

Introduction

The essays collected here are revisions of lectures given at East Carolina University during the Spring semester of 1978, and they are their authors' answers to the question around which the lecture series was organized: 'What use are the sociological classics today?'

Every teacher of sociology will recognize the question since every sociology student asks it, sooner or later, one way or another. It is a legitimate question and it deserves a serious response, though faculty often have trouble remembering the answers. What is worse, we typically organize sociology curricula so that students are virtually informed that the classics are now irrelevant. Such a message is of course unintended, but the tacit learnings of hidden curricula, as Polanyi (1966) and Kuhn (1970) among others have made clear, are often the most important parts of a student's education. Thus most undergraduates in this country probably never seriously study a major work of sociology, and in student research the masters appear most frequently, when they appear at all, as footnotes embellishing work whose true inspiration is to be found more in the computer lab or in the administrative directives of applied sociology. Even courses in the history of the discipline, or theory courses which take the historical approach, are ordinarily little more than breakneck surveys of names having no clear relationship to anything else in the curriculum. Knowledge of the masters becomes, in Whitehead's devastating refrain, mere information 'from which nothing follows' (1949, p. 18).

Our lecture series was intended to help correct this state of affairs, and the essays of this volume should be read as in the first instance addressed to beginning majors in sociology – juniors, seniors, first-year graduate students – though to be sure the problem is not confined to the campus (Wiley, 1979). If the classics have a future, though, as the title of the book affirms, it will be because the new generation of sociologists recognizes their importance and uses them as they should be used.

We assumed that if anyone could convey a sense of that importance it would be those sociologists who have won the general respect of the discipline as students and critics of the classics, and with that criterion in hand the roster of speakers practically suggested itself. The general theme of the series was expressed this way in our letters of invitation:

The lecture series is intended to provide an occasion for sociologists knowledgeable about the classics to demonstrate that, and how, the classics are contemporary and important, not only as means for becoming familiar with the style of a master craftsman (that too, but that is not all of it), but also because the frames of reference employed, the questions asked, the conceptualizations developed, or the specific hypotheses explored remain worth knowing here and now – and in the future. Feel free to deal with this issue as you see fit, but at least two topics seem unavoidable. First is the matter of contemporaneity, the demonstration that the thought of the author is not just an item of historical interest. A 'What Is Living and What Is Dead' in his sociology thus seems appropriate, with perhaps some discussion of current research. Also, consistent with the future-orientation of the series, I am sure you will want to say something about what *ought* to be living or dead: neglected aspects of his work that deserve revival, overworked or banalized themes that need reformulation, misinterpretations that should be corrected, etc. A second, though not a necessary, topic would deal with the gap between theory and practice, i.e. some discussion of how the author's work might be used to confront those problems which are today most often the province of relatively atheoretical 'applied' sociologies. The audience to which the paper should be addressed will be advanced under-graduate and beginning graduate sociology students who will already know something of the author: they will all have had the usual history course and will in addition have been prepped on the author before your presentation (we have organized a seminar around the lecture series). The audience to which you will be *speaking* (both during the morning's formal presentation and in the afternoon faculty–student seminar) will include, in addition to sociologists from our own and nearby campuses, faculty and students from several other departments, so you might want to add a few words locating your author in the larger intellectual landscape.

The responses to our letters of invitation were, almost predictably, wholly positive and even enthusiastic: to know a classical work thoroughly, it would seem – one is tempted to say 'of course' – is to be somewhat evangelical about it. Perhaps that is one mark of a classic. In any event, the talks and now the papers which followed our invitation all testify to the seriousness with which our speakers undertook to answer the honest question our students had asked. These are not simple papers – that would be to falsify the classics, as is too often the case in textbooks – but they are

accessible, and that is all that can be asked, all that we did ask
and everything that we hoped for.

The first seven papers below discuss specific masters and are
arranged in no particular order except for a slight nod to chron-
ology: Professor Zeitlin's essay on Marx is placed first because
Marx is the earliest classical figure, while Professor Cahnman's
paper, placed second, extends its analysis, at our request, back to
some of the earliest precursors. The last two papers, again at our
request, are summary papers, Professor Coser's exemplifying how
the classics can be used in empirical research, Professor Parsons's
exemplifying how the classics can be used to generate new theory.
The styles and approaches of the papers are as different and
individual as are their authors, which is as it should be. It is the
bad essays that are all alike; every good essay is good in its own
way.

Beyond this sketch of their provenance little more need be said
about these papers: they speak for themselves, and very well.
During the course of editing this volume, though, I have read each
chapter several times, and I cannot resist one last observation.
To echo Talcott Parsons about the classics themselves (p. 189),
each time I went back to them I *always* found something new.
In making the thought of the masters more accessible to students,
these authors have made them more accessible to us all.

Acknowledgements

The 'we' used in the Introduction is literal, not editorial. The original concept and initiative for this project were wholly those of our departmental chairman, John Maiolo, and I would like to thank him for having me serve as director. Funds came from East Carolina University, and its provost, John Howell, is to be thanked not only for his official support but for his personal participation as well. Numerous colleagues from my own department, and from other departments and campuses, helped in a variety of ways, and they already know how grateful I am. They will also recognize the spirit in which I omit their names in order to list instead the students of the special seminar who by their diligence and spontaneity made our sessions so enjoyable, and who by their willingness to tackle any job saved my neck more than once: Rebecca Faison, Jean Huryn, Elizabeth Jones, Jules Rivera, Gail Spencer, Nancy Sconyers, Franky Lee Turner, Mary Susan Whalen, Barry Willis and John Zimmerman. Shirley Taylor Smith and Jo Ann Sutton, with Robin Hammond, typed the manuscript for this book in addition to doing, as departmental secretaries always do, practically everything else required to make an academic project work. Delene, my wife, and Joe, my son, not only endured my absences and abstractions but provided, as always, support and inspiration. Victor Lidz of the University of Pennsylvania was most generous in editing Talcott Parsons's paper, and Michael Holdsworth of Allen & Unwin has been a gracious and understanding editor. The book is dedicated to Melvin Williams, founding chairman of our department, on the occasion of his retirement. The dedication is made by the collective 'we' of his department, but also most warmly and sincerely by the purely personal 'I'.

1

Karl Marx: Aspects of His Social Thought and Their Contemporary Relevance

IRVING M. ZEITLIN

The past several decades have yielded important clarification of Marx's philosophical outlook. Marx and especially Engels often employed the word 'materialist' to describe their method of studying man, society and history. However, the term 'materialist' caused a fundamental misunderstanding, and Marx's dialectical approach was soon transformed into the very caricature he criticized in others. Indeed, the full lesson of Marx's mediation between Hegel's idealism and Feuerbach's materialism has yet to be learned today.

Marx spoke of a 'rational kernel' buried in the 'mystical shell' of Hegel's philosophy. What, in a word, was that 'rational kernel'? It was the critical insight that humans are active, creative beings who constitute their world, and thereby themselves, by means of their practical activity. The human world, Hegel and other idealists had understood, is a 'superorganic', historically evolved cultural cosmos in the modern anthropological sense. However, the trouble with this view was that Hegel described social and historical processes in highly abstract metaphysical terms. The real world of human activities and struggles was scarcely discernible behind the Hegelian categories. Hegel had severed reason from its natural-social roots in man, turning it into a disembodied, independent, creative historical subject. 'Reason' (or 'the Ideal', or 'the Spirit') became the guiding immanent principle of history, while the real world was merely the external form of the Idea. For Marx this was an upside-down view of things.

Yet Feuerbach's materialistic critique of Hegel was equally unsatisfactory. For he transformed the human being into a wholly passive and determined *object*. Feuerbach and other mechanistic materialists had produced the one-sided doctrine according to which humans are the product of circumstances, pure and simple. However, Marx reminded them that 'it is humans who make and change circumstances'. Thus Marx sought to overcome the extreme one-sidedness of both the idealist and materialist doctrines in a new dialectical synthesis of his own.

Today contemporary social science has yet to liberate itself from these extremes. In certain currents of social psychology, for example, there exists a powerful idealistic tendency. Humans are portrayed as disembodied, symbolizing, self-indicating and other-indicating role-players. Yet these role-players are anything but active and creative beings since they simply internalize and absorb whatever society decides to implant in them. From this 'oversocialized' standpoint there is no human nature that is not wholly a product of society. The human is portrayed as if the stuff of his being were totally ideational. At the same time he is denied any real conscious creativity since he is wholly passive and conditioned. He is all 'me', in George Herbert Mead's terms, and no 'I'.

This idealistic caricature of the human being has its materialistic counterpart in the highly influential theories of B. F. Skinner – the Feuerbach of today. In all essential respects the present-day behaviorism of B. F. Skinner is hardly to be distinguished from the classical doctrine of J. B. Watson. 'We can follow the path taken by physics and biology', writes Skinner,

> by turning directly to the relation between behavior and the environment and neglecting supposed mediating states of mind. Physics did not advance by looking more closely at the jubilance of a falling body, or biology by looking at the nature of vital spirits, and we do not need to try to discover what personalities, states of mind, feelings, traits of character, plans, purposes, intentions, or the other prerequisites of [so-called] autonomous man really are in order to get on with a scientific analysis of behavior. (1975, pp. 12–13).

Skinner goes on to inform us that the stimulus–response model never solved the basic problems of behavior and was never very convincing 'because something like an inner man had to be invented to convert a stimulus into a response' (1975, p. 15). But does Skinner's conception of 'operant conditioning', replete with positive and negative reinforcers, actually achieve greater success in eliminating an 'inner man'? Let us see. He writes that 'negative reinforcers are called aversive in the sense that they are the things organisms "turn away from" ' (1975, p. 25). Skinner thus seems not to have noticed that his theory is afflicted by the same contradictions he found in classical behaviorism. For while he denies that organisms have any autonomy whatsoever, he nonetheless conceives of them as turning away from negative reinforcers. Clearly an 'inner man' of some kind is present in this scheme too. How otherwise shall we account for the organism's turning away?

Skinner zealously strives to get rid of the 'inner man' and all that it implies, namely, an organism with a will and consciousness of its own. 'Man's struggle for freedom,' he writes, 'is not due to a will to be free, but to certain behavioral processes characteristic of the human organism, the chief effect of which is the avoidance of or escape from so-called "aversive" features of the environment' (1975, p. 39). Let us therefore note that Skinner succeeds no better than his behavioristic predecessors in eliminating the inner man. For even in Skinner's conception of things man has sufficient *consciousness* to distinguish between positive and negative features of the environment; sufficient *will* to wish to escape from its aversive features; and sufficient *autonomy* to succeed in escaping from aversive features.

For Skinner, 'freedom', 'dignity', 'consciousness', 'autonomy', 'will', and so on, are pure fictions. All of these terms imply that man is an active, creative being. But this is precisely what the behaviorists wish to deny. 'A person does not act upon the world', says Skinner, 'the world acts upon him' (1975, p. 202). Since man is a wholly determined, passive object anyway, Skinner contends, we lose nothing by stripping away the functions previously ascribed to that fictional entity called 'autonomous man', and transferring them to the controlling environment.

So we see that Skinner follows closely in the footsteps of Ludwig Feuerbach. The image of man common to both these thinkers is that of a being wholly controlled from the outside. In Skinner's utopia man will be no less controlled than ever before; but in the new society the environment will no longer be an unplanned determiner. Instead, it will be an environment governed by what Skinner regards as advanced, scientific behavioristic principles.

Several questions suggest themselves about both the theoretical and political aspects of Skinner's proposal. If men are wholly passive and determined creatures, then who will serve as the active conditioners in Skinner's new society? If everyone learns only through conditioning, how will the conditioners learn? Who will condition the conditioners? Or does Skinner mean that everyone will condition everyone else? Skinner asks us to remember that man's environment is 'largely of his own making' (1975, p. 205).

But how does a passive, totally determined being make his own environment? Because these and other problems, contradictions and ambiguities are nowhere resolved in Skinner's theory, we may safely conclude that he has advanced no further than the mechanistic materialists of the nineteenth century and that all of Marx's criticisms of that doctrine apply with equal force to present-day behaviorism and to theories of a similar kind.

We see, then, that Marx's mediation between Hegel and Feuerbach is of more than historical interest. His methodological point was to grasp human nature as authentically as possible. Marx was among the first to formulate an adequate conception of man as a *social* being. As early as the *Paris Manuscripts* he states that man's life 'even if it may not appear in the direct form of a communal life carried out together with others – is an expression and confirmation of social life' (Marx, 1961, p. 105).

However, what has been almost entirely overlooked is Marx's view of man as an integral part of the organic world. 'Man', Marx stresses again and again, is a natural being, but a unique one.[1] As a human being he not only retains his natural needs (hunger and sex) but acquires new ones – *love*, to single out the most essential for his happiness. 'If you love without evoking love in return', he writes, 'if through a living expression of yourself as a loving person you do not make yourself a loved person, then your love is impotent – a misfortune' (Marx, 1961, p. 141). It is clear that the *Paris Manuscripts* as a whole represent Marx's conception of human nature and human needs. It is this conception that became his implicit criterion for assessing the goodness of social systems. More, Marx's understanding of alienation embraces, among other things, the process of *repression* in the Freudian sense.

This has been clearly brought out by Herbert Marcuse's reinterpretation of Freud. At the very center of Freud's theory one finds an irremediable antagonism between the organic needs of the human being and the requirements of the civilizing process. The development of the ego and super-ego necessarily involves a subordination of the individual's organic needs (the pleasure principle) to the demands of the socializing agencies (the reality principle). The result is a repression of man's natural impulses and needs with all that this entails – deep unhappiness, mental and emotional disturbances, and the like. A tragic contradiction prevails in which the advance of civilization exacts from man huge bio-psychic cost. This is the conclusion Freud drew in his late writings, notably in *Civilization and Its Discontents*.

However, as Marcuse has reminded us, this necessary process does not, in and of itself, account for the deprivation and pain that man has suffered historically (1955). This is evident from the fact that the societies of the past and present have never distributed scarce resources in accordance with individual human needs. On the contrary, scarcity has always been controlled by the privileged elements of society and distributed in accordance with their interests. Therefore, it is not the 'reality principle' pure and simple that accounts for man's suffering. Added to the necessary repression required by *any* form of human organization, man has endured the controls of specific institutions of *domination*. These have not been necessary, strictly speaking, and have therefore exacted from man *surplus repression*. The pleasure principle has been hedged in and suppressed not simply because man's struggle with nature has required it, but also and primarily because the privileged interests of those who dominate society have enforced it.

This is an important extrapolation by Marcuse from Freud's own concepts. For it preserves Freud's general insight and prevents the extreme flattening out of man's nature that one finds in certain sociologistic doctrines. At the same time the extrapolation alerts us to the fact that man suffers more than he must owing to the effects of specific forms of social organization which are unnecessarily repressive. This idea is certainly implied by Marx's concept of alienation, a condition in which man 'does not fulfill himself in his work but denies himself, has a feeling of misery rather than well-being, does not develop freely his mental and physical energies, but is physically exhausted and mentally debased' (1961, p. 73). Doubtless what Marcuse calls surplus-repression is an element of alienation. In a passage reminiscent of the *Paris Manuscripts* and probably inspired by them, Marcuse writes:

For the vast majority of the population, the scope and mode of satisfaction are determined by their own labor; but their labor is work for an apparatus which they do not control, which operates as an independent power to which individuals must submit if they want to live. And it becomes the more alien the more specialized the division of labor becomes. Men do not live their own lives but perform pre-established functions. While they work, they do not fulfill their own needs and faculties but work in *alienation*. Work has now become general, and so have the restrictions placed upon the libido: labor time, which is the largest part of the individual's life time, is painful time, for alienated labor is absence of gratification, negation of the pleasure principle. (1955, p. 41)

There is a definite compatibility, therefore, between Marx and a reinterpreted Freud.

The greatest value of Marx's *dialectical* view of man lies in his recognition of both the active and the conditioned sides, of the natural and the social dimensions. Man, for Marx, is a being with natural-social needs. The fulfillment of those needs is the measure of a good society.

The Problem of Order

It follows from Marx's recognition of man's active side, that he can never become a totally socialized and conditioned being. There always remains a residue of resistance in the human being to the repressive rules, roles and relationships imposed upon him. Even Skinner, as we have seen, has to admit that it is *in* man's nature to try to avoid and escape the 'aversive' features of his environment. The question arises, then, as to how social order is maintained in the face of this human characteristic.

From the time of Aristotle political theorists had maintained that moderate property-ownership and, hence, economic independence for the majority of society's members, was a precondition of the stable polity. A large middle class can mediate successfully between the extremes of wealth and poverty and can moderate the tensions between them. A situation of this sort may have existed in the English countryside prior to the Enclosure movement. Poor as some of the English peasant-proprietors may have been at that time, the vast majority had unrestricted usufruct of the land they tilled, and they owned their instruments of production. In these circumstances everyone or almost everyone had a stake in the existing order, and Aristotle's principle was realized in practice.

But with the Enclosures and the beginnings of capitalism, there occurred certain changes in the social structure which rendered Aristotle's logic obsolete. For now one witnessed the phenomenal growth of a class of propertyless proletarians. Since they owned nothing, they could have no stake in the system. If such a class had remained small, it would have constituted little or no threat to the existing order. But when this class became a nation within a nation, to paraphrase Disraeli, it was bound to create conflicts and antagonisms.

So the question is this: how is social order maintained in a society containing a very large class of persons with no material interest in the prevailing system? Marx's reply is highly complex. To begin with there is the Hobbesian element. Doubtless fear of the

Leviathan, of the coercive state apparatus, played a role in engendering the compliance of the dominated class. In addition, the fact that the wage-laborers were totally dependent for their livelihood on the owners of the means of production meant that fear of losing their jobs also contributed to their compliance. The extreme dependence of the working class was also noted by Durkheim. He spoke of the 'forced division of labor', a condition in which, owing to the fundamental inequalities between employers and workers, the contractual relationship between them was objectively coercive and unjust (Durkheim, 1933, pp. 374f.). Similarly Max Weber wrote that capitalism presupposes a class of workers who offer their services 'in the formal sense voluntarily, but actually under the compulsion of the whip of hunger' (1961, p. 209).

Besides the 'whip of hunger' and the fear of the Leviathan there is still another reason why dominated groups generally tend to obey and comply. Although the organized ruling minority has the vastly superior might of the state at its disposal, and can therefore repel challenges to its rule by force, this is done only as a last resort. As a rule it succeeds in stabilizing its dominance by making it acceptable to the ruled masses. This is accomplished by means of what Marx called the ruling ideology. Every ruling class endeavors to justify its exercise of power by resting it on some higher moral principle. Marx's 'ruling ideology' is thus equivalent to Weber's 'legitimation', Mosca's 'political formula', Pareto's 'derivations', Sorel's 'myths' and Gramsci's 'ideological hegemony.'

The ruling ideology is not merely propaganda. Nor is it a great fraud with which to trick the people into obedience. The ruling ideology appeals to the common values, beliefs, sentiments and traditions which result from a people's common history; it thus makes the people receptive to the formula employed by the dominant group to legitimize its rule. Nationalism is an obvious example. Nationalist ideology has frequently enabled ruling groups to mobilize the masses for military adventures and wars from which they stood to gain nothing. Ideologies change with the socio-historical circumstances. But throughout history the consent of the governed has been based on a ruling legitimation formula of some kind. The majority of the people consent to a given political system because it appears to be rooted in the religious and moral beliefs that are widely accepted by them. The degree of consent depends upon the extent and ardor with which the oppressed group believes in the ideology which the dominant group employs to justify its power.

A ruling ideology cannot depart too far from the culture of the governed without generating conflicts that threaten the very foundation of the existing order. The principles underlying the legitimation formula must be rooted in the consciousness of the people. When such principles penetrate deeply enough, the rulers, however corrupt and oppressive they may be, achieve unswerving devotion.

This, in brief, is the way Marx approaches the 'problem of order'. Marx's approach was subsequently elaborated by several other classical theorists and then fully incorporated into contemporary social science. In these terms, Marx's contribution is very much alive and relevant, though no longer exclusively Marxian.

Social Classes and Stratification

For Marx, landowners, capitalists and laborers are the three major classes of the English society of his day. Each of these classes has its own distinctive form of revenue. Individual class members live from rent, profit and wages, respectively. It might therefore appear, says Marx, that it is the identity of revenue which defines the boundaries of classes and sets them apart. But there are, after all, innumerable distinctions of interest and position in society. So source of revenue cannot be the defining characteristic of class since it would create as many classes as there are occupations, professions and interest groups in society. Clearly this will not do. We must seek elsewhere for the key criterion of social class.

There is something which the members of a single class share, which separates them from other classes and which generally overrides the differences of interest within a class. This something is a common relationship to the means of production: the landowners own the land; the capitalists dispose over the industrial means of production; and the proletarians sell their labor power.

It has become increasingly clear that this conception of social class is inadequate for a comprehension of twentieth-century conditions. It is equally clear that the most fruitful extension and revision of Marx's concepts may be found in the work of Max Weber.

Weber concurs in many essential respects with Marx's characterization of capitalism. Although capitalistic forms existed in previous historical epochs, Weber agrees that capitalism as described by Marx is a modern phenomenon, and that it has become the dominant mode of production since the middle of the nineteenth century. Weber also accepts Marx's view that capitalism presupposes 'the appropriation of all physical means of production – land, apparatus, machinery, tools, etc., as disposable property of autonomous private industrial enterprises' (Weber, 1961, p. 208). Like Marx, Weber stresses in addition the need for 'free labor'. 'Persons must be present', he writes, 'who are not legally in the position, but are also economically compelled, to sell their labor on the market without restriction' (loc. cit.). Thus 'free labor' – in the double sense of being free from forced servitude but also free (i.e. separated) from any and all means of production – is for Weber as for Marx a precondition of modern capitalism.

Weber employs all of Marx's major class concepts: class consciousness, class conflict, class interest, and so on. For Weber the following were the main social classes of modern society:

(1) the working class as a whole – the more so, the more automated the work process becomes;
(2) the petty bourgeoisie;
(3) the propertyless intelligentsia and specialists (technicians, various kinds of white-collar employees, civil servants – possibly with considerable social differences depending on the cost of their training);
(4) the classes privileged through property and education. (Weber, 1968, Vol. I, p. 305)

Herein, in this list, we can begin to see how Weber departs from Marx's conception of classes. Marx had anticipated the 'sinking' of the petty bourgeoisie into the ranks of the proletariat. But Weber, like others writing early in the twentieth century, noted that this was not in fact happening – or at least not as dramatically as Marx had supposed it would. Moreover, Weber witnessed the phenomenal growth of the 'new middle class' – specialists, technicians and other white-collar employees. This was a development which Marx never foresaw. The remarkable expansion of this class touched the very heart of Marx's theory. For in his scheme of things these propertyless persons shared the same relationships to the means of production as did the manual workers. Marx's followers accordingly expected all of these propertyless workers to develop a sense of common interest – a common class-consciousness. But in the course of the twentieth century it became increasingly clear that the white-collar employees did not look upon production workers as class brothers at all. Under nineteenth-century conditions Marx may have been justified in ignoring stratification within the working class; but for Weber, the theorist *par excellence* of growing bureaucratization, it was obvious that differences in education, training and property other than means of production all had considerable importance in shaping the social psychology of classes.

Thus what we find in Weber is a refinement of Marx's categories. If Marx's view of classes under capitalism was by and large devoid of status considerations, Weber recognized that such a view was unsuited to the twentieth century. Accordingly he stressed that the control of all types of wealth is a source of power; and that social honor or prestige based upon education, skill, or whatever may also be transformed into power. For Weber, then, classes, status groups *and* political parties 'are phenomena of the distribution of power'.

Although Weber analytically distinguishes 'class' from 'status group', his definition of class by no means constitutes a watering down of the class concept. He emphasizes that one's class situation tends to determine one's 'life chances' and that members of a class tend to share a common fate; and although he stresses the pivotal role of wealth in general – not only 'capital goods' – he maintains that ' "Property" and "lack of property" are . . . the basic categories of all class situations' (Weber, 1968, Vol. II, p. 927). In these terms Weber's conception of class situation is not as remote from Marx's as some commentators have suggested.

However, Weber goes on to show that within the broad categories of propertied and propertyless, other important distinctions may be discerned, notably differences in social honor or prestige. Prestige, for Weber, is associated with the style of life of a status-group. Within any given class one will find several such status-groups. The varying degrees of prestige accorded them may rest on the source and size of their income, their political positions in the community, their education, specialized training, or other evaluated social characteristics. Among the wealthy and propertied we find old and new rich, and other status distinctions based upon the source of one's wealth; among white-collar workers we find status gradations based upon occupation, education, expertise, and so on; and within the blue-collar class we find status differences resting on occupation, skill, size of income, and the like. Status differences, Weber believes, must be taken into account in class analysis because they tell us how social groupings within a class regard themselves and are regarded by others.

Furthermore, careful analysis of a class situation often reveals that it is not one situation but several. Among the propertyless, for instance, it will not do to lump white-collar and manual workers together simply because they share a common relationship to the means of production. Not only are their self-conceptions quite different; so are their work situations.

For Weber, there was still another dimension of social structure which had paramount importance for an understanding of twentieth-century industrial societies. Marx, focusing attention on the concentration of capital, neglected non-economic forms of power. But Weber, recognizing the powerful bureaucratic tendencies of modern society, demonstrated that the concentration of power was not confined to the economic sphere. There were several strategic areas of social life in which one could observe (1) the concentration of the means of power in the hands of small minorities and (2) the consequent separation of the majority of men from those means. This was the inevitable meaning of advancing bureaucratization. For Marx and the Marxists the most essential question was: who controls the means of production? For Weber, it was necessary to ask, in addition, who disposes over the other strategic means of controlling and dominating men? Weber does not deny the importance of control over key economic resources. He maintains, however, that this is not sufficient for an understanding of the structure of social power in general. He thus generalizes Marx's theory, arguing that control of the means of political administration, means of violence, means of scientific research, means of education, and so on, are also major means of dominating men. He writes:

> Organized domination which calls for continuous administration, requires that human conduct be conditioned to obedience towards those masters who claim to be the bearers of legitimate power. On the other hand . . . organized domination requires the control of those material goods which in a given case are necessary for the use of physical violence. Thus, organized domination requires control of the personal executive staff and the material implements of administration. (Weber, 1958, p. 80).

In this way Weber convincingly suggests that Marx's 'separation' of the worker from the means of production is only one facet of a general social process. 'If 'separation' is one side of the coin, concentration of power is the other. Marx's concentration of the means of production is generalized by Weber to other means of power, notably the political-administrative, the military and the scientific-technical. By thus providing an important complement to Marx's analytical framework, Weber adapts it to twentieth-century conditions.

Social Change: Is Classical Marxism an Evolutionary Theory?

The nineteenth century was the heyday of social-evolutionary theories. Edward Burnett Tylor, Lewis Henry Morgan, Auguste Comte, Herbert Spencer and numerous others all subscribed to a doctrine according to which the human race progressed through successive stages. Doubtless we owe a great intellectual debt to these extraordinary thinkers. From them we have acquired a vast substantive knowledge about a wide range of human societies and cultures. The question remains, however, whether their conception of social evolution is scientifically sound.

Nineteenth-centry evolutionary theories shared certain premises, stated and unstated, which may be summed up in the following statement: *change is natural, directional, immanent and continuous and derived from uniform causes.*[2] These premises were shared by such otherwise diverse thinkers as Hegel, Saint-Simon (and Comte), Tocqueville, Spencer, Morgan and Durkheim. For Hegel the development idea expressed itself in the spirit of freedom which grew from its modest beginnings in the ancient Orient until it attained its highest form in the Prussia of his day. In Saint-Simon and Comte the idea is evident in their Law of Three Stages, according to which human knowledge passes from the religious through the metaphysical to the positive (or scientific) stage. In Tocqueville we find societies increasingly embodying the spirit of equality, thus moving from aristocracy to democracy. For Spencer the direction of evolution is from the relatively homogeneous 'military' society to the complex 'industrial' one. Morgan advanced three basic states of development: 'savagery', 'barbarism' and 'civilization'. And Durkheim, finally, placed the subject of social solidarity in an evolutionary framework arguing that society normally moves from a 'mechanical' to an 'organic' stage of solidarity. Many more thinkers could be mentioned in this connection to illustrate the prevalence in the nineteenth century of evolutionary systems. As Robert A. Nisbet has reminded us in his illuminating monograph *Social Change and History*, all of these systems and their underlying premises are drawn 'from the metaphor of growth, from the analogy of change in society to change in the growth processes of the individual organism' (Nisbet, 1969, p. 166).

Are these evolutionary theories to be regarded as scientific accounts of social change? If, following Robert Nisbet, we define social change 'as a succession of differences in time in a persisting social entity', then we would have to reply to this question in the negative. For no evolutionary theory has so far succeeded in demonstrating a series of developmental steps in the change of a single social entity. Typically, evolutionary theorists select their evidence for stages from different societies and from a variety of historical periods. Then they arrange their data in a sequential pattern resembling the actual historical record in the West. The result, as Nisbet has noted, is not a theory of the actual course of development in a single social entity, but rather a ' "series" as in a movie film. It is the eye – or rather, in this instance, the disposition to believe – that creates the illusion of actual development, growth, or change.' And Nisbet continues:

It is all much like a museum exhibit. (It might be observed in passing that the principles of museum arrangement of cultural artifacts have not been without considerable influence on the principles of cultural evolution.) The last one I saw was an exhibit of 'the development of warfare'. At the beginning were shown examples of primitive warmaking – spears, bows and arrows, and the like. At the end of the exhibit were examples (constructed miniatures) of the latest and most awful forms of warfare. In between, constructed in fullest accord with the principles of logical continuity, was the whole spectrum or range of weapons that have been found or written about anywhere on the earth's surface at whatever time. All of this, observers were assured, represented the development of warfare. But the development of warfare where? Not, certainly, in the United States, or in Tasmania, or in China, or in Tierra del Fuego, *or in any other concrete, geographically identifiable, historically delimited, area. What 'develops' is in fact no substantive, empirical entity but a hypostatized, constructed entity that is called 'the art of war'*. (1969, p. 197, italics added)

This is a telling criticism. The social evolutionists, far from having proved the validity of their theories, have merely given expression to the dominant intellectual and cultural ideas of their time. The entire evolutionary theory and method rested on the prior acceptance of the idea of progressive development. Thus evolutionary theory suffers from an inherent circularity which it has never overcome. Nisbet includes Marx among the evolutionists. But the view that Marx belongs in this category bears closer scrutiny.

Not surprisingly, Marx was also influenced by the dominant intellectual ideas of his day. Traces of evolutionism are evident throughout his writings and those of his colleague Frederick Engels. In *German Ideology* they described several stages of ownership forms – tribal, ancient, feudal and capitalist. In the *Critique of Political Economy* and in *Pre-Capitalist Economic Formations* (a part of the *Grundrisse*), Marx delineated the Asiatic, ancient, feudal and capitalist modes of production. In common with the evolutionists of their time, Marx and Engels constructed their developmental stages by selecting forms from diverse times and places.

The impression that Marx and Engels viewed society as developing in stages is further strengthened by their enthusiastic reception of Lewis Henry Morgan's *Ancient Society* and by Engels's heavy reliance on that work in his *Origin of the Family, Private Property and the State.*

Besides, Marx and Engels frequently employed progressivist-evolutionary language, and apparently saw some parallels between organic and social evolution. In his funeral oration over Marx's grave in 1883, Engels stated that 'Just as Darwin discovered the law of development of organic nature, so Marx discovered the law of development of human history' (Marx and Engels, 1951, Vol. II, p. 153). In 1888, in his preface to an English edition of *The Communist Manifesto*, Engels writes that Marx's ideas are 'destined to do for history what Darwin's theory has done for biology'. Analogies between historical processes and evolutionary biology are scattered through *Capital.* In Marx's preface to the second edition in 1873 he states that capitalism is 'a passing historical phase' and quotes from a Russian review of the first edition. The review praised Marx's work for demonstrating that the unfolding of economic life is analogous with biological evolution, and 'disclosing the special laws that regulate the origin, existence, development, and death of a given social organism and its replacement by another and higher one'. And Marx approvingly comments that the reviewer has accurately portrayed his 'dialectical method'. Marx's treatment of England as the most advanced capitalism of his time also suggests that for him the 'less developed' countries were ultimately destined to mirror the conditions of the 'more developed'.

And yet, it is probably a mistake to look upon Marx's organismic metaphors as anything more than rhetoric. Indeed, Marx himself eventually recognized that his metaphors had misled interpreters of his work. In a letter to Mikhailovsky, Marx rejected the latter's attempt to transform his sketch of the origins of capitalism in Western Europe into a supra-historical theory 'of the general path every people is fated to tread, whatever the historical circumstances in which it finds itself' (Marx and Engels, 1953, p. 379). In this letter and in a later one to Vera Zasulich Marx expressly excluded Russia from the picture of the genesis of capitalism found in *Capital*; and he emphasized to his correspondents that that picture had been intended for England and Western Europe only (Marx and Engels, 1953, p. 412).

A careful examination of Marx's writings tends to confirm that he had always intended his stress on socio-economic processes as a historically specific proposition relating to the West European origins of capitalism and not to societies in general. Marx subscribed neither to evolutionism nor to any other supra-historical philosophy. He firmly rooted his social theories in the historical record, in concrete, empirical-historical evidence. And he intended his theories to be judged by that criterion.

The major aim of Marx's theoretical framework was to guide the exploration of the manifold and historically changing connections between the economy and all other facets of society. His method enjoins the investigator to give serious attention to the 'mode of production'. This includes the following four factors, which are all to be regarded as causally active:

(1) the direct producers in their cooperative relations and the technological know-how with which they carry on production;
(2) the instruments and means of production;
(3) the property and other power relations governing access to and control of the means of production and its products;
(4) the natural base and the way it conditions the productive process.

The 'mode of production' is the 'foundation' of human society inasmuch as man's economic activity is everywhere essential and indispensable. But nowhere does Marx assert that the mode of production is the universally decisive factor in determining the various forms of society. It is strictly a matter for empirical investigation whether economics, politics, religion, or whatever will be the decisive element for change or non-change in any particular case.

For Marx, then, there is no universal 'prime mover' of history, there are no 'iron laws', no universally necessary or inevitable stages. It is this reading of Marx that will enable contemporary social scientists to recover the scientific value of Marx's legacy.

Notes: Chapter 1

1 Marx, 1961, p. 156. I have provided a fuller discussion of the convergences between Marx and Freud in Zeitlin, 1973, ch. 19.
2 In the present discussion I rely on Nisbet, 1967, pp. 166–88.

2

Hobbes, Toennies, Vico: Starting Points in Sociology

WERNER J. CAHNMAN

Sociology at the present moment offers a confused picture. To be sure, among the fifteen thousand sociologists in the United States and Canada – not to speak of those in other countries – there are many competent professionals who produce well-conceived pieces of research. But many of these pieces of research lack significance because they take their departure from a method in search of a topic rather than from an attempt to elucidate a topic with whatever methods would seem serviceable. At best we have before us a bewildering array of isolated findings, significant or insignificant as they may be, but without the guidance of a theory. We have no image of mankind and the way it travels. If one listens to theoretical discussions, one hears of conflict theory versus system theory or of Marxism versus functionalism, but on closer investigation these dichotomies appear less than convincing. Conflict is not a theory but a fact and 'system' is a formal concept that can be filled in with a variety of contents. Marxism, for example, is indeed a system, but one built upon the notion of conflict, not in opposition to it. And again, functionalism, referring to the relationship of parts to a whole, including a Marxistically conceived interdependence of parts and a whole, is a virtual synonym for system, not an antonym or alternative. In such a fashion, we are moving in circles.

In addition, we are worshipping idols. There is hardly a theoretical paper published by sociologists that fails to quote Weber and/or Durkheim, while other equally important authors are ignored. There is nothing wrong about learning from such giants in sociology as Weber and Durkheim except their uncritical acceptance. Weber's work, if properly understood, is an imposing torso in need of being supplemented, analyzed and summarized, while Durkheim's work, on closer look, appears as a brilliant doctrine so much enamored of itself that it more often than not does violence to the facts on which it supposedly rests. Perhaps more important, the work of both men is hardly ever viewed historically, in its time and place and as the end-result of earlier work extending over generations.[1] Unless we see a broad advance on the front of historical interpretation, we are not likely to arrive at an adequate theory in sociology. In other words, the future usefulness of authors in sociology, whether contemporary or classic, may well depend on our appreciation of their antecedents.

With this consideration in mind, I wish to refer to older sources of thought and to derive from them guidelines that might prove to be helpful in coping with the contemporary predicament in sociology. I take my point of departure from two philosophical writers of the seventeenth and eighteenth centuries, Thomas Hobbes and Giambattista Vico. These two men are very different. Hobbes is a rationalist and a theoretician of natural law; he stands with Spinoza at the fountainhead of the Enlightenment, without, however, succumbing to the illusion of the Enlightenment about the perfectibility of man. Vico is a Neapolitan Catholic, a man of the baroque period with its comprehensive vistas, a foe of mechanistic and materialistic thinking and a precursor of romantic and historical thought. Vico, in his time, argued against Hobbes, but I intend to show that his philosophy is complementary rather than contradictory to the philosophy of Hobbes. Specifically, I propose to show how the positions of Hobbes and Vico converge on, and are combined in, the work of Ferdinand Toennies. The future of the older classics, then, is implicated in the future of the work of Toennies; but the promise of Toennies for the future of sociology rests in its turn squarely on his implicit combination of the two seemingly opposed older traditions.[2] We are going to refer first to Hobbes, then to Toennies and finally to Vico.

Man in the Philosophy of Hobbes

The world in which Hobbes found himself, and which in increasing measure is our world, was no longer a static Aristotelian world which needs a mover to be moved. The moving force, for Hobbes as for Galileo, whom Hobbes admired, was now the energy which is contained in the world itself. In the human world that energy is provided by the emotions.[3] Hobbes, in formulating his thoughts, knew about the new discoveries in the physical sciences; in addition, he was thoroughly familiar with Thucydides' soberly realistic *History of the Peloponnesian War*, which he had translated from the Greek (1839a, Vol. VIII). Further, he had before his observing eye the experience of the civil war in England. In this turbulent period, which he described and analyzed in his book *Behemoth* (a Hebrew word for animals), Hobbes saw the social world, not unlike the physical world, in motion (1969b). Loyalties shifted. The parties in the civil war were arraigned against each other; belief and custom were eroded; contentious opinion, hunger for power and greed for gain were taking their place; everybody was for himself and peace and security were ardent desires, but not realities. Hobbes concluded from that experience that man is driven by a lust for power and that this lust is held in check only by the fear of harm and, ultimately, of death.

In order to prove his point, Hobbes conducted a Galilean thought experiment. Imagine, he argued, how men would behave if they were 'but even now sprung out of the earth and suddenly, like mushrooms, come to full maturity without all kinds of engagement to each other'.[4] There would be no bonds, no privileges, no obligations. It would be a state of nature without culture. In these circumstances, which would result in a 'war of each against all', men would have to construct an alternative to the state of nature by subjecting themselves to moral rules and by authorizing, as individuals, some man or group of men to be their sovereign representative and to guarantee the peace. Hobbes comprehends society, then, as if it were a contractual relationship among individuals to ensure the peace. The ideally assumed contract, even if not actually concluded, is the *ratio essendi* of government without which society could not emerge from a chaos of conflicting interests.

To disregard this ideal assumption would be misleading. Hobbes did not intend to derive contemporary societies from an antecedent state of violence among individuals and groups, which he admitted did not exist always and everywhere, although he was aware of the condition of the American Indians whom he called 'the savage people in many places of America', and their inability to establish peace among themselves (1968, ch. 13, p. 187, and 1969a, ch. 14, p. 73). Nor did he deny that states may come about by conquest rather than by contract or, at any rate, by conditions that could not 'in conscience be justified' (Hobbes, 1968, p. 722). Hobbes argued not historically, but rationally, although he never entirely 'ceased to connect his abstraction with the development of human civilization out of savagery and barbarism'.[5] What he asserted is that governments cannot be based on the sense of belongingness which used to be the principle of the aboriginal family. Hobbes is concerned with human relations outside of familial bonds. In this context, he maintains that the 'laws of nature' are immutable and eternal and, considering that human nature was constant in its assertiveness, that it was imperative that it be effectively curbed. Hence, he thought that the establishment of enforceable law and effective government was a prime requirement of civilized life. It follows that Hobbes differs from the Aristotelian notion of man as *zoon politikon*, that is, as a 'naturally' social, even political, kind of being, forming organized communities, as if by destiny, in the manner, as it were, of bees and ants (whom Aristotle numbered among political creatures).[6] According to Hobbes, man's unguided inclinations are destructive, so that society must be shaped by an act of will. Hobbes viewed human society as the work of man, an artifice, not an attribute of nature.[7]

The Sociology of Toennies – Fundamental Concepts

Toennies, who was a Hobbes scholar before he became a sociologist, adopted the constructional procedure which he employs from his understanding of Hobbes.[8] Toennies's theory is constructional in one view, even if it is historical in another view. Toennies used the Hobbesian conception of human conduct as a starting point; his inclusion of Hobbes's analysis of the workings of human nature into a more complex system of sociological theory is ingenious. The outlines of the theory, which one must be aware of before the Hobbesian inclusion can be appreciated, are as follows.

In the Toenniesian system of special sociology, the transhistorical and static aspect of society is dealt with in what Toennies calls 'pure' sociology while the historical and dynamic aspect is dealt with in 'applied' sociology. Within this system, fundamental concepts are established in 'pure' sociology: they are structural, namely, *Gemeinschaft* and *Gesellschaft* on the one hand, and social-psychological, namely, essential or existential will (*Wesenwille*) and rational or arbitrary will (*Kuerwille*), on the other.[9] In essential will, means and end are not separated, so that, for instance, we mount a horse not to reach a goal but because we find the ride enjoyable. While in *Gesellschaft* we associate with others to pursue a single end, like reaching a destination or acquiring an economic goal, we are in total and unquestioned communion in *Gemeinschaft*. While the prototype of *Gesellschaft* is exchange, as in contract, the prototype of *Gemeinschaft* is attachment, as in kinship (Cahnman and Heberle, 1971, pp. 76–7). Kinship refers to sexual love, brotherly and sisterly love, and especially to the relation of mother and child. A mother's love of her child is not irrational as Wundt, following Schopenhauer, assumed when he identified will with 'drive without thought', but it is true that a mother's love arises from an intentionality that is not reflective. Essential will, leading to *Gemeinschaft*, is based on communal, or shared, feelings and experiences, such as liking, habituation and memory (Toennies, 1965, p. 13, 1970, pp. 93–100; Loomis, 1963, pp. 108–17). Although these feelings and experiences extend from kinship to friendship, the point is that essential will remains genetically anchored because it denotes an intentionality that is not separated from vital processes. It should be noted that the dichotomy of *Gemeinschaft* and *Gesellschaft*, although by other names, has a long history. For one thing, it is contained in the dichotomy of *philia* and *koinonia* in the *Nikomachian Ethics* of Aristotle, with *philia* pointing to intimate togetherness and *koinonia* to association for a purpose.

Gemeinschaft and *Gesellschaft* are not concretely separate structures, as essential will and arbitrary will are not concretely separate kinds of will. Toennies states that he does 'not know of any condition of culture or society in which elements of *Gemeinschaft* and elements of *Gesellschaft* are not simultaneously present'.[10] As fundamental concepts, *Gemeinschaft* and *Gesellschaft* do not stand for actual societies, as the 'state of nature' does not circumscribe a point in history. Conceptually, *Gemeinschaft* and *Gesellschaft* are limiting points of a continuum. The totality of social reality hangs between these opposite poles, as physical reality hangs between the poles of inertia and motion.[11] Consequently, it donates a profound misunderstanding to say that these fundamental concepts are 'oversimplified'[12] or 'used as perennial frames into which the many-sided, complex and elusive facts of reality are squeezed', as some authors maintain (Wirth, 1926, pp. 412–22). It is likewise misleading to introduce third categories, like Schmalenbach's 'Bund', meaning a league or covenant of agemates, or Parsons's collegiality, as inherent in the professional role, to complement the Toenniesian fundamental principles (Cahnman, 1973, pp. 11–15). Surely, reality contains innumerable subdivisions, modifications and combinations, shades, grades and mixtures, but these variations are qualifying, not fundamental in character.

However, what is firmly stated and sharply delineated in pure or constructional sociology (Cahnman, 1973, pp. 103–24) is fluidly interpreted and variously combined in applied or historical sociology. There is a dialectical tension between the two sociologies, as there is a dialectical tension within each of them between the fundamental concepts *Gemeinschaft* and *Gesellschaft* and between their correlates essential will and arbitrary will. Again, within applied sociology, there is tension between the variegated historical manifestations of the interplay of social forces to which these concepts refer. By a dialectical, as against a positivistic, scheme, then, we refer to a view of human relations as a continuing and contradictory process rather than as an assemblage of separately demonstrable facts. Admittedly, the task is complex. 'Pure' concepts must be illustrated by concrete examples, but the examples, in turn, only approximate the clarity of the conceptual formulation. For instance, relations within a family are more likely to be based on 'essential will' and hence more readily lead to *Gemeinschaft* than relations within a joint stock company or a government office, but to what extent this is the case is a question for research. Even a seemingly thoroughly integrated family merely approximates the 'pure' concept of a family as *Gemeinschaft*, just as an actual line merely approximates a mathematical line. For, as Toennies puts it, in *Gemeinschaft und Gesellschaft* concepts are 'nothing but artifacts of thought, tools devised to facilitate the comprehension of reality' (1970, p. 133; Loomis, 1963, p. 14; Cahnman and Heberle, 1971, p. 44). These 'things of thought' are common denominators or normal (norm) concepts and their objects are ideal types; 'they are never found complete and pure in reality'. In order to comprehend reality, 'the transitions, constraints and complications' must be introduced, as Toennies observes in *Thomas Hobbes: Leben und Lehre* (1971, pp. 89–90; Cahnman and Heberle, 1971, pp. 39–40). In *Gemeinschaft und Gesellschaft* he continues:

As free and arbitrary products of thought, normal concepts are mutually exclusive; in a purely formal way nothing pertaining to arbitrary will must be thought into essential will, nothing in essential will into arbitrary will. It is entirely different, if these concepts are considered empirically. In this case, they are nothing else but names comprising and denoting a multiplicity of observations or ideas; their content will decrease with the range of the phenomena covered. In this case, observation will show that no essential will can ever occur without the arbitrary will by means of which it is expressed and no arbitrary will without the essential will on which it is based. (Cahnman and Heberle 1971, p. 44)

In other words, what Toennies says is that essential will and arbitrary will as well as *Gemeinschaft* and *Gesellschaft* are not distinguished in the way the botanist distinguishes trees and grasses or the zoologist vertebrates and invertebrates. Toennies does not employ the descriptive naturalist's method of distinction, but the chemist's method of isolation (*Scheidung*, not *Unterscheidung*; ibid., p. 91). He speaks of not concretely distinguishable categories, but of intellectually distillable elements. Going a step further, one might say that while the fundamental concepts initially are formulated in an either-or context in pure sociology, they are considered in a more-or-less context in applied sociology. Consequently, what the pure theorist isolates, the applied analyst carries back into the stream of life. These two operations are complementary, not contradictory and, what is more, both operate within the same universe of discourse because pure and applied theory each deal with social relations as positive relations. The fundamental concepts refer to positive social norms and positive social values; negative constellations, such as wars, riots, lockouts, strikes, crime, delinquency, marital discord and, even more so, the radical negation of social bonds that occurs in suicide, are in Toennies's parlance asocial in character. They are pathologies. Pathology is thus a third category in Toennies's scheme, in addition to *Gemeinschaft* and *Gesellschaft* and opposed to both. There are pathologies of *Gemeinschaft*, like crimes of passion, and pathologies of *Gesellschaft*, like crimes of calculation, crimes that arise sooner in the *Gemeinschaft*-like context of a rural hamlet and crimes that arise sooner in the *Gesellschaft*-like context of a metropolitan area: they are negations of their positive counterparts. Pathology, then, while not a fundamental concept, is a mirror image of fundamental concepts and as such has its place in the Toenniesian system (Cahnman and Heberle, 1971, p. 91; Cahnman, 1973, pp. 15–16).

Toennies and Hobbes: Aspects of Modernity

Toennies recognized in the Hobbesian model of society the concepts of arbitrary will and *Gesellschaft*, meaning a rationally constructed social order. But Toennies realized that these twin concepts provide but a partial view of human nature and he suggests that Hobbes himself may have been aware of it. In a usually overlooked passage of his book on Hobbes, Toennies comments that the view of human nature as essentially and universally rational stands in contrast to another view of Hobbes which is less absolute, namely, that humanity had arisen from animality and that it continues to contain it.[13] At this point, an evolutionary spark appears embedded in Hobbes's mechanistic thinking. It is true, though, that this second view is not fully worked out because Hobbes's attention is focused on the triumph of culture over nature, a process which in a Toenniesian context is seen as leading to *Gesellschaft*. Toennies maintains that the Hobbesian scheme needs to be complemented by the concept of *Gemeinschaft* (1965, p. 164); in addition, a process of 'aging' is implied in the development of a predominantly *Gemeinschaft*-like to a more *Gesellschaft*-like society.

If one thus completes the Hobbesian argument, which belongs to 'pure' theory, by an 'applied' sociology, that is, by a historical consideration, one recognizes that *Gemeinschaft* and *Gesellschaft* are present in every societal structure – yet their relative strengths may vary and have actually varied over time. In Toennies's view man is by nature a social being in *Gemeinschaft* and an initially asocial being in *Gesellschaft*; but *Gesellschaft* makes for social relations through convention and law. The relation between these two fundamental concepts and their application can be viewed in a variety of ways. In his paper 'The nature of sociology' (*Das Wesen der Soziologie*) Toennies says that both theses, that man is a social being and that he is an asocial being, are valid and applicable and that they complement each other (Cahnman and Heberle, 1971, p. 91). In his paper 'A prelude to sociology' (*Einleitung in die Soziologie*) he adds that it would be inaccurate to say that the organic, or historical, and the mechanical, or rationalistic view are both 'right' and that they are to be combined in a synthesis (Cahnman and Heberle, 1971, pp. 81–2). The organic view, he means to say, precedes the rationalistic view logically and historically: *Gesellschaft* is derived from *Gemeinschaft* in the same sense in which arbitrary will is derived from essential will, reflection from emotion. But this statement, seemingly the starting point, actually is the conclusion; in Toennies's mind the argument runs the other way round, in line with the philosophy of Hobbes, which starts from an analysis of *Gesellschaft*, that is, from the need for societal order. In other words, as Toennies explains it in 'A prelude to sociology', wherever organic unity exists, thought, rational deliberation, arbitrary will are likely to corrode it; but the self-same arbitrary, or reflective, will must strive to establish unity where unity has been abandoned. Thus multiplicity either arises from unity which exists prior to the parts or multiplicity is the starting point and unity, or union, is the desired goal (Cahnman and Heberle, 1971, pp. 75f.).

Clearly the conscious construction of societal cohesion where there is a lack of it is the normative thrust of the Hobbesian argument. Hobbes observed the corrosion of *Gemeinschaft*. He recognized in their initial stages the ills that are still with us: the spirit of permissiveness among intellectuals, the abuse of the churches and other public institutions for private purposes, the venality of people in all classes of society, the power of the purse of the big trading cities as well as of individual entrepreneurs and the exploitation of the poor (Hobbes, 1969b, pp. 2–4, 126). Toennies took these statements as an indication that Hobbes was aware not only of the beginnings but of the very nature of the capitalistic mode of production. He further contended that Hobbes had recognized in his mind's eye the continuing dissolution of *Gemeinschaft*-like relations and unions, especially insofar as their consequences for women are concerned, and their replacement by *Gesellschaft*-like relations, that is, by the accommodation of individual interests.[14] The Marxists, using the terminology of political economy rather than that of sociology, called the new society not *Gesellschaft*, but capitalism. C. B. MacPherson, in his challenging book, called it the society of 'possessive individualism'.[15] American sociology, consciously or inadvertently, has continued in Toennies's approach although freed from the Hobbesian assumption that society can only be organized by means of a centralized government – an assumption which Toennies had already rejected. There are other agencies of social control, especially in America. The transformation of tradition-bound villagers into restless urbanites, the drift from established custom to social movement and the attempt to cope with the disturbances that arise from these changes have become the focus of attention in a variety of investigations by American sociologists, starting from Thomas and Znaniecki's *The Polish Peasant in Europe and America* (1918) and the urban studies of the Chicago school and now pursued in the analysis of deviance and especially in studies of development, particularly in Africa. The guiding spirit of the Chicago school, Robert E. Park, provided a Toenniesian formula for studies related to the urban environment: he assumed that the element of competition in the biotic-ecological complex would have to be checked by a new 'moral order' which he conceptualized as 'consensus', the combination amounting to the notion of *Gesellschaft*.[16]

An effort at societal unity, indeed, has to be made because from where we stand now the new moral order that is required can hardly be seen emerging. What we do observe is that the individual initially has been freed from feudal bonds, then from customs and usages and finally from each and every obligation that goes beyond the satisfaction of individual needs. Arbitrary will, the striving for isolated goals, now rules supreme and a vast emptiness occupies the mind. As a consequence unrest is spreading in ever-widening circles and the time has come for the rational reconstruction of society. But how will such a reconstruction be achieved? By means of a 'consciously conceived ethic, as Toennies hoped?[17] What will be the content of that ethic? The recognition of the need for a more effective 'government' in a Hobbesian mold? An agreement on the procedures which lead to 'consensus' through public debate? An achievement of 'consensus' through a new coercive power, namely, public opinion? A combination of a variety of approaches? These are questions which science can pose, but hardly answer.

Hobbes and Vico: the Verum Factum

As we move from Hobbes to Vico, we enter a different world. Yet the similarities as well as the dissimilarities between Vico and Hobbes have occupied Italian scholarship in recent decades. Vico polemicized against Hobbes at various points in his writings, but two of the foremost Italian Vico scholars, Fausto Nicolini and Eugenio Garin, have pointed out that it is not likely that Vico knew much of Hobbes's work first-hand and that he seems to have relied in large part on the biased interpretation of Hobbes by the Kiel professor Georg Pasch.[18] Following the spotty information he received from Pasch and others, Vico mistook Hobbes's emphasis on human 'will' in the construction of governmental institutions as an assumption of 'arbitrariness' in the way the world is run and a reliance on 'chance' in human conduct in the Epicurean understanding of these terms. Yet Vico uses the expression *homo homini lupus*, which is commonly considered Hobbesian in connotation, in several of his writings.[19] A contemporary author, Ferruccio Focher, in comparing Vico and Hobbes, points to Hobbes's contention that two principal parts of human nature, reason and passion, correspond to 'two kinds of learning, mathematical and dogmatical', and that the latter kind, which is the conventional historian's manner of proceeding, has no claim to scientific standing.[20] At the same time, Focher is aware of Hobbes's high appreciation of serious historical scholarship, as evidenced in his translation of the work of Thucydides. Focher's main point in dissolving the seeming contradiction is that linguistic approaches to the critique of sources and their interpretation in historiography, which originated in the eighteenth century and of which Vico is a principal originator, remained unknown to Hobbes and were therefore not utilized in the Hobbesian argument (Focher, 1977, pp. 96–104). Viewed in the light of that contention, Vico is not so much an antagonist of Hobbes as his successor.

Focher's point is well taken, but not decisive. In order to demonstrate Vico's successorship, it must be shown that the different point of departure in Vico's thinking, in addition to his different methodology, enabled him to arrive at a more comprehensive resolution.[21] Giambattista Vico, a trained lawyer and a teacher of rhetoric at the University of Naples, grew up in a Cartesian intellectual atmosphere, that is, in an environment where Hobbes and Spinoza as well as Descartes were widely discussed, but in which he remained opposed to the mechanistic world-view he felt they represented. Vico established in his *New Science* a historical approach as a counter-image to their mechanistic world-view, but I shall attempt to show that the *New Science* in effect is a complement rather than a contradiction to the Hobbesian construction, the difference in the philosophical points of departure notwithstanding. Vico objected to the Cartesian assumption that judgements claiming to be true must consist of 'clear and distinct ideas', as in mathematics, and that consequently mathematical certitude was the only permissible certitude in the pursuit of knowledge. The Cartesian assumption has dominated the sciences ever since, and inasmuch as many sociologists have conceived of sociology as a 'science' it has exerted a vast influence in sociology also. Vico especially objected to Descartes' disregard of history because it was lacking in mathematical certitude. The geometrical method of Descartes appeared to Vico as tantamount to 'disregarding the nature of man, which is uncertain because of man's freedom'.[22] Moreover, in Vico's view, man's freedom makes for a new certitude because we 'make ourselves', that is, we are doing what is done in history. A Neapolitan of the thirteenth century, Thomas Aquinas, in using Aristotelian distinctions, had contrasted nature as *ordo quem ratio considerat* with human action in society as *ordo quem ratio considerando facit,* in other words, nature as the work of God with history as the product of man (Croce, 1964, pp. 27–8). Vico, not a Thomist, transformed the Thomistic formula into the statement that *verum et factum convertuntur*, meaning that our freedom in action permits us to know the truth of that which we have made.[23]

Vico: Historical Sociology

As we proceed from Descartes to Hobbes, the vista widens. While constructing law and government is not identical with making history, it is remarkable that Hobbes, in connecting mechanics and geometry with the science of government, asserted that we have knowledge not only about the geometrical figures whose lines we draw, but also about right and wrong, fairness and injury, because we have 'made' the laws and agreements on which they are based (1839b, ch. X, sections 4, 5; Toennies, 1971, p. 113). Vico adds to the Hobbesian contention the observation that the new science of history – or shall we say, of historical sociology – has more reality to it than geometry because 'the institutions having to do with human affairs are more real than points, lines, surfaces and figures are' (Vico, 1948, para. 349); Vico agrees with Hobbes that men, dominated by passions, such as ferocity, avarice and ambition, 'would live like wild beasts in the wilderness' if they had not 'made the civil institutions by which men live in human society' (Vico, 1948, paras

132, 133). The difference is that the Hobbesian scheme is meant to be a thought experiment, not a historical fact, the agreement between Vico and Hobbes that humanity arose from an 'animal-like condition' notwithstanding. Vico's statement, on the other hand, is clearly historical.

Vico provides the historical dimension to the Hobbesian construction, including the Toenniesian complementation of *Gesellschaft* by *Gemeinschaft*, because even in the term *Gemeinschaft* the constructional character overlays the historical derivation. Originally, Vico imagines – and the term 'imagination' is important – savage giants, that is, wild men with bestial natures, to have roamed the forests in the pursuit of their desires, until they were tamed, 'tied', as it were, not by the state, but by religion. They were subdued by the clap of thunder and the stroke of lightning, terrifying manifestations of the uproar of nature which they understood to indicate divine displeasure with their bestial conduct. Their bestiality consisted not only in their killing each other, chiefly in competition for women, but also in the rape and abuse of women, the neglect of offspring and the abandonment of the dead. To abolish these horrifying crimes, the family was first constituted in the caves where the thunderstruck fugitives had come to dwell. Thus, religion, marriage and burial, according to Vico, mark the beginnings of civilization or, as we might prefer to say, of social organization (Vico, 1948, paras 333, 337, 504). These three institutions, religion, marriage and burial, are common to all civilized nations. It follows that custom brought a hallowed order into the aboriginal chaos and *Gemeinschaft* was initiated by the compulsion of religious awe, long before a condition of *Gesellschaft* prompted the establishment of governmental authority. That is what Vico has in mind when he objects to the position of the theoreticians of natural law, namely, Grotius, Selden and Pufendorf, and implicitly Hobbes. Vico maintains that these authors argue from 'the latest times of civilized nations' rather than from the beginning (Vico, 1948, paras 318, 329, 493 *et passim*). Indeed, the genetic approach, the grasp of the 'initial phenomenon', as Goethe put it, a case history as we might call it, is indispensable for the comprehension of the phenomena which present themselves to us in the here and now. It is Vico's contention that we understand what happens now from its beginnings and what is going to be from what has always been. Vico's theorem, that doctrines or theories must begin where the matters they treat begin (Vico, 1948, para. 314), is notable as the basic statement in historical sociology.

Vico's historical reconstruction of the societal order, then, complements rather than invalidates the Hobbesian statement. To be sure, the idea of a *Gemeinschaft*-based rather than a *Gesellschaft*-

based natural law had occurred to Toennies (1965, p. 217; Cahnman and Heberle, 1971, p. 205), although more as a *desideratum* than as a factuality. Such a *Gemeinschaft*-based natural law, Toennies argues, would consider prerogatives and obligations not as separate but as complementary categories, which is precisely what happens in the family, both in the historically emerging and in the ideally constructed family. However, as it is dubious whether and to what extent the principle of the family can be applied to the larger society, a *Gesellschaft*-based legal order is likely to remain the preponderant feature in modern societies, a variety of attempts to introduce ingredients of mutuality notwithstanding. Hobbes's grasp of this basic fact is compelling. The need to confirm 'liberty in law' cannot be gainsaid in the enormously extended context of contemporary societies. But the theorem that doctrines must begin where the matters they treat begin opens a new vista.

In the account of history, matters do not begin with government. Vico has demonstrated that the sociology of religion and the sociology of the family, which arises from the sociology of religion, must take first place in the scheme of historical sociology (Vico, 1948, paras 333, 336, 337, 504; 177–9, with references to Hobbes). Religion, that is, the initiator and protector of the family or, concretely expressed, the God that is alive and potent in the hearth fire around which the family gathers, has first established and then maintained society, as Vico emphasizes in one of the concluding paragraphs of the *New Science* (Vico, 1948, para. 1109). Burial is required in completion of the religion–family complex because of the bond with which religion 'ties' us to our ancestors – religion in Latin means to 'bind' or to 'tie'.[24] It follows that the institution of the burial of the dead and, going beyond Vico, the initiation of permanent settlements in the vicinities of the graveyards of revered ancestors, complete the establishment of society. The next step is the city, that is, the rise of civilization as an over-arching loyalty, encompassing and containing the loyalty to a family or a clan. In that sense, Fustel de Coulanges' *La Cité antique* appears as the crowning effort in a Vichian historical sociology.[25] In Fustel's book humanity, starting from the family, constructs its social world in larger and ever more inclusive forms, through clans, phratries and cities to the *imperium mundi* which is Rome. One can observe a remote echo of Vichianism even in Durkheim's *Les Formes élémentaires de la vie religieuse*.[26] Durkheim, a student of Fustel de Coulanges, grasped the interrelatedness of symbolism and social structure and the persistence of that relation over time. However, Durkheim confounded comparability with identity in applying the Arunta experience to the *république laique*. He thereby turned the scholarly statement that religion is social into the political assertion that 'society is God', a contention which Vico would have rejected. We have, however, a most stimulating discussion of the concept of civilization in a Vichian mold in the symposium on *Civilisation – le mot et l'idée,* edited by Lucien Fèbvre and others, and containing the extensive report by Marcel Mauss, Durkheim's nephew and successor, on 'Les civilisations – éléments et formes'. Mauss's report takes up the Vichian theme of civilization as a comprehensive phenomenon.[27] French scholarship in the social sciences had been directed toward Vico by the historian Jules Michelet, a translator of Vico, and the interpreter of Vico for several generations.[28]

Vico's Method

Vico's method is linguistic rather than mathematical in nature; within linguistics, the approach is genetically conceived. Vico holds that the savage giants of the beginning could utter only unarticulated sounds; out of these grew song and the elevated speech which is called poetry. Poetry in Vico's understanding is not a form of art, it is the very language itself of ancient man. Neither is the poetry of the ancients a sophisticated account *post festum* or an allegory, and it is certainly not an expression of individual sentiment. It is a depiction of the world in images rather than its description in thought. In the history of mankind, as in the growth of the mind from infancy to maturity, the pictorial comprehension of reality comes first, the intellectual generalization afterwards (Vico, 1948, paras 218, 363, 377, 34). What the ancients express in corporeal images bears the name of mythology, but it is actually *vera narratio,* historical truth, though told by means of legend and saga – *mythos.* To be sure, mythology, in Vico's scheme, comes in time before poetry, but it is expressed through poetry; mythology records the actions of men and women whereby, as in the songs of Homer, a person may stand for a collectivity, a class, a city, a generation (Vico, 1948, bk 3: 'Discovery of the true Homer'). Thus a universal truth is created linguistically, from the experience of reality, not constructionally as in mathematics. The poetic characters which stand for reality are imaginative genera or symbolic expressions, replacing the mute language of signs and physical objects which guided the entrance of bestial man into the social world. In the present context of our deliberations, there would seem to be no need to assume a fundamental difference between mythology and poetry.

In poetry, then, peoples speak as in a single voice. Individuality, philosophy, systematic thought and intellectual argument come later, when collectivities are dissolved and a widely used 'vulgar' language is practiced in which the laws of a diversified society are written. Yet language preserves the memory of origins and popular usage retains poetic images. Vico quotes examples that may not always be correct, but they illustrate the historical methodology he is using. So, to cite only one of these examples, *nomos*, law or regulation, retains a reference to pasturage, for landed estates were once allocated by heroic kings to subjected clans, with mutual obligations as a corollary. Examples of the corporeal images which we continue to use are head for top, mouth for opening, heart for center; we refer to the vein of a rock, the whistling of the wind, the murmuring of the waves. Thus the oldest and newest phenomena are linguistically connected and thereby elucidated, though not equated (Vico, 1948, paras 52, 354, 405, 607). By means of philology, Vico attempts to formulate a scientific approach to the comprehension of historical process. Words carry a meaning through time. We learn to understand the nature of institutions from the record of their coming into being (*nascimento*; Vico, 1948, paras 147–52). We comprehend the flower from the bud.

Along Vico's path we move, as in a mental voyage, across the eighteenth century, from the ideas of the Enlightenment and the theories of natural law to the philosophies of romanticism and historicism, as carried forward chiefly by German scholars and philosophers. Vico differs, though, from Herder and the romantic linguists and jurists.[29] They use language and custom as unique expressions of respective 'folk-minds' whose unity lies not in their comparability but in their orchestration, as when a violin corresponds to a cello in a symphony. The comparative methodology of Vico also goes far beyond the use which Max Weber, not a romanticist but a historical sociologist, makes of counter-examples when he contrasts the civilizations of China and India to those of Europe and America. More closely related to Vico is the sophisticated heir to romantic thought, Wilhelm Dilthey, who explicitly refers to Vico.[30] Dilthey's hermeneutic approach is Vichian when he points out that nature is a phenomenon 'external' to man and hence comprehensible only mathematically, while society is 'our world' and therefore accessible to *Verstehen*, that is, to immediate mind-to-mind understanding as applied in interpretive research. It is possible to compare Vico to the newest efforts in linguistics, such as Noam Chomsky's, if and inasmuch as the common features of all linguistic expression are emphasized. But structural linguistics is synchronic rather than diachronic. Structural linguistics overlooks the stages of development and thereby neglects the very historicity which is of the essence in Vico's theoretical scheme.

The 'Corso que Fanno le Nazioni'

Vico's fame rests with the concept of the 'ideal eternal history' – the *corso que fanno le nazioni* – a scheme which comprises diversity in universality (Vico, 1948, bk 4: 'The course the nations run'). Societies move from youth to maturity to decline and, again, to renewal, from crude beginnings to the high noon of thought; from evolution to dissolution. The process that is envisaged is ideal because it is a 'thing of thought'; it permits modification, but it is eternal because it is providential as well as flexibly repetitive; and it is historical because it is specific in its application to the events and situations that are investigated. Vico's thought construct of an 'ideal eternal history' is something forever present and forever unfolding, as if it were a part of creation and thus inseparable from the life of man. Vico envisages three successive ages of gods, heroes and men (Vico, 1948, para. 31) and correspondingly three kinds of customs, three kinds of natural laws, three kinds of civil states or common-wealths; and for the purpose of justifying these institutions, juris-prudence, authority and reason (Vico, 1948, paras 915f.). To illus-trate these sequences, there are three successive kinds of government – divine, aristocratic and legal; three successive kinds of languages – mute religious acts, heroic blazonings and articulate speech; and so throughout the trichotomies of Vico's order of the human universe. Once the cycles have run their course, a renewal takes place and a new cycle begins. Italian scholars, especially G. Fassò, have pointed out in that context that Vico uses the term *verum factum* rarely in the final edition of the *New Science*, replacing it with the term *verum certum*. By the term *verum certum*, Vico is assumed to refer to the rationality, that is, the universality and predictability of the *corsi* and *ricorsi*, or to their 'providentiality', if the concept is rendered in a Christian key.[31]

The notion that human history moves in cycles is old. It has been particularly congenial to the Greeks, although in a static way, as in the renewal of the seasons; it is found in Plato, Aristotle, Polybius and also, more flexibly later, in Machiavelli; finally, in our day, in Pareto, Spengler, Sorokin and Toynbee. In all these schemes, history is conceived more in images of growth and decline rather than of actual change. Vico has been compared to Hegel, but the Hegelian scheme of thesis–antithesis–synthesis, and consequently the teleolo-gical prospect in Hegelian philosophy of moving ever higher along the spiral of history, is lacking in the sequence of *corsi* and *ricorsi* that is envisaged by Vico. For Vico, the decline of institutions and civilizations is as real as their rise, and providence guides them both. However, both Vico and Hegel share a dialectical methodology;

their sequences are repetitive in a varied way, so that, for instance, three stages in the history of medieval and post-medieval Christianity correspond to, but are not identical with, three stages in the history of Roman and Greek antiquity.

Trichotomy and Dichotomy

The sociologist would wish to translate Vico's divine providence into recurring patterns of events, no matter who directs them, but he must enter a proviso regarding the theory of the three stages. The proviso is as follows: the trichotomy of a religious, heroic and civic age, which is encountered not only in Vico and Hegel, but also in Ferguson, Turgot, Comte, Lewis Morgan and others, appears to be modelled after the concept of the Holy Trinity which, in turn, goes back to ancient Egyptian wisdom. But there are other holy numbers in the tradition of the peoples, so that one is inclined to assume that the threefold division of reality amounts to a cultural compulsion in the civilisation of the Occident. One could construct four (tetragrammaton), five or seven subdivisions with equal assurance. Perhaps a dichotomy, spanning life from birth to death and from evolution to dissolution, and hence indicating limiting points rather than subdivisions, is more in line with the structure of reality. Such an interpretation would demonstrate the similarity between Vico's view and Toennies's fundamental concepts and thus bring Vico in line with classical sociological theory.[32]

A further deliberation will confirm the convergence. We cannot quote at this point the numerous examples from Greek and Roman history which Vico uses to illustrate the theory of *corsi* and *ricorsi*. Suffice it to say that Vico consulted all the literary sources that were available to him – not only jurists, historians and philosophers, but apart from Homer, whom he thinks of as a collectivity, also individual poets like Virgil, Horace, Lucretius and others. Indeed, the historical sociologist would agree with Vico that the creative writer and artist must not be neglected in the search for sources: he gives us not a literal, but an enhanced view of reality. From legendary and poetic sources and linguistic remnants, as we have indicated above, one may even imagine what happened far back in time, when the explicit testimony of contemporaries ceases to speak. From the factual data and their interpretation Vico assumes, to quote from my own earlier writing, that

> the ferocious vagrants of old, embroiled in a 'war of each against all', threw themselves at the mercy of the settlers who received them as dependants, clients and serfs (Vico, 1948, para. 258). Con-

quest, then, while not excluded, is not a necessary condition of submission. Indeed, following Vico's axiom 79, there is a sequence: the protected associates in the first stage become the plebeians in the urban stage and the subjected provincials in the imperial stage. What happens is that the fugitives from violence become *famuli* who attach themselves to the *fama* (glory, reputation) of the heroes and are accepted as members of their families; they are forerunners of the serfs subdued by conquest. Only a family has a god present in the hearth fire and hence enjoys independent status; one can understand, therefore, that the Roman plebeians, in pursuance of the Law of the Twelve Tables, demanded *connubia patrum*, that is, solemn nuptials, sanctioned by *auspicia,* with equality before God and man and the rights of citizenship as a consequence. (Cahnman, 1976, p. 834)

The example is taken from Roman history. We do not need to decide at this point whether submission occurs, in ancient Italy or elsewhere, without conquest, or whether submission antedates conquest, both of which are Vico's assumptions, because in either event, along the very lines of Vico's reasoning, we arrive at a dichotomous rather than a trichotomous view of the course of events. In following Vico and some of his spiritual descendants, such as Fustel de Coulanges and Marc Bloch, or among contemporary social scientists Louis Dumont, we move from hierarchy to egalitarianism (Dumont, 1970). Between protectors and serfs, patricians and plebeians, citizens and strangers, or in the European Middle Ages between lords, peasants, burghers and priests, and in India between the various castes, a gradation of duties and privileges is found which implies a rank order, but at the same time assigns an independent and incomparable value to each participating group in a total society. This initial principle of societal organization in the course of time gives way to an egalitarian system, which in the West arises out of Hebrew prophecy and Christian teaching, and proceeding via the proponents of natural law and the innovators in science, arrives by means of the destruction of ranks at a system of stratification according to the economic categories of property, income and conspicuous consumption. These three measurable categories are the criteria of the division of classes in an egalitarian society. Even property qualifications may eventually be cast aside, so that only the dynamic differentiations remain. Weber, and finally Merton, have guided us in the understanding of that process which Weber called the 'disenchantment' of the world. What Vico designated as an 'age of men' is ushered in at the end of the *corso,* where solidarity has given way to tolerance and public institutions are used for the satisfaction of private appetites. Individualism, then, rules supreme until break-down within or conquest from without brings a reversion to a new barbarism. Such conditions prevailed in the waning centuries of antiquity and, if indications are not deceptive, confront us today. Vico's way of putting it is forceful: 'Men first feel necessity, then look for utility, next attend to comfort, still later amuse themselves with pleasure, thence grow dissolute in luxury, and finally go mad and waste their substance' (Vico, 1948, para. 241). So, what is indicated here is a fivefold (not a threefold) sequence of subdivisions amounting to a continuum from necessity to waste. The Vichian trichotomy is thus reduced to a dichotomy, both in terms of a societal construct and in terms of a sequence of stages. The 'ideal eternal history' is transformed from a theory of successive stages to a unified theoretical system, without losing its historicity.

Conclusion

One must call to mind at this point that Toennies, like Vico, sees the Middle Ages and the newer centuries as a civilizational unit, moving dichotomously from a prevalence of *Gemeinschaft* to a preponderance of *Gesellschaft*.[33] Hobbes, from whose philosophy the Toenniesian scheme is derived, envisages man's moving from an animal-like condition and a sense of belongingness, through individualism, to the more firmly established state of a rationally organized society. Hobbes's counter-image, though, is not *Gemeinschaft*, but dissolution. Hobbes's approach is constructional, while Toennies combines the constructional and historical, or the rationalistic and empiristic aspects. Vico, as we have shown, adds a more intensely argued historical dimension to these chiefly analytic schemes. He offers a guide to historical sociology. All three authors, although proceeding from different points of departure, agree that the varied world of human experience must be comprehended within a conceptual context of limits. History provides the dates, sociology the concepts by which the data are analyzed. Applying the approach thus indicated to the problems of contemporary society, or of any society, a viewpoint is provided by which to order the bewildering array of phenomena that are encountered day by day. This is what a theory should do.

Notes: Chapter 2

1 I have attempted to put Max Weber into a historical context in the paper 'Max Weber and the methodological controversy in the social sciences', in Cahnman and Boskoff, 1964, pp. 103–27.

2 Toennies was aware of Vico, as documented by his comment in 1926, p. 36.
He compared Vico with those philosophers of antiquity who assumed a
deterioration of human life and conditions rather than a continued progress. Toennies was surely aware of Schelling, Schopenhaeur, Gierke,
Maine and Fustel de Coulanges, that is, of a tradition comparable to
Vico's approach. However, the Enlightenment aspect of Toennies's thinking remains unimpaired by these considerations.

3 The English works of Hobbes (1839a) in the Sir William Molesworth
edition comprise 11 volumes, the *Opera philosophica quae latine scripsit
omnia* (1839b), 5 volumes. Easily accessible is the Pelican paperback edition of Hobbes's main work, *Leviathan* (1968), edited by C. B. MacPherson,
as well as the early work, *The Elements of Law Natural and Politic*
(1969a) and Hobbes's last book, *Behemoth or the Long Parliament* (1969b),
both edited by F. Toennies, 1889. Richard Peters's Penguin paperback
volume (1956) offers an introduction into Hobbes's system of thought.
Among the extensive Hobbes literature, two recent publications by C. B.
McPherson (1962) and J. W. N. Watkins (1965) are especially stimulating.
Toennies's basic evaluation. *Thomas Hobbes: Leben und Lehre* (1971),
with an introduction by K. H. Ilting, has not yet been translated into
English.

4 Hobbes, 1839a, Vol. 11, pp. 108-9. Compare the famous passage about the
states of war and peace as the limiting concepts of human relations in
Hobbes, 1968, ch. 13, pp. 185-7.

5 Quoted from Ferdinand Toennies, 1965, p. 213; now in Cahnman and
Heberle, 1971, p. 203. Compare K. H. Ilting's introduction to Toennies,
1971, p. 22.

6 Hobbes, 1968, ch. 17, p. 225; compare Cahnman and Heberle, 1971,
pp. 48-61, where Hobbes's argument concerning the requirements of
societal order is reviewed.

7 Hobbes says in the very first sentence of the introduction to *Leviathan*
that a commonwealth or state is an 'artificial animal' and one that is made
by 'the art of man'.

8 In the preface to the second edition of *Gemeinschaft und Gesellschaft*
Toennies confirms that he had taken his departure from Hobbes (Cahnman and Heberle, 1971, p. 31).

9 The corresponding conceptualizations of *Gemeinschaft* and *Gesellschaft* as
well as *Wesenwille* and *Kuerwille* are developed in the first and second
chapters of Toennies (1970), English translation by Loomis (1963). This
basic work, written in the enthusiasm of youth, was published when the
author was 32 years of age. The fundamental concepts contained in the
book were elaborated and clarified in four major subsequent papers and in
numerous other writings; they are selectively combined in Cahnman and
Heberle, 1971. The four major papers published between 1899 and 1924 are
indispensable for the understanding of Toennies. An analysis of all aspects
of the work of Toennies is offered in Cahnman, 1973. Other pertinent
literature, including literature not available in English, is quoted in both
volumes. Several chapters from Toennies's otherwise untranslated book,
Einführung in die Soziologie (1965), are included in Cahnman and Heberle,
1971.

10 Cahnman and Heberle, 1971, p. 10. Corresponding to the *Gemeinschaft-
Gesellschaft* continuum, human will or intentionality should also be conceived as a unity, with essential will and arbitrary will as limiting
points. Compare Toennies, 1970, p. 87; Loomis, 1963, p. 103; and Cahnman and Heberle, 1971, p. 6.

11   Compare Funkenstein, 1976, esp. pp. 194–5. Funkenstein fails to mention Toennies in his extensive bibliography.

12   Janowitz, 1976, pp. 82–108, esp. pp. 85–90. Janowitz repeats his misinterpretation of Toennies in a recent publication (1978). Compare my paper 'Toennies in America' (Cahnman, 1977).

13   Toennies, 1971, p. 190. Reference may be made to Hobbes, 1968, p. 187, where Hobbes observes that 'savage people' have no government 'except the government of small families, the concord whereof dependeth on natural lust'. Hobbes makes here a concession to the concept of *Gemeinschaft,* but rejects its applicability to the conduct of government.

14   Toennies, 1971, pp. 39–40, 206, 267. Future research will have to take up the consequences for women, that is, for love and sex and generally for the family, of the increasingly *Gesellschaft*-like human relations in contemporary society.

15   Hobbes observed and analyzed the upcoming 'bourgeois' society, but MacPherson's contention that Hobbes's analysis served the interests of that society is an inference that is not born out by the text of Hobbes's writings. If it were not for that inference, MacPherson's argument (1962) would closely resemble the one of Toennies.

16   Robert E. Park's scattered opus is assembled in Park, 1952. See also Park and Burgess, 1972, pp. 165–6. The sentence 'Every society represents an organization of elements more or less antagonistic to each other, but united for the moment, at least, by an arrangement which defines the reciprocal relations and respective spheres of action of each' circumscribes a *Gesellschaft.* One of the most Toenniesian papers of the Chicago school is 'Urbanism as a way of life' (Wirth, 1964, pp. 60–83). Compare also Robert Redfield, 1930.

17   The expression is taken from the last lines of Toennies's book *Die Sitte,* now translated by A. F. Borenstein as *Custom: An Essay on Social Codes* (1961).

18   Nicolini, 1931, pp. 30, 46, 1942, pp. 67–99, 1949a, pp. 25–43; Garin, 1962. These scholars argue that Hobbes was not well known in Naples at the turn of the seventeenth century and that whatever knowledge existed was distorted by second-hand information. It seems that Vico gained much information from the writings of Georg Pasch (1661–1707). Georg Pasch was professor of moral philosophy, then of practical (Lutheran) theology, at the University of Kiel. His major books, *Schediasma de curiosis huius saeculi* (1695) and *De novis inventis* (1700), are considered superficial pieces of analysis by Nicolini. Pasch compares Hobbes to Machiavelli, Lucretius and a number of other authors. However, Fisch and Bergin (Vico, 1944, pp. 30, 46) comment that some of Vico's references to Hobbes are not in Pasch, so that it seems that he may have known Hobbes's Latin, but not his English, works.

19   The expression *homo homini lupus,* frequently quoted in connection with Hobbesian thought, especially *De Cive,* ch. VI, and *Leviathan,* ch. XIII, occurs in earlier juridical writings of Vico, especially *De constantia jurisprudentis* according to Focher (1977, p. 9).

20   Focher, 1977, pp. 73f., referring to Hobbes, 1969a. According to Hobbes the dogmatic historians were given to rhetoric, which he opposed to logic.

21   Vico has become accessible to the English reading public through Bergin and Fisch's translation (Vico, 1948) now available, somewhat abridged, in a Cornell paperback edition (3rd printing 1975). Bergin and Fisch have also translated *The Autobiography of Giambattista Vico* (Vico, 1944). A plethora of Vico interpretation is contained in Tagliacozzo and White,

1969, and Tagliacozzo and Verene, 1976; also in vol. 43 of *Social Research*, Nos 3 and 4 (Autumn and Winter 1976). Readers of Italian may consult the *Bolletino del Centro di Studi Vichiani* (Naples: Libreria Internazionale Guida).

22   Vico, 1709, quoted in Michelet, 1971, vol. 1, p. 354. The entire sentence is as follows: 'The Cartesians investigate the nature of objects on account of the prospect of certainty which they contain; they disregard the nature of man which is uncertain because of man's freedom' (my translation).

23   The principle of the *verum factum* is clearly formulated in Vico, 1948, para. 331, as 'a truth beyond all question: that the world of civil society has certainly been made by men and that its principles are therefore to be found within the modification of our own human mind'. Compare Berlin, 1976, pp. 79–114, for the modifications of the concept.

24   Vico reminds us of the meaning of the word 'religion' in Vico, 1948, para. 503.

25   Fustel de Coulanges, 1956. Fustel does not quote Vico in his book, but it must be assumed that he was familiar with Jules Michelet's translation of Vico. He was in contact with Michelet in Michelet's last years. Fustel's students appear to have been aware of his Vichianism; they are reported as having mocked him with a chant: 'Qui est-ce qui a pillé Vico? C'est Fustel!' cf. Guiraud, 1895, pp. 324–34. Indeed, Fustel's theme seems indicated in Vico, 1948, para. 341, where Vico states that 'man in his bestial state desires only his own welfare; having taken a wife and begotten children, he desires his own welfare along with that of his family; having entered upon civil life, he desires his own welfare along with that of his city; when its rule is extended over several peoples, he desires his own welfare along with that of the nation; when the nations are united by war, treaties of peace, alliances and commerce, he desires his own welfare along with that of the entire human race'. I am obliged to the late Professor Benjamin Nelson and to Professors Louis Dumont and Yash Nandan for advice and assistance in matters of French sociology.

26   Durkheim, 1961. Durkheim refers to Fustel de Coulanges in the preface to the first volume of *L'Année sociologique*; in the preface to the second volume he points out that religion takes first place in the analyses contained in the *Année* because religious phenomena are those from which all other phenomena are derived. Benjamin Nelson refers to the Vico–Durkheim connection in his 1976 review paper.

27   Febvre *et al.*, 1930. The most important contribution in that volume is Marcel Mauss's treatise, 'Les civilisations – éléments et formes', pp. 87–106. One of the participants in the forum discussions was Alfredo Niceforo, professor of statistics at the University of Naples. A further extension of the topic of civilization is found in Braudel, 1966. In the preface to the second edition, Braudel acknowledges his indebtedness to Marc Bloch and Lucien Fèbvre.

28   About Jules Michelet, see note 25 above. Compare Pons, 1969.

29   The affinity of German romantic thought in philosophy and historiography with Vico's approach, especially with the appreciation of mythology and with the concept of *nascimento*, has repeatedly been stressed, but never closely investigated. Croce (1964, pp. 249ff., 323 *et passim*) pointed to the similarities, even if he may have overemphasized the idealistic tendencies in Vico's thought; a German (Austrian) author whom Croce held in high esteem, Karl Werner, was emphatic in the contention that Vico's ideas, even without direct acquaintance of German scholars with his writings, had been carried forward to completion in German linguistic and ethno-

logical studies and, as far as the *verum factum* is concerned, in the identity philosophy of Schelling (Werner, 1879, pp. 58–9, 320–5). Even more pertinent were Schelling's lectures on the philosophy of mythology. The closest affinity is with Herder, recently noted by Berlin (1976, pp. 143–216). Focher, 1977, pp. 107–26, compares Vico and Droysen.

30 Note Dilthey's (1957, Vol. 7, p. 148) sentence which reminds one of Vico: 'The mind understands only what it has itself created.' The reference to Vico is in ch. XV. The best recent work on Dilthey in English is Makkreel, 1975.

31 Compare Focher, 1977, pp. 45–61, 102. Focher further points out that philosophy provides the concrete substratum for the scientific understanding of historical processes (pp. 97f.). Focher's contention is borne out by Vico (1948, para. 138): 'Philosophy contemplates reason, whence comes knowledge of the true; philology observes that of which human choice is author, whence comes consciousness of the certain.'

32 About the meaning of dichotomy in Toennies, see Cahnman, 1973, introduction, p. 12.

33 Cahnman and Heberle, 1971, pp. 288, 318. These passages are translations from *Fortschritt und soziale Entwicklung* (1926) and *Geist der Neuzeit* (1935).

3

Max Weber and
Contemporary Sociology

DENNIS H. WRONG

Max Weber has no peers in the breadth of his influence on modern sociology. His ideas on bureaucracy, structures of political authority, social stratification, the ethical codes governing economic activities, religious world-views and legal systems are still *used* in concrete investigations of these subjects. My major aim in this chapter is to review briefly Weber's influence on several centrally important fields of study within sociology. Yet, in addition to the continuing relevance of his work to major subfields, Weber must be assessed as one of a small group of 'classical' nineteenth- and early twentieth-century social thinkers who are regarded as *general* sociological theorists.

Theory is not, however, a sort of special effects department within sociology to be displayed and celebrated only on ritual occasions when we wish to impress others – and for that matter, ourselves – with our capacity to rise above the timebound preoccupations and the frequently routinized operations of everyday research pursuits. The best research is linked to and penetrated by larger theoretical concerns. But we also seek a unified general perspective on human nature and society as well as on the world we live in, shaped by the convulsions of modern history of which sociology itself is a distinctive intellectual product. Theory at this level answers to a need that is independent both of specific investigations and of the history of sociology or social thought considered as a special subfield of sociology devoted to recounting the achievements of illustrious ancestors.

The failure of our multiple particular researches conducted with ever more precise and complex methods to cumulate into a coherent overall vision of the world largely accounts for the immense flowering of interest in recent years in the so-called classical sociologists of which this lecture series is itself evidence. And the new interest has been especially pronounced in the cases of Marx and Weber, both of whose work was pre-eminently historical in focus, guided by what the Marxist philosopher Karl Korsch called the 'principle of historical specificity'. In Weber's case, much of the voluminous recent scholarship devoted to him has involved revisions and correction of earlier images, especially in the English-speaking world. To a considerable extent this effort was made necessary by the partial and uneven translation and publication of his major works – indeed, some important writings have still not appeared in English. But selective theoretical and ideological perception has also played a major role, probably more so than in the case of the other classical sociologists except for Marx, where rather different considerations account for the almost endless process of reinterpreting him.

Indeed, a major theme of recent discussions of Weber has been his relation to Marx and Marxism, discussions that have revised the simplistic view of Weber as an 'idealist' critic of Marxist 'materialism' based on *The Protestant Ethic and the Spirit of Capitalism*, the first of Weber's major writings to be translated into English and to become widely known. The Parsonian interpretation of Weber exaggerated the differences from Marx in many areas and sometimes tended to present Weber as a kind of anti-Marx. One of the first overviews of Weber's sociology in English, antedating Parsons's 1937 discussion in *The Structure of Social Action*, was that of Albert Saloman, whose writings on Weber are largely remembered for his description of Weber as the 'bourgeois Marx' and his later claim that Weber's sociology was 'a long and intense dialogue with the ghost of Karl Marx'. The label retains a certain appositeness, but the characterization of Weber's sociology is not really tenable. Weber's stature in the Anglo-American world has become so great that Marxists and neo-Marxists today are prone to try to assimilate him to Marx, seeing him as expanding upon a number of themes first adumbrated by Marx which have become more salient in this century, such as the greater bureaucratization of capitalism and the state and their increasing interpenetration. This perspective was ably presented by Hans Gerth and C. Wright Mills in their introduction to the first book-length selection in English of Weber's sociological writings, which appeared in 1946. In more recent versions one sometimes detects an inclination to dispose of Weber by annexing him to an essentially Marxist outlook, but that Weber and Marx are less at odds than was formerly believed, at least at the level of their substantive interpretations, seems to me to be undeniable.

Some Marxists of a doctrinaire cast of mind, unable simply to dismiss Weber as a bourgeois ideologue – though efforts to do so continue – have tried to cope with him by claiming that his most valuable ideas are directly borrowed from Marxism. On the other hand, disillusioned Marxists or neo-Marxists, whose hopes have been irretrievably shaken by two world wars, the creation in Russia and elsewhere of new political and social tyrannies in the name of Marxism and the stolidly non-revolutionary temper of the working class in capitalist countries have often tended to cannibalize Weber, drawing heavily on his vision while reformulating it in more congenial neo-Marxist or Hegelian terms. I have in mind particularly the original Frankfurt school theorists. As Raymond Aron, the man who introduced Weber into France, wrote of Herbert Marcuse's famous attack on Weber at the 1964 Heidelberg conference honoring the centennial of Weber's birth:

> Have events proved Max Weber wrong? It is quite obvious that they have borne him out, as even Herbert Marcuse admits ... Herbert Marcuse cannot forgive Max Weber for having denounced in advance as a utopia something that up to now had indeed turned out to be utopian: the idea of a liberation of man by the modification of the system of ownership and a planned economy. (1967, p. 250)

That is what sticks in the craw of Marxists to this day even more than Weber's ironic definition of himself as a 'class-conscious bourgeois'. For he engaged Marxists on their very own terrain with superior intellectual resources, often reached similar conclusions about past and contemporary history, and yet unreservedly rejected their historical optimism. Marxism, even in its complex and subtle variants that are influential in Western universities today, remains a political faith affirming the unity of theory and practice, however unconsummated that unity is presently conceded to be by 'Western' Marxists shorn of any illusions about the oppressive practice of all existing communist states. Although Weber died just a few years after the Bolshevik seizure of power, he foresaw almost immediately that it would prove to be a historical disaster for the Russian people, producing 'mounds of corpses'.[1]

Weber was equally blunt in rejecting the revolutionary means as well as the utopian ends cherished by Marxism: 'He "who wishes to live as modern man" even if this be "only in the sense that he has his daily paper, railways, electricity, etc.," must resign himself to the loss of ideals of radical revolutionary change: indeed he must abandon "the *conceivability* of such a goal".' [2] Recent events in France in 1968, in Chile and Portugal in the 1970s and the appearance of what has come to be called 'Eurocommunism' have in different ways powerfully confirmed this conclusion. Today's 'Marxists of the chair', a species at long and welcome last becoming established in the American university, often expound a Marxism that owes more to non-Marxist thought than to the original doctrine. In particular, the eschatological hopes invested in the proletariat have been considerably diluted or abandoned to the point where some latter-day self-described Marxist theoreticians remind one of the death-of-God theologians who made a brief stir in the 1960s. They have tacitly accepted the diagnosis of modern industrial civilization that Weber advanced with bleak but unsurpassed clarity over sixty years ago. Yet Marx remains for them an iconic figure while Weber continues to arouse their ambivalence.

Western Marxists who long ago rejected the world of the Gulag Archipelago often remain reluctant even to acknowledge that world as a form of Marxist 'praxis', if not the only imaginable one. Self-declared Marxists, after all, rule states containing over a third of the world's population, whereas Weberians control no more than a few professorships. An American Marxist professor once complained to me rather bitterly of an eminent colleague: 'He thinks it fine to love Tocqueville, but you're not supposed to love Marx.' Such an attitude was certainly not uncommon in American sociology until fairly recently, but I found it hard to refrain from remarking – though I did refrain – that in the world at large people have been killed for not loving Marx, or for not loving him in the prescribed way. To be sure, people have also been killed for loving him, though not quite as many; the numbers in both cases, however, run to the millions. But no one has ever been killed for not loving Tocqueville or Max Weber.

Twenty years ago I described Max Weber as 'the one great man we sociologists can plausibly claim as our own', a judgement with which I concur if anything more than ever today. But the word 'plausibly' was deliberately inserted in the statement with Marx in mind, for it is possible to deny that Marx was essentially or fundamentally a sociologist but not that he was a great man, who, whatever the fate of the movements launched in his name, achieved an encompassing grasp of wide swaths of human history without, like so many of his contemporaries and his own epigoni, sacrificing concrete detail to the conceptual demands of an abstract scheme. In reaction against such schemes, Weber was deeply suspicious of wide-ranging developmental theories, but the scope and depth of his own historical work achieves as much as Marx's the level of universal history. Marx and Weber are therefore likely to continue to be linked together less as antipodal figures than as sources of inspiration for the large-scale comparative-historical sociology toward which the more ambitious social scientists in a number of countries are increasingly moving now that the view that the natural sciences present an appropriate model for the social sciences to emulate has been epistemologically dethroned.

One is moved to speculate that if Marx had been born several decades later in the less embattled political climate of the Wilhelminian *Rechtstaat*, he would have achieved the professorship to which he initially aspired, though he would doubtless, like Weber, have been a controversial figure standing at the borderline between scholarship and politics. If Weber, on the other hand, had been born early in the last century, it is hard to believe that he would not have been driven into exile by the Prussian authorities when one recalls his outspoken contempt for cant and bombast, his willingness to attack fiercely the educational authorities on behalf of controversial scholars denied deserved appointments or preferments, and the fears aroused among his friends that his unrestrained denunciations of the Kaiser's war policies would be regarded as treasonable even in the surprisingly free atmosphere of wartime Imperial Germany. Such speculation is, of course, a vain pastime according to the very tenets shared by Marx and Weber which would deny that it makes any sense to imagine persons apart from their actual historical context while assuming that they retain essentially the same identity.

The present revival of broad comparative history which recognizes both Marx and Weber as ancestors is an interdisciplinary project involving both sociologists and historians who have overcome the traditional barriers that have long divided them. In its fidelity to the actual historical record, the new comparative history even at its most ambitious bears little resemblance to the all-embracing systems of such nineteenth-century sociologists as Comte and Spencer, who tried to impose abstract nomological straitjackets on the disorderly and variegated materials of actual history. If we turn, however, to the discipline of sociology as presently conceived in the United States, Weber's influence is considerably more pervasive than that of Marx. The deliberately provocative but only slightly overstated assertion of a recent writer suggests one reason for this:

Remembering that we are speaking in strictly quantitative terms rather than qualitative ones, the sociology of Weber compares to that of Marx as, let us say, *The Brothers Karamazov* does to

Little Red Riding Hood. No one can deny that *Little Red Riding Hood* is a profound tale. But there really is not very much of it. (Dotson, 1974, p. 186)

I am aware that efforts to create a 'Marxist' criminology, political sociology, theory of the family and sex roles, sociology of education, and a host of other recognized fields of study within sociology are prominent today. However, most of these efforts deal with subjects on which Marx and Engels had little or nothing to say or occasionally held views at variance with those advanced by their present-day followers. The wish to elaborate alleged 'Marxist perspectives' on crime or the family follows from the fact that Marxism, as distinct from the actual writings of Marx, strives for the closure of a total world-view – or *Weltanschauung* in the German word which possesses untranslatable overtones. The same is not true of Weber's work. His concepts or themes are picked up where helpful in analyzing particular problems but there is no pressure toward closure giving rise even to a distinctive Weberian school of theory let alone to an outlook embracing both a theory of society and a political program.

Weber's intellectual concerns, in fact, were so diverse and far-ranging that there has been a tendency to regard him as an extra-ordinary polymath whose work remained highly fragmented and lacking in coherence and continuity. Recent Weber scholarship has done much to correct this view. In assessing Weber's impact on American sociology, however, I shall consider it in relation to the established specialties of the field rather than according to the natural lines of division in his work that have been carefully drawn by recent Weber scholars. I shall nevertheless note where the use made of Weberian concepts has involved considerable wrenching of them out of their context in the total corpus of his work. By 'established specialties' I mean simply those subfields of sociology that are the subjects of course offerings, textbooks and anthologies of readings, and that are recognized as distinctive 'areas of competence' by the American Sociological Association.

Formal Organizations

It is scarcely an exaggeration to say that the very existence of this field stems from Weber's conception of bureaucracy. Some contribution to its emergence was made by the field of public administration and by the industrial sociology of the 1930s and 1940s which was centered in the Harvard Business School and was theoretically influenced by Pareto and Durkheim. Today industrial sociology in the United States has been almost entirely absorbed into the field of formal organizations. The study of formal or complex organizations is one of the most highly developed areas of contemporary sociology in its integration of theory and research, but as a recognized specialty it does not predate the 1950s. Published Columbia doctoral dissertations by Peter Blau, Alvin Gouldner and Philip Selznick got the field under way[3] and all of them took as their point of departure the Weberian model of bureaucracy available for the first time to an English-speaking audience in translations published in the late 1940s.

Weber, of course, did not invent the concept of bureaucracy: Hegel and Marx used it, Saint-Simon at least implied it, and such nineteenth-century novelists as Gogol, Balzac and Dickens (not to speak of Kafka early in the present century) satirized it. Weber's achievement was to extend it from the realm of government to other areas of social organization, to identify bureaucratization as a master trend in modern society, and – most important to American sociologists – to define it formally as a generic type of social structure. American social scientists took the Weberian model as a point of departure for the empirical observation and analysis of a huge variety of special-purpose organizations which, not surprisingly, were often found to deviate from the attributes of the model.

Apart from its legitimating a new field of empirical research, the early users of Weber's concept were actuated by two extra-sociological aims. First, the Weberian model could be used to defend the welfare state of the New Deal – and even the idea of 'socialism' – against its conservative political opponents who made an epithet of the label 'bureaucrat' in their diatribes against 'red tape', desk-warming civil servants feeding at the public trough, and the like. Weber's emphasis on the efficiency of bureaucracy as a means to the achievement of clearly defined collective goals served as a defense against its detractors: 'The decisive reason for the advance of bureaucratic organization has always been its purely technical superiority over any other form of organization. The fully bureaucratic mechanism compares with other organizations exactly as does the machine with nonmechanical modes of production' (Gerth and Mills, 1948, p. 214). At the same time, Weber's insistence that bureaucratization was not confined to government but encompassed the corporate economy as well drew the sting from the arguments of the defenders of 'free enterprise' against state intervention in the economy.

A second aim, following from the first, was to reformulate the idea of bureaucracy in order to make it less incompatible with the

American democratic and egalitarian ethos. This involved the divesting of the Weberian concept of its heavy emphasis on hierarchical authority, impersonal relations and the suppression of individual initiative. The accounts by the Harvard industrial sociologists of the emergence of an 'informal structure' of social relations in large organizations, modifying and bypassing the formally prescribed rules and lines of authority, were widely employed for this purpose. Weber's relative neglect of 'staff' as opposed to hierarchical 'line' positions in organizations and his failure to discuss the collegial ties central to the professions were also stressed in this connection, especially by Talcott Parsons.

These uses and modifications of Weber's model tended to ignore the duality of his own outlook toward bureaucracy as, on the one hand, an indispensable rational instrumentality under the conditions of modern life, and, on the other, as a 'living machine' which 'in union with the dead machine . . . is laboring to produce the cage of that bondage of the future to which one day powerless men will be forced to submit like the fellaheen of ancient Egypt' (1968, p. 1402). American liberal-democratic social scientists found Weber's historical pessimism, based on the fear of a trend toward total bureaucratization, no easier to stomach than did Marxists. The 'counterculture' of the 1960s, on the other hand, has given far greater resonance to Weber's despair over the 'iron cage' of modern society, though it often assumed oppositional stances that he would have regarded as sentimental and unrealistic.

Indeed, the negative side of Weber's view of bureaucracy has in recent years almost completely overshadowed the positive side. What one writer has called 'bureaucracy baiting' has become as characteristic of the left as of the right.[4] Bureaucracy is presented as an implacable force opposing both personal freedom and popular democracy. Weber's emphasis on the essential passivity of bureaucracies, their availability to any political leaders strong and determined enough to use them, is ignored in this view. Nor has the possibility of combining democratic leadership and control with a reliable and efficient civil service, advocated by Weber in the last few years of his life, received anything like the attention given to his more pessimistic statements about the spread of bureaucratization.

Specialists in the study of formal organizations have often distorted Weber in a different way. Their procedure of treating the Weberian concept as a tool with which to study particular bureaucratic organizations abstracts the idea of bureaucracy from Weber's historical sociology. He did not develop the concept for the purpose of comparing different bureaucracies – government agencies, factories, hospitals, custodial institutions, and the like – but rather to contrast bureaucratic organization as such with its non-bureaucratic counterparts and to note the increasing expansion of the former in modern industrial societies. Mommsen has made this point very succinctly:

> It is small wonder that some sociologists found that Weber's concept of bureaucracy – in so far as it overemphasizes the role of subordinance, discipline, and formal rationality – does not altogether fit the empirical reality of present-day bureaucracies. It may well be said, however, that this was intentional, that is to say that the 'ideal type' of 'bureaucracy' was deliberately designed by Weber in such a way as to serve as a yardstick which would be used to ascertain in exact terms the tremendous cultural significance which the rise of modern bureaucracies possesses for conscientious citizens living in liberal societies of the western type ... If all this is taken into account it could be somewhat misleading to criticize Weber's 'ideal type' of 'bureaucracy' as a one-sided concept. For it was deliberately 'one-sided', in order to serve as an epistemological tool for cognition on a truly universal-historical level. (1974, p. 19)

Social Stratification

Marx, of course, long ago placed classes and class structures at the very center of sociological and historical analysis and his views have loomed large in most theoretical discussion ever since. The first two generations of American sociologists dealt with class stratification and several of them devoted respectful though not uncritical attention to Marx. Empirical research on class and inequality began in the 1920s and mushroomed in the 1930s and 1940s. One is even surprised to realize that it was as late as the 1950s that social stratification became fully established as a sociological specialty: the first book of readings was the 1953 Bendix–Lipset volume, the first textbook was published in 1954, the second a year later, and two more in 1957 (Bendix and Lipset, 1953; Cuber and Kenkel, 1954; Mayer, 1955; Kahl, 1957; Barber, 1957). Yet sociological interest in stratification, often then as today reflecting liberal-radical political concerns, was already so intense in the 1930s that anyone who, like myself, first encountered sociology in the 1940s was scarcely aware that these books of the 1950s were actually the first of their kind.

As in the case of formal organizations, the institutionalization of stratification as a field came only a few years after the translation of Weber's writings on the subject. The very title of the Bendix–Lipset reader – *Class, Status, and Power* – echoes Weber's tridimensional view of stratification and two of the four textbooks mentioned earlier were organized according to Weber's conceptualization. However, in contrast to the study of formal organization, the persisting presence at least in the background of Marxism as a positive or negative influence, and the existence of a research tradition going back to the 1920s, would probably have ensured that stratification achieved the status of a specialty roughly at the time it did even without Weber. American social scientists have long displayed an understandable, if sometimes obsessive, interest in social mobility, a subject scarcely dealt with at all by Weber or, for that matter, by Marx. The title of an undergraduate course I still teach at NYU, 'Class and Caste', reflects another longstanding concern of American sociologists. Like an archaeological relic, it points back to the preoccupations of several decades ago, for 'caste' refers not primarily to the Hindu caste system but to the application of this label to American race relations, especially in the South, a prime object of study by stratification researchers in the 1930s.

The Weberian triad of status, wealth and power is indispensable to the study of social inequality and class structure, although the interdependences among the three are as important a subject of investigation as the distinction itself. This has not always been recognized by American sociologists whose quick acceptance of the triad was not free of selective distortion. The concept of 'status-group' is sometimes employed as a counter to the economically based Marxist concept of class, although Weber never contended that status-groups were *more* important in modern society than classes, which he, like Marx, grounded in the economy, merely that they were distinguishable. Weber's emphasis on status was also sometimes invoked in support of a quite different use of the term: its equation with the prestige rankings of individuals or positions (usually occupations) derived by the favored methods of survey research. But Weber wrote of status-groups, not of status as an attribute of individuals or positions, and he did not identify status-groups with a rank order reflecting an underlying consensus on values in society. Far from implying consensus, conflict between status groups was in Weber's view just as prevalent as class conflict. Incidentally, one of the two Weberian terms which have passed into popular usage, 'life-style', comes from his description of status-groups (the other is, of course, 'charisma'). But Weber meant by 'style of life' the shared values and customs that gave a group its sense of collective identity, not a way of living freely selected because of its congruence with individual psychological needs as the term is usually employed today.

Political Sociology

Nearly all of the classical sociologists were concerned at some level with politics, even though – or perhaps because – the hallmark of the sociological perspective as it arose in the nineteenth century was to claim historical, causal and normative priority for society over the state. This, in conjunction with the later almost simultaneous development of political science as a discipline, retarded the emergence of political sociology as a sociological specialty. As Seymour Martin Lipset, who has probably done more than anyone else to win official status for political sociology as a specialized area of competence within sociology, has observed: 'The term political sociology has come to be accepted within both sociology and political science as encompassing the overlap between the two parental disciplines' (1967, p. 438). The fact that the major areas of research in political sociology were originally explored within older specialties also accounts for the delayed recognition of political sociology in the United States: for example, the association of voting studies with the field of public opinion and mass communications, of community power research with stratification and urban sociology, and of studies of social movements with collective behavior. In any case, there were no readers in political sociology as such before the 1960s, although there were several on voting behavior and on social movements. Except for Rudolph Heberle's *Social Movements* which appeared as early as 1951 and was subtitled 'An Introduction to Political Sociology', the only two general textbooks in political sociology were published in the 1970s and the two authors of one of them are British.[5]

In short, political sociology, like formal organizations and social stratification, began to emerge as a specialty not long after publication of the first translations of Weber's sociological writings. (His many commentaries on the political issues of his time remain untranslated, as does Mommsen's important study of his political views.) Weber's concept of legitimation, his threefold typology of legitimate authority, his definitions of the state and of power and his treatment of bureaucracies as power structures (which influenced his contemporary, Robert Michels) have had a far-reaching effect on the theoretical formulations of political scientists as well as political sociologists. Weber alone of the 'classical' sociologists, including Marx, did not treat the state and politics as secondary phenomena subordinate to autonomous 'social forces'. Of nine-teenth-century social thinkers, only Tocqueville bears comparison with Max Weber in this respect and his insights were less system-atically developed. Traditional Marxism, like its bourgeois counter-parts, has a dusty Victorian ring and has required strong infusions from later thinkers, including Weber, in order to retain the appearance of relevance to our time, not to speak of its embar-rassments in confronting the record of the movements and regimes it has itself inspired. Max Weber of all the classical sociologists seems most to be our contemporary, for the troubled history of the twentieth century has cast doubt, to put it mildly, on the classical ascription of primacy to the social over the political. Totalitarianism has merely deviated furthest in achieving the com-plete ascendancy of the latter over the former.

The three fields I have reviewed – formal organizations, strati-fication and political sociology – are the substantive core of what has come to be called macrosociology: the study of the larger collectivities and their interrelations within whole societies. If we follow Weber's own method of 'objective possibility' and imagine away his influence on these fields, two of them would be gravely impoverished conceptually, and one of them, formal organizations, would in all likelihood not exist at all as a separate specialty. Doubtless all sorts of people would be engaged in studying large organizations of all kinds, but their efforts would probably be spread over several specialties including some in disciplines other than sociology.[6] To put it as bluntly and simply as possible, eliminate the concepts of 'bureaucracy', 'status-group' and 'legiti-mation', and macrosociology would be theoretically polarized be-tween a crude Marxism and a crude functionalism with an even greater predominance of close-to-the-ground atheoretical empiricism than exists at present.

Organizations, social classes and state structures are not, of course, sufficiently autonomous entities for us to be able to consider them for very long in isolation from one another. Classes are the largest 'horizontal' divisions within societies: loose, solidary communities coalescing around shared values and interests. In-creasingly, large organizations have become the warp cutting vertically across the woof of the class structure, binding societies into tighter, more coherent unities. State structures are a system or complex of intermeshing large organizations which extend across and down the loom or frame-setting boundaries to a particular society. All three are tightly interwoven and yet each can be distinguished as a separate and partially independent pattern. The nineteenth-century belief that the state and other salient institutional structures are merely instruments or byproducts of more fundamental 'social forces', such as the class structure, is as untenable as the older belief that the state both shapes and most fully expresses the social order, as well as more recent claims, usually heavy with pathos, that modern men and women are mere puppets (if, often, willing ones) manipulated by numerous organizations invisibly coordinated – at least in extreme versions of this view – to form a total monolithic system. Max Weber's careful explorations of the trend toward bureaucracy, the formation of class and status communities growing out of market situations and ethnic and kinship ties, and the concentration of both force and ultimate legitimacy in the over-arching structure of the state provide us with a starting point toward understanding the varying interactions among all of these structures and processes in different historical situations. Weber's work provides no more than a starting point, but we have yet to move much beyond it at the level of macrosociological theory.[7]

The three fields influenced by Weber that I have reviewed are all primarily concerned with social organization. If a sociology of economic life ever develops as a recognized specialty, it will join them in owing a large debt to Weber. The sociology of culture rather than of social organization is a larger component of the other specialties in which Weber's influence has been great. He is with Durkheim one of the two major theorists of the sociology of religion. Without reducing religious ideas to simple reflections of the social location of the classes and communities that upheld them, he explored their intimate connection with the concrete situations in which their creators and carriers found themselves. If *The Protestant Ethic* was in part a polemic against 'historical materialism', Weber's later comparative sociology of religion displays many points of convergence with Marxist-inspired perspectives. Weber was highly sensitive to the continuities between the secular political ideologies of modern history and older religious world-views, to the ways in which the 'ghost of dead religious beliefs ... prowls about in our lives'. The application of his typologies of religious leaders and belief systems to the modalities of political faith is still far from complete. Weber was formally educated in the law and his earliest scholarship dealt with legal institutions. Since much of it remains untranslated, or has been translated only recently, his influence on the sociology of law, especially in comparative historical scholarship, is bound to increase. His writings on the sociology of music and of architecture are major contributions to these undeveloped fields.

What, finally, of so-called general theory in sociology? I have chosen to concentrate on Weber's influence in special fields because that is where he has had the greatest immediate impact and all of his writings that present general concepts of social action or that deal with the methodology of the social sciences were intended to guide substantive inquiry by codifying, rather than prescribing for, the actual practice of scholars in history and the social sciences. Weber's later work concentrated on the elaboration, especially in *Economy and Society*, of a comprehensive typology of social action, norms, groups, belief-systems and institutional structures for which he accepted the label 'sociology' that he had previously resisted. His approach has been criticized as taxonomy rather than true theory because it does not produce generalizations asserting invariant – that is, transhistorical – relations between types of action and social structures. This criticism presupposes the hypothetico-deductive conception of science that has been widely assailed in recent years even in its application to the physical sciences on which it purports to model itself. Where the social sciences are concerned, we have at last in the Anglo-American world caught up with the famous *Methodenstreit* in German historical and social science scholarship of the decades before the First World War, though not without repeating many of the errors and excesses committed by the participants in that debate to which Weber addressed himself in his methodological writings.

To Weber, general concepts were mainly instruments rather than the final goals of social science scholarship,[8] for, as Guenther Roth, the editor and partial translator of the English edition of *Economy and Society*, has observed: 'The sociology of *Economy and Society* is "Clio's handmaiden"; the purpose of comparative study is the explanation of a given historical problem' (1968, p. xxxi). This is so because, in contrast to the subject matter of much of natural science, what we most urgently want to know about human affairs is usually historically specific. Why did the Vietnam War give rise to a vigorous protest movement whereas the Korean War little over a decade before did not? Why did the birth rate go up in the 1950s and down in the 1960s? Generalizations about the conditions under which wars become unpopular or the factors influencing fertility are of some help, but even in a rigorously quantitative field like demography we cannot escape confrontation with the gritty particulars of a given time and place. Now that our sociology has been largely cured of the 'waiting for Newton syndrome' (Wrong, 1978, pp. 34–7), Weber's 'historicism' can more readily be perceived as a strength rather than a weakness.

A recent use of Weber that distorts his aims in a different direction from that of positivist science-building is the taking of his definitions of social action and social relations in the first part of *Economy and Society* as the point of departure for working out a general epistemology of the social world of everyday life, for the construction, in effect, of a thoroughgoing microsociology. Alfred Schutz was a pioneer in this effort and has been a major influence in ethnomethodology and other brands of social phenomenology. But Weber was not a philosopher or epistemologist *manqué,* let alone a phenomenologist, and his 'Some categories of an understanding (*verstehende*) sociology', the title of the recently translated essay that was the forerunner of Part One of *Economy and Society,* was intended both to demolish the reification of collective concepts and yet to make possible a transition from the directly present world of 'everyday life' to the analysis of large-scale institutions and processes of historical change, a transition that phenomenologists have been either unable or unwilling to make.

Weber does not easily lend himself to the categorizations favored by writers of textbooks and taxonomists of sociological theories. Specious though such pedagogic labelling often is, at least a modicum of plausibility exists for calling Marx a 'conflict theorist', Durkheim and Parsons 'functionalists' or 'consensualists', and various people 'exchange' or 'phenomenological' or 'symbolic interactionist' theorists. Weber fails to fit under any of these familiar rubrics nor under those that stress epistemological standpoints ranging from strict positivism to pure hermeneutics. 'Historicist' perhaps suits him best, but most sociologists have felt uncomfortable with the label (Collins, 1975). Their historical knowledge, especially in America, has usually been limited and in Weber they confront a man whose works, in Mommsen's words, 'display an abundance of historical knowledge which has so far not been surpassed by anyone else, with the possible exception of Arnold Toynbee' (1974, p. 3). American sociologists have often regarded sociology as a kind of intellectual short-cut providing nomological formulae under which historical particulars can be subsumed, thus eliminating the necessity of understanding them directly in their complex particularity. Weber's vast and detailed knowledge seems to reproach sociologists for their *hubris,* especially since he makes little claim to derive from it universal generalizations, in contrast to Toynbee's 'challenge and response' theory of civilization which can be identified with a familiar tradition of theorizing and criticized for its vague, metaphorical character.

Sometimes sociologists read into Weber generalizations that are not actually there. One again and again encounters the assertion that *The Protestant Ethic* is a sociological study attempting to demonstrate that religious beliefs influence economic activities. It can justifiably be maintained that this broad proposition was both a presupposition and a conclusion of Weber's *later* comparative studies of the world religions, but *The Protestant Ethic* argues no more than that the ideas of certain sixteenth- and seventeenth-century Protestant divines influenced the attitudes toward economic pursuits of their adherents. *The Protestant Ethic*, in short, is an interpretive essay on the origins of the capitalist spirit in early modern European history[9] rather than an attempt at sociological generalization of either a transhistorical or developmental sort – a bold and ambitious historical interpretation, to be sure, but no more – and no less – than that.

Weber at one time resisted the label 'sociologist' and preferred to call himself a comparative historian. It can be argued that the core of sociology is the comparative analysis of social structures and historical change (or of social structures *in* historical change), that the best historical work is at least implicitly comparative rather than limited to the analysis of single cases, and that the artificiality of disciplinary boundary-lines between history and the social sciences is becoming increasingly apparent. However, even some sociologists strongly committed to comparative historical work would regard these assertions as conceding too much to historical singularity and would qualify them by claiming a larger role both for transhistorical statements and for generalizations about types of structures and processes within broad historical limits (Collins, 1975). Weber himself eventually defined his later work as sociology and in *Economy and Society* he unmistakably undertook to distill from the flux and variety of history general as well as historically individualized typologies, including, of course, the well-known classifications of universal social actions, relations and groups in Part One of the book. Most sociologists can be located at different points on a continuum between the poles of generalizing and individualizing interpretation and conceptualization; there is unlikely ever to be agreement on a 'correct' location. For the continuum itself reflects the heterogeneity of the questions we put to social reality. Weber stands closer to the individualizing pole – even his typologies in *Economy and Society* are, as Roth puts it, 'historically saturated'.

But Max Weber was more than a scholar of prodigious learning. Even his most specialized and objective writings communicate an underlying tension and moral passion, a 'pathos of objectivity' in Gerth and Mills's incisive phrase. Moreover, he never confined himself to 'scholarship as a vocation' but was constantly drawn to politics even if in the end his career as a political man was an abortive one. Thus he demands to be assessed according to the ultimate values that gave his life and work a unity despite the apparent fragmentation of his omnivorous intellectual concerns.

There is much justification for regarding Weber as an existentialist *avant la lettre*. To his close friend Karl Jaspers Weber himself was an existentialist hero, and Jaspers claimed that his own existentialist philosophy was inspired by the example of Weber as 'the man who embodied human greatness', who 'lived in the only way possible for a man of integrity in those times: breaking through all illusory forms he disclosed the foundations of human Existenz' (Jaspers, 1964, pp. 193, 257). Weber's indebtedness to Nietzsche, generally regarded now as one of the fathers of existentialism, has been increasingly recognized by his more recent interpreters. Weber's conception of the relationship between values and knowledge can now be seen as much more existentialist than positivist. His insistence on 'value freedom' or 'ethical neutrality' as a prerequisite for any social science worthy of the name has long been upheld by American sociologists as the first commandment of their calling. Younger sociologists involved in the protest movements of the 1960s attacked value neutrality as a self-serving defense of professional interests, as an excuse for political indifference and simply as a sham violated in the actual research of many who proclaimed it. Neither side in this rancorous dispute, now thankfully showing signs of moving to higher intellectual ground, did justice to Weber's position whether in claiming to affirm it or to reject it.

Weber did not argue for the exclusion of value judgements from social science because he regarded them as blind, irrational eruptions of human emotion posing a threat to the majestic authority of pure science. It was rather the other way around: he wished to preserve values as the realm of individual freedom subject to the dignity of responsible choice uncoerced by the constraints of the world of fact revealed by science, even in the face of a full and stoical awareness of these constraints. This was, of course, a Kantian position reflecting Weber's neo-Kantian philosophical heritage. But Weber differed from the Kantians in denying that there were objective values in which rational consensus was possible. He insisted rather that there was a plurality of irreconcilable values, that the world was one of 'warring gods' and that to align oneself with one of the gods meant to deny the claims of another who might be equally attractive and powerful. This position is existentialist or Nietzschean rather than Kantian: we are condemned to the often painful and even tragic choice between rival values and we cannot slough off the burden of choice by claiming that it is not ourselves but the world as understood by science that dictates our conduct.

More recent criticisms of Weber's assertion of the dichotomy of fact and value have not mistaken him for a positivist but have correctly understood his existentialism and have challenged the 'decisionism' it entails at the level of action. Jürgen Habermas, for example, contends that Weber denies the possibility of rational consensus on values implied in language itself, if only realized in an 'ideal speech situation' undistorted by unequal power relations among the speakers (1973, pp. 95–102). Weber's insistence on the 'ethical irrationality' of the world and the consequent irreducible arbitrariness of value choices limits reason and empirical knowledge to a purely instrumental role and makes superior power the only basis for implementing one set of values at the expense of another set. Anthony Giddens has noted that Weber equated values with *ends* – the termini of concrete, situated actions – and ignored their role as *standards* guiding the selection of particular ends.[10] Weber fails therefore to recognize the contributions made by empirical knowledge and rational argumentation to agreement on value standards.

These standpoints are essentially Kantian. They affirm the reality of formal criteria for adjudicating differences in values in what amounts to a renovated, linguistically sophisticated version of the categorical imperative. But Weber's existential decisionism is rooted in his sensitivity to the harsh exigencies of choosing between courses of action, choices that cannot be inferred from prior commitment to normative principles or value standards given the constraints of the contingent situations in which they must be made. Giddens is correct in maintaining that Weber identifies the relation of knowledge to values with the relation of means and ends in motivated conduct rather than with the justification of value standards. But Weber's sense of the inescapable antinomies of choice is precisely the ground of his existential vision, his 'tragic sense of life'. A conclave of sages from different cultures might conceivably agree that both resistance to foreign conquerors and caring for aged parents are 'ultimate' moral obligations, but the choice between these imperatives in a particular situation may still require a decision that is independent of both reason and evidence, as in Sartre's famous paradigm of existential choice: the young man who sought his advice in 1940 on whether he should join the Free French or stay home and take care of his devoted mother (1947, pp. 28–32). However resolvable value conflicts may be at the level of what Habermas calls 'discursive redemption', such conflicts cannot necessarily be resolved *situationally*. Weber's involvement in politics was obviously reflected in his view of the dilemmas of choice and his recognition at the same time of the 'damned duty' of choosing. 'World history is not a seminar' [11] and in practice some values can only be advanced at the cost of others.

For politics, Weber favored an 'ethic of responsibility' in preference to an 'ethic of intention' (or of 'absolute ends' as it has often – misleadingly, I think – been translated). An ethic of responsibility takes into account the consequences and further ramifications of realizing a particular end and also appraises an end in terms of the costs of attaining it. Empirical knowledge therefore enters into the consideration of ends to be pursued regardless of their status in some 'ultimate' scheme of values. Here Weber places less of an existentialist emphasis on the autonomy and irreducibility of the choice of ends and gives weight to the interaction of ends and means and their frequent interchangeability, treating knowledge and values as complementary rather than as sealed off from one another. Such a position is closer to that of John Dewey in his *Theory of Valuation* than to existentialism with its stress on unconditioned choice (Dewey, 1939, pp. 24–50). Dewey, indeed, can be seen as having spelled out systematically the full logic of Weber's ethic of responsibility. Significantly, a major concern of Dewey's was to criticize the extreme separation of values from facts in both logical positivist and non-naturalistic intuitionist theories of value (1939, pp. 6–13, 55–7). The affinity between Weber and Dewey casts doubt on the received view of Weber as the uncompromising exponent of an unbridgeable gulf between facts and values.

It is impossible to confront Weber without a sense of the man behind the work. He is the only one of the classical sociologists who has been the subject of a psychobiography (Mitzman, 1970), whose life and character have been made into a cultural symbol in a brilliant if tendentious study by a literary scholar (Green, 1974), and whose love letters, no less, are shortly to be published. Even Marx's life and personal history have not attracted comparable interest, largely because Marx's message was ultimately an affirmative one embraced by an entire movement whereas the tension and ambivalence of Weber's thought points in the direction of personal stoicism rather than collective commitment. The spell cast by the passion and the pathos Weber projects has been a source of irritation to his critics. Leo Strauss, for whom all of modern history was decline and fall, called him a 'noble nihilist' and complained that 'he had to combine the anguish bred by atheism (the absence of any redemption, of any solace) with the anguish bred by revealed religion (the oppressive sense of guilt)' or else 'life would cease to be tragic and thus lose its depth' (Strauss, 1963, pp. 430, 445–6).

Donald MacRae, a proper Scotsman, who has written a little book deliberately intended to 'demystify' Weber, remarks that 'practically all that is written on Weber is written in awe' with the result that 'when one is knocking one's forehead on the floor one's vision is certainly limited and probably blurred' (MacRae, 1974, p. 91). Marxists, starting with Georg Lukács who belonged to Weber's Heidelberg circle in his youth and whose later work still bore traces of Weber's influence, have regarded Weber's pessimism as evidence of the decadence and impending dissolution of the bourgeois civilization they hope to inherit.

Arthur Mitzman is not a Marxist, but there is a sense in which his judgement is clearly true: 'At the heart of Weber's vision lies only the truth of his epoch, his country and his station, the truth of a bourgeois scholar in Imperial Germany' (Mitzman, 1970, p. 3). That epoch and country are dead and gone, having produced a historical tragedy that Weber himself sensed in the tainted air. Even the memory of the tragedy is now fading. But why then Weber's continuing spell? I write unashamedly from within the circle of the bewitched, also as one who in middle age feels historical nostalgia for the time of his parents' childhood, the years of Weber's manhood, and, moreover, as one with little inclination to apologize for his own 'bourgeois values'. Part of the answer lies in one remark of Donald MacRae's with which I can agree: 'Our century has apparently dedicated itself, only half knowingly, to acting out the ideas and dreams of [early twentieth-century Europe] in deadly earnest' (1974, p. 92). By the late 1970s we are perhaps entitled to conclude that the acting out has almost ended. This too is a source of Weber's relevance, for he anticipated the trajectories of our belief, disbelief and unbelief. A world of 'specialists without vision and sensualists without heart' today sounds painfully more like a description of the way we live now than like the possible future described by Weber in 1905. And we have had a good deal of unsatisfactory experience with the 'entirely new prophets' and 'great rebirth of old ideas and ideals' that he expected to arise in reaction to the world of modernity. Although the imperatives facing us are scarcely the same, we are unable to improve upon his conclusion that 'nothing is gained by yearning and tarrying alone' and that what remains is for us to 'set to work and meet the "demands of the day", in human relations as well as in our vocation'.

Notes: Chapter 3

I should like to thank Buford Rhea for his scrupulous editorial attention to the original draft of this chapter. I have followed nearly all of his valuable suggestions in revising and expanding it. I am also grateful to Bryan Turner of the University of Aberdeen for several helpful comments.

1 In 1918 or 1919 Weber met Joseph Schumpeter in a Vienna coffeehouse. Schumpeter observed that he was delighted by the occurrence of the Russian Revolution because it would provide a laboratory test of the viability of socialism. Weber responded angrily, insisting that the revolution would lead to unparalleled human misery and would prove to be 'a laboratory filled with mounds of corpses'. Infuriated by Schumpeter's detachment, he rushed out of the cafe leaving his hat behind. See Jaspers, 1964, p. 222.

2 Giddens, 1972, p. 46. The entire statement sounds like Weber, but Giddens gives only partial quotation marks, citing as his source Mommsen's 1959 untranslated book on Weber's politics.

3 All three were students of Robert K. Merton who in 1952 was senior editor of the first reader in organizations: Merton, Gray, Hockey and Selvin (eds.), 1952.

4 Miller, 1978, pp. 205–22. For a recent qualified defense of bureaucracy by a socialist, see Pachter, 1978, pp. 304–6.

5 Dowse and Hughes, 1972; Orum, 1978. Several readers, most of them including 'political sociology' in their titles, appeared in the 1960s.

6 In England, for example, courses on formal organizations as such are rarely given in departments of sociology. Industrial sociology, however, remains a recognized subfield, reflecting the continuing salience of labor–management relations and conflicts in British society. Sociologists who specialize in the study of organizations hold teaching positions and even chairs in the fairly recently established schools of management and business, of which there are four in England and two in Scotland.

7 Collins, 1975, is an ambitious attempt to develop a general theory which centers on stratification, formal organizations and the state, and acknowledges a very large debt to Max Weber.

8 Collins (1975, pp. 34–7) criticizes the 'historic sociology' of Weber, his predecessors and heirs.

9 See Mommsen, 1974, pp. 10–13. This point is also made by Torrance, 1974, pp. 131–2.

10 Giddens, 1977, pp. 89–95. I have also drawn on fuller discussions of Weber in two lectures by Giddens at New York University in April 1977 and at Balliol College, Oxford, in April 1978.

11 Lowenthal, 1976, p. 266. Lowenthal's article is a critical analysis of Habermas's idea of legitimation crisis and he invokes Weber's insistence on the 'irreducible plurality of values' against Habermas's more consensual view (pp. 267–72).

4

Sociology's Quest for the Classics: The Case of Simmel

DONALD N. LEVINE

In a recent film whose title reads like the report of a microsociological investigation but which in fact deals with encounters between inhabitants of this planet and beings from outer space, certain characters appear inexorably driven to reach a curiously shaped mountain in Wyoming (Spielberg, 1977). They search for this mountain for reasons they do not fully understand but following impulses they believe to be terribly authentic and supremely 'important'.

Their saga reminds me of the quest of certain members of the sociological community to attain closer contact with what are commonly referred to as the classics of the sociological tradition. This quest is truly peculiar. It characterizes no other intellectual discipline I know of. It is indeed, to adopt the term for such quests used by actor François Truffaut in the film just referred to, a 'sociological phenomenon'.

The phenomenon can be located temporally with some precision. During the two decades preceding 1960 there were only two books published in the United States on the history of sociological theory and almost no serious secondary analyses of the classic authors. Sociologists seemed driven to *avoid* the classics, following with apparently fanatic devotion the injunction suggested by the Whiteheadian epigraph to Robert K. Merton's widely influential book of essays first published in 1949: 'A science which hesitates to forget its founders is lost.'

In stunning contrast, the decade of the 1960s produced a mounting effort to recover the sociological classics, an effort whose force has by no means yet been spent. Since 1960 well over two dozen books on the historical foundations of sociology have been published. What is more, fresh translations, editions and secondary analyses of classic authors have constituted one of the fastest grow-ing industries within sociology. Between 1972 and 1978 no fewer than ten full-length books in English were published on Emile Durk-heim alone (not to mention the new rage for Durkheimian studies in France).

What is striking about all this activity is not merely the upsurge of interest in the classic authors but the serious reversal of judgement about the worth of their works. In a review published some years ago I described this shift of opinion in terms congruent with the imagery which opened this essay: 'Like mountains in a range', I wrote,

> the makers of the sociological tradition become more imposing the farther back we stand from them. Dimly sensed as a collectivist mystic, Durkheim later flashed into view as a peak of analytic discipline. Max Weber, long a misguided economic historian, only slowly emerged as an overarching intellectual summit. Amorphous Simmel eventually came into focus as a genial source of streams of rigorous propositions. Obscured by closer shapes for a while, Spencer appeared (in Parsons's more distant perspective) to be bearing 'very much the framework of a satisfactory sociological scheme'. Mount Saint Marx thundered into view yet again, vibrant with new roots and branches. (Levine, 1975, p. 654)

These words were used then to introduce some remarks on the revival of interest in Comte; they may stand now to introduce a discussion of Georg Simmel, that remarkably gifted and creative philosopher and sociologist who lectured in Berlin at the turn of the century.

In Simmel's case the reversal of judgement of which I speak is easily documented. At the time of my doctoral research on Simmel in the mid-1950s he was widely regarded as an archaic amateur. The dominant ethos in sociology at the time held that the only sociological knowledge worth having was produced by applying rigorous empirical procedures to generate what were then and are now awesomely regarded as 'data'. From that perspective, Simmel was far too un-empirical to be taken seriously. On the other hand, the much smaller number who struggled to pursue theoretical questions in sociology found Simmel's habit of thinking too playful, whimsical almost, and rejected him as a serious theorist. Pitirim Sorokin had declared that Simmel's sociological enterprise was misguided in aim and flawed in execution, and that 'to call sociologists back to Simmel . . . means to call them back to a pure speculation, metaphysics, and a lack of scientific method' (Sorokin, 1928, p. 502, n. 26). Theodore Abel, in an energetically argued critique, had faulted Simmel for propounding an approach which was at variance with his actual substantive analyses, an incongruity which 'deprived him of [making] valuable contributions to sociology' (Abel, 1929, p. 48). Talcott Parsons, in what eventually came to be viewed as an authoritative monograph, declared that Simmel (like Spencer whom he earlier declared obsolete) espoused a conception of sociology that was 'unacceptable for reasons which cannot be gone into here' (Parsons, 1968a, [1937], p. 773).

In the last two decades, however, all this has changed. Reversing the harsh negative assessment of Simmel's work he had formulated thirty years earlier, Abel would go on to proclaim that Simmel 'could justifiably be regarded as the founder of modern sociology' and to confess that it had taken many years of development in sociology since Simmel's death to enable the profession to appreciate his importance (Abel, 1959, p. 474). Introducing the paperback edition of his famous book, Parsons would write that 'the most important single figure neglected in *The Structure of Social Action*, and to an important degree in my subsequent work, is probably Simmel' (Parsons, 1968a, p. xiv, n. 10). And Merton, whose serious intercourse with the classic authors may have been subdued for a time but was never repressed, went on to devote a good part of two year-long graduate seminars to combing Simmel's work for ideas pertinent to a general theory of social structure. In his extensive codification of group properties which followed that investigation, Merton noted that 'Georg Simmel's writings were, beyond comparison, the most fruitful for the purpose' (Merton, 1968, p. 346, n. 46).

Given such facts – given this renewal of interest in and belated appreciation of Simmel in particular and of the sociological classics in general – one is disposed to ask: what accounts for this phenomenal quest for the classics in sociology today, especially when nothing comparable is occurring in any of the other intellectual disciplines? Why, like the good citizens of Indiana mysteriously imprinted with an urge to flock to Devil's Mountain, do so many sociologists feel compelled to turn back to recover something 'terribly important' in the chief figures of the sociological tradition?

At this point the film analogy breaks down. As sociologists know, when mystifying behaviour is empathically examined it can usually be related to quite understandable human intentions. Rather than appeal to extra-terrestrial forces to account for sociology's quest for the classics, one can delineate a number of plausible human reasons. One could, for example, refer to certain idiosyncratic features of the history of the field such as the fact that, unique among the disciplines, sociology experienced a major ecological disjunction in the course of developing: its most profound intellectual foundations were laid in continental Europe, whereas it developed as a profession chiefly in the United States. The current return to the classics consequently can be seen as a belated effort of anglophone sociologists to recover important contributions that had never been incorporated properly into their professional stock of knowledge. Or one could focus on patterns of recruitment and socialization into the discipline, noting that many who are drawn to the subject matter of sociology are alienated by its dominant methodological approaches and thus seek to construct careers following conventional patterns of humanistic scholarship. Inasmuch as the present context obliges us to consider the future of the classics, I shall stress instead certain ailments in the present condition of sociology for which continuing attention to the classic authors may be regarded as a form of ongoing therapy.

The ailments in question reflect a condition of severe fragmentation. Although all the disciplines have become highly specialized in our time, most if not all of them have evolved from an initially coherent conception of their field and retain some center of gravity: within the social sciences, for example, the operations of the market in economics; the structure of government and the uses of power in political science; the nature of 'culture' and of non-literate cultures in anthropology. Sociology, by contrast, has been a highly fragmented and pluralistic field all along, to the point that a lack of shared orientations became an acute symptom within the profession in this generation. Sociology's quest for the classics may accordingly be viewed as an effort to constitute a common set of symbols in order to satisfy serious moral-emotional and cognitive needs.

There is a need for acceptable symbols to internalize in forming a firm professional identity; the revivification of the classic figures provides eminently suitable imagoes of that sort. There is a need for common symbols to link the members of the profession in some minimally solidary manner; the popularization of the classic figures affords almost the only available basis for collective solidarity in the field today. As Robert Jones suggested in an entertaining paper, the 'founding fathers' of American sociologists have come to be sacralized in the form of collective representations of 'ancestral spirits which both express and maintain the clan's sense of social unity' (n.d., p. 6).

There are significant cognitive needs as well. There is a need to find edifying grounds for defining research problems and connecting those problems to the concerns of a broader intellectual enterprise. To a large extent, research problems today are selected on the basis of a fetishistic attachment to techniques; idiosyncratic personal passions; material opportunities; or esoteric subject matter specialties.

The classic sociologists are of particular help as an antidote to this condition because each of the classic sociologists articulated both a general conception of the sociological enterprise and a set of fundamental problems to which his various specialized studies were subordinated.

There is a need, finally, to respond in some fashion to the expectations both of those who entered the field and of the larger intellectual community that sociology, as presumptive heir to theology and moral philosophy, may have something worthwhile to say about the human condition in 'modern' society. This was a central concern of the classic authors and again may account for some of their renewed appeal and future significance.

This rather oblique *entrée* to my discussion of Simmel's work – in keeping, it might be noted, with the oblique manner in which Simmel himself characteristically opened up the discussion of topics – was designed to find some basis for the narrow selection I must make in discussing Simmel's future in our intellectual life. We are dealing, after all, with a man who wrote some two dozen books and well over two hundred articles on subjects that include moral philosophy; the philosophy of history; the nature of conflict, competition and exchange; forms of superordination and subordination; secrecy and secret societies; jealousy, envy, faithfulness and gratitude; fashion, honor, aristocracy and poverty; the nature of culture; individualism and freedom; the effects of money on personal relations; the effects of metropolitan living on mental habits; the miser and the spendthrift; the character of adventure and the concept of fate; feminine culture and the status of women; Venice and Florence; the symbolism of bridges, doors and handles; the art of Rembrandt and Rodin; the intellectual personalities of Kant, Goethe, Schopenhauer and Nietzsche; the metaphysics of love, religion, life and death. I propose to approach this mountain of material by asking what resources are offered by Simmel's work to satisfy the two chief cognitive needs mentioned above. First, what does Simmel furnish to the quest for general principles to ground and organize the sociological enterprise? Secondly, what insights does Simmel provide to help us understand the human condition in modern society?

Simmel's Conception of Sociology

Many have denied that there are any viable organizing principles in Simmel's sociological work. He has been viewed widely as no more than a 'talented essayist', one who dropped assorted *aperçus* as he turned from topic to topic but whose writings are not to be searched for a coherent theoretical outlook. Such an interpretation, I submit, can be sustained only by a studiously superficial reading. On five different occasions spanning his whole scholarly career (1890, 1894, 1896, 1908a, 1917) Simmel took pains to articulate a carefully argued conception of the field of sociology. He even posted a warning at the entrance to his magnum opus *Soziologie* advising the reader to *keep that conception in mind* while reading the book 'or else', he wrote, 'these pages might appear as a heap of disconnected facts and reflections' (1908a, p. i). Paradoxically, despite his reputation for being so unsystematic Simmel may well have produced the most unified conception of any of the classic sociologists, since his sociology is not only internally unified by a single guiding conception but is also consistently linked with the meticulously elaborated ideas of his metaphysics and epistemological thinking, as I have indicated elsewhere (1959, 1971, pp. xiii–xliii).

Although it is a simple matter to find the language Simmel used to formulate that guiding conception, admittedly it may be less easy to fathom what he meant by saying that the proper subject matter for sociology is the *forms of human association*. 'Form' was perhaps the central analytic concept in Simmel's thought, just as 'society' was for Durkheim and 'rationality' for Weber; and readers of all three have been frustrated by the fact that, despite the centrality of these concepts for those authors – or as I would prefer to put it, precisely because of the centrality of these concepts for those authors –one finds the terms used in a variety of ways in different contexts, at times in ways which even appear contradictory. (On the ambiguities in Durkheim's 'society' see Lukes, 1972; on the ambiguities in Weber's 'rationality' see Levine, forthcoming.)

Some of this confusion may be reduced by recalling that the distinction between forms and contents was deliberately used in a highly flexible manner by Simmel. At the most abstract philosophical level, 'contents' is a concept signifying those aspects of reality which are determined in themselves but as such do not exhibit any kind of knowable structure. 'Forms' are the synthesizing principles provided by human subjects which select elements from the raw stuff of experience and shape them into meaningful unities. Since experience can be organized in a number of different universes of forms, or 'worlds', what appears as content in one context may appear as form in another.

When this distinction is applied to the world of human association, contents refer to those *drives, purposes and ideas which lead people to associate* with one another in different ways; forms are the *patterns exhibited by the associations* they get into. For example, two parties may relate through the form of a contract for a variety of reasons: to run a business together, to provide and receive a course of education, or to run a political campaign. Conversely, for these same purposes, parties may relate through an entirely different form of association, such as authoritarian domination or on the basis of sentimental attachments.

What did Simmel seek to accomplish – and what might we still gain – by focusing on this distinction? First, it gave him a way to establish sociology as a distinctive intellectual discipline rather than as a comprehensive science of all the facts of social experience. For a discipline to have a distinctive subject matter, Simmel believed it required a distinct analytic focus. The other social science disciplines tend to be organized around an interest in some content area of social life. They ask what kinds of phenomena occur when people are engaged in the pursuit of business (economics), or learning (education), or power (political science). For sociology to have its own province, Simmel felt it had to proceed by adopting a novel analytic focus, one which would involve abstracting from the various 'content' spheres *what is common to relational forms* such as contract, authoritarian domination, or love. Such a conception may indeed provide a unifying framework for those who today consider the proper work of sociology to be the study of such phenomena as exchange, conflict, stratification, friendship networks, formal organization, social movements and other kinds of 'forms'. (It may also locate and relate those branches of sociology which today are oriented more to 'content' areas, such as the sociologies of religion, science, work and leisure.)

A second feature of Simmel's distinction between the forms and contents of social life is its linkage with a plausible ontological claim about the nature of 'society'. Simmel rejected both the holistic notion that society exists as a superorganic entity endowed with independent existence and/or moral properties *and* the atomistic notion that individuals alone are real and that there are no distinctive supra-individual regularities. Instead, he advanced the view that 'society' consists of the patterned interactions which individuals create when they associate with one another to achieve their various purposes. This leads him to see social forms both as the products of human creative activity and as established sources of satisfaction for and constraint on human action. It also gives him a ready perspective on the dynamics of social change, which is seen to occur when existing forms no longer satisfy the purposes of those whose lives they shape. Such a conception is clearly congenial to those efforts in contemporary sociology which seek to transcend the limitations of a relatively fixed organismic system model and to direct attention to *form-creating processes* in such terms as 'social construction' (Berger and Luckmann, 1967), 'morphogenesis' (Buckley, 1967), applied 'frames' (Goffman, 1974), or 'structuration' (Giddens, 1976).

It should further be noted that Simmel sought to distinguish social forms not only from the contents of social life but from other kinds of forms as well. In writings outside his sociology he dealt with forms of personality, and with forms of culture like religion, science, philosophy and art. Simmel was thus the first social scientist to articulate *a consistent differentiation among psychological, social and cultural levels of analysis.* Psychic motivation and cultural patterns thus belong in his scheme in two separate places: as contents when the perspective is sociological, and as forms when attention shifts to questions of personality structure or cultural patterns.

With these points in mind, it may be easier to grasp what Simmel had in mind by making the problem of sociology one in which the forms of association are to 'be identified, ordered systematically, explained psychologically, and studied from the standpoint of their historical development' (1971, p. 27). However, although Simmel's sociology can readily be demarcated by formulations of this sort, it is hard to keep track of this underlying conception when reading Simmel's writings, which are essayistic rather than rigorously expository in style, full of detours and distractions, and anything but overtly systematic. Indeed, the phenomena treated in *Soziologie* are so disparate in character that one is hard pressed to determine their equivalence as Simmelian topics. In what sense can the following be regarded as parallel facts to be glossed by the single term 'forms of association' – superordination and subordination (ch. 3), conflict (ch. 4), the stranger (ch. 9), secret societies (ch. 5), group expansion and the development of individuality (ch. 10) and quantitative aspects of groups (ch. 2)?

In the terms of contemporary sociology, we would be inclined to say that these represent quite diverse categories of phenomena: that superordination-and-subordination designates a social *relation;* conflict a type of social *process;* the stranger a kind of social *role;* secret societies a kind of *collectivity;* group expansion a *developmental pattern;* and group size a dimension of social organization, hence a *structural variable.*

At this point an effort is required to introduce a greater degree of systematic order to his thought than Simmel himself provided. We can do this by formalizing what is only implicit in the full range of Simmel's sociological writings: to analyze the forms of association means *to look at the structural aspects of phenomena from a variety of angles.* The study of social forms, following Simmel, can focus on relationships, or interaction processes, or roles, or collectivities, or developmental patterns, or structural variables. All of these represent structural regularities abstracted from diverse purposive areas of human life. A relationship, like superordination–subordination, is a form considered with respect to the kind of connection linking a number of statuses. A process, like conflict, concerns the kind of activity that goes on among the incumbents of those statuses. A status-role, like the stranger, concerns the properties of one party to a relationship. A collectivity, like a secret society, concerns the properties of one party to a relationship when that party consists of a plurality of units. A developmental pattern, like group expansion and the development of individuality, is some regularity concerning formal changes exhibited by groups over time. A structural variable, like size, is some dimension of organization, changes in which are accompanied by changes in other aspects of organization.

What all this amounts to is a suggestion that *if one were to take seriously Simmel's overall program for sociology, his work just might provide a rather interesting synthetic paradigm.* Four of the categories just mentioned – relationships, processes, individual status-roles and collective status-roles – represent stable configurations. One of them represents structural changes, and the other refers to structural variables. Accordingly, a complete examination of one of the forms of association, such as conflict, would include the following:

(1) What are the properties of the kinds of relationships in which statuses are connected in an oppositional way, such as enmity or mutual hatred?
(2) What are the characteristics of the various types of conflictual interaction processes?
(3) What are the properties of the individual status-role involved in such relationships? What is the nature of 'the enemy'?
(4) What are the properties of collective status-roles involved in such relationships, such as armies or parties?
(5) What are the characteristic patterns of the transformation of conflictual processes or relationships over time? Under what conditions, say, does enmity lead to separation or to reconciliation?

Viewed, finally, as a structural variable:

(6) What are the effects of different degrees of conflict on other relational forms?

In order to complete this sketch of a Simmelian approach to sociology, we must devote some attention to the terms in which Simmel describes the properties of forms. Again, bringing more order to Simmel's work than he was inclined to, we can identify six variables which seem to be particularly salient in his sociological analyses: size, distance, position, valence, self-involvement and symmetry.

(1) *Size*. In this chapter on the quantitative aspects of groups Simmel presents numerous propositions about the effects of the size of a group on the interaction among its members. Whether the parties to an interaction are two or three or a hundred substantially affects the character of that interaction. Certain formations can be realized only below or above a particular number of group elements, and the mere fact of being of a certain size imposes specific kinds of structural arrangements.

(2) *Distance*. All social forms are defined to some extent in terms of the dimension of interpersonal distance. There are many kinds of distance; a systematic ordering of Simmel's writings would note that he uses the term variously to refer to degree of interactional proximity, degree of emotional involvement, degree of cognitive familiarity, degree of cultural similarity and perhaps other variables as well. Some social forms, like conflict, bring distant people into close contact. Others, like secrecy, increase the distance between people. Certain forms, like fashion, and the stranger, are characterized as entailing distinctive combinations of both nearness and remoteness.

(3) *Position*. Distance may be vertical as well as horizontal. I use the term position here to distinguish relative distance along a vertical dimension. It would seem important to distinguish the terms because people who occupy highly unequal statuses may be relatively remote *or* close in any of the senses entailed by the concept of horizontal distance. One effort which represents a model of Simmelian investigation is that of Roger Brown and his associates, who have been examining variations in modes of address explicitly in terms of what they call horizontal and vertical distance. They have uncovered what appears to be a universal pattern: that in every known society, when status unequals address one another, the linguistic form that is used by the superior to address an inferior is the same form used mutually by people who are close to one another in dyads of equal status; while the form used by an inferior to a superior is, in dyads of equal status, that used reciprocally by people who are distant from one another (Brown, 1965, ch. 2).

(4) *Valence*. By valence I refer to the dimension of positive or negative sentiment involved in forms of interaction. Much confusion in sociological analysis has stemmed from the failure to distinguish this variable from that of distance. A moment's reflection will make

it clear, however, that people who regard each other positively may be very distant from one another, while those who are close may and often do have strongly negative feelings toward one another. Renewed attention to the latter configuration helps account for the fact that a book titled *The Intimate Enemy* became a best-seller a few years ago.

(5) *Self-involvement.* Another variable treated in Simmel's analyses is the amount of personal involvement required by different forms of association. In general, Simmel stresses the fact that persons enter into social relations with only certain parts of their personality. An individual always stands both within and outside of any particular interaction. But forms vary a great deal with respect to the quantum of involvement of the self they must incorporate. Lewis Coser, who has worked with Simmel's ideas perhaps more productively than any other sociologist, has taken a page from this aspect of Simmel's work to inspirit his account of 'greedy institutions' – those institutions which seek exclusive and undivided loyalty from their members by pressuring them to sever ties with others who might make competing demands. His essays on the captives of such greedy institutions deal with such statuses as eunuchs, court mistresses, Jesuits, Leninists and the priesthood (Coser, 1974).

(6) *Symmetry.* Finally, the degree of mutuality or symmetry is a variable of some prominence in Simmel's analyses. It is the essence of certain forms that they entail complete reciprocity: economic exchange, personal adornment and the milling behavior of crowds, for example. In other forms, such as superordination–subordination, the relationship may be highly asymmetrical. One mode of asymmetry concerns the significance of the matter of who initiates an interaction. The relationship of gratitude, for example, is crucially affected by the fact that once one has received something good from another, one can never after make up for it completely: the gift from the person to whom we feel gratitude, because it was first, has a voluntary character which no return gift can have, since the latter is constrained by a sense of ethical obligation. Conversely, Simmel speaks of the constraint experienced by someone who has spontaneously offered help to another, one who through a kind of 'moral induction' thereafter feels a sense of responsibility to continue lending help to that beneficiary.

One other feature of Simmel's sociological approach deserves particular mention here. This is what I have called the principle of *dualism*: Simmel's assumption that social formations can be represented most revealingly as simultaneous embodiments of opposed categories (1971, pp. xxxv—xxxvii). At issue here is not merely the Hegelian–Marxian idea that contradictions constitute the driving force of historical change, a viewpoint sublimated into Simmel's notion of the chronic tension between established forms and vital needs, but even more fundamentally the idea that *the condition for the persistence of any aspect of life is the coexistence of a diametrically opposed element*. The dualistic character of social forms is thus a fundamental feature of the human condition, one which is not to be transcended and which stems both from man's ambivalent instinctual disposition and also from society's need to have some ratio of discordant to harmonious tendencies in order to attain a determinate shape.

Simmel's dualistic mode of interpretation manifests itself in several ways. At times he defines forms in terms of opposed tendencies or qualities which they synthesize. Thus, fashion is a form which combines conformity and individualization. Jealousy, and conflictual relationships generally, are constituted by the polar elements of antagonism and solidarity. Subordination combines both a tendency to want to be dominated and a tendency to oppose one's superordinate. Private welfare is a form which involves giving both 'too little and too much' to those in need.

At other times dualistic constructs are employed by Simmel as heuristic devices which enable us to allude to what is in reality some 'inner unity'. In this vein one defines a form not as a synthesis of opposites but as a midpoint between them. Thus, confidence in another person presumes beliefs which lie somewhere in the middle on a continuum between complete knowledge and total ignorance about the other. Similarly, the middleman performs a single role that is most conveniently represented as involving a combination of connecting and separating functions. More generally, 'man's position in the world is defined by the fact that in every dimension of his being and his behavior he stands at every moment *between two boundaries*' (1971, p. 353).

In marked contrast to this analytic style the prevailing orientation in American sociology looks for dominant patterns, univalent metrics and unilineal logical derivations. There are, however, some signs of ferment which may render the dualistic modes of analysis practiced by Simmel more congenial. One of these is a flurry of interest in what has been called dialectical sociology – a totally vague construct to be sure, but one which at least suggests the desirability of considering contradictory tendencies in the analysis of social formations (albeit in a framework which often posits the dubious assumption that contradictions are inherently unstable). Another is Merton's publication of a number of papers under the title *Sociological Ambivalence*, work which can be represented as dualistic in a number of ways. Merton invites us to characterize social relations not in terms of the dominant pattern they embody but in terms of compresent norms *and* counternorms. He also stresses the dualistic character of attitudes and faults certain survey research instruments for 'not expressly [including] statements of the negative as well as the positive bases of evaluation' (Merton, p. 20; see also Levine, 1978).

Simmel's conception of sociology is incomplete in its own terms and at best cannot possibly encompass all the ways in which sociologists might want to look at the human world. As a source of bold ideas and a framework for integrating a great deal of sociological inquiry, it holds the promise of stimulating such creative work in the future as it has in the past (see Levine *et al.*, 1976).

Simmel's Conception of Modern Society

Next to the notion that Simmel lacks a coherent theoretical orientation perhaps the most common other stereotype about Simmel is that he is wholly ahistorical. Like the former stereotype this view too has some basis in reality. Much of his writing does proceed by analyzing general formations which have been abstracted from concrete historical settings. Simmel seems, moreover, to deviate from the example of the other classic sociologists whose guiding substantive interest was the question, How does the type of social order peculiar to modern (equals industrial, capitalist, urban, and/or rationalized) society differ from earlier types of social order? In apparent contrast to Simmel, each of the other classic sociologists is remembered chiefly for his distinctive formulation of the essential character of modern Western society.

Here again, however, a closer reading may indicate that Simmel has a carefully conceived approach to this question and that his approach may in some ways be superior to many others. Simmel's views on this problem are scattered in four different writings, most of which have remained unknown in American sociology: in his first work, *On Social Differentiation* (1890), which has never been translated (although parts have been translated from their revised versions as chapters of *Soziologie*); in *The Philosophy of Money* (1900), translated for the first time in 1978; in his well-known essay 'The metropolis and mental life' (1903; translated in 1950, pp. 409–24, 1971, ch. 20); and in a set of later essays on the philosophy of culture (1968, ch. 2, 1971, chs 15, 16, 17, 24).

Although the first of these writings is presented as a series of studies on general forms of interaction, to a certain extent each of its four substantive chapters can be read as an effort to delineate a particular evolutionary pattern. They all depict patterns of evolutionary development from 'more primitive epochs' to the present which represents some mode of increased individuation. There is the transition from a form in which jural responsibility is invested in groups to one in which liability is assigned to individual persons (1890, ch. 2); from the relatively small-scale organization of groups containing homogeneous members to an expanded scale of association in which group members differ from one another (1890, ch. 3; 1908 rev. version translated in 1971, ch. 18); from a condition in which shared beliefs embody the lowest common denominator of mental activity to one which permits individualized intellectual achievement (1890, ch. 4); and from a relatively compulsory pattern of group affiliations based on the accidents of birth and propinquity to one in which persons associate voluntarily on the basis of shared interests, such as organizations of workers, or merchants, or women, and thereby create more individuated constellations of group affiliation (1890, ch. 5; 1908 rev. version translated in 1955, pp. 12–95). The burden of this monograph, then, is a portrayal of modern society as a highly differentiated social world wherein individuals are liberated from a variety of jural and customary constraints in ways which enormously expand their freedom of action.

In his long treatise on money published ten years later, a work which must surely rank among the greatest unread works in the entire literature of the social sciences, Simmel developed a more profound and differentiated conception. Although this work, too, is presented as a general theoretical analysis, one which seeks 'to derive from the surface level of economic affairs a guideline that leads to the ultimate values and things of importance in all that is human' (1978, p. 55), the principal lines of social-historical interpretation presented in its second or 'synthetic' part clearly set forth a kind of deep structural analysis of modern society.

The first of these lines of interpretation follows the basic direction staked out in *On Social Differentiation* but goes on to consider how the widespread use of money as a general medium of exchange serves to advance the processes of liberation treated in the earlier work. Just as the enlargement of spheres of social contact liberates individuals by removing them from the conventional constraints of local communities, so money promotes freedom in the sense of liberation from external constraints: indirectly by enlarging the effective sphere of exchange relations through an expanded market, and directly, by facilitating transactions in which the obligations by which persons are bound to one another can be limited to a very precise and specific exchange. The modern money economy creates a situation in which one is dependent on a host of other people for services but free and independent of them as *particular persons*, and in which a worker is constrained to provide not himself as a person nor the entirety of his labor but only specific services or products.

Like the secular processes of social differentiation, moreover, money promotes freedom not only in the 'negative' sense of liberating persons from external constraints but also in the 'positive' senses of the term: freedom to attain satisfactions and freedom to develop one's individuality. Just as the shift from associations based on kinship and local territorial bonds to voluntary interest associations provides both new freedoms to pursue one's goals and to realize the unhampered development of one's unique personality, so money provides the freedom to do and the freedom to be. Again, it does this both indirectly, by facilitating the formation of innumerable voluntary associations organized around particular objective interests, and directly in a number of ways. Money enhances the freedom to do in that, of all objects, money offers the least resistance to an agent. It is the most possessable of all things, and hence completely submissive to the will of an ego. It can be acquired in countless ways. The amount of it that one can possess can be increased indefinitely, and its uses are without number.

Money enhances the freedom to be one's true self by providing an effective means of differentiating between the subjective center and the objective achievements of a person. The individual's performance may be paid for with money while her or his person remains outside the transaction. Or else individual persons can be supported (by monetary contributions from many others) while their specific performances remain free from financial considerations and constraints. Further in this vein Simmel argues that the separation of workers from their means of production (for which a 'money economy paved the way'), while viewed by some as the focal point of social misery, may rather be viewed 'as a salvation' insofar as it provides conditions for the liberation of the worker as a human subject from the objectified technical apparatus of productivity (1978, p. 337).

The attainment of so much freedom is not without peril, however. A second line of interpretation pursued by Simmel examines some of the negative effects of all this liberation. Citing the maxim that 'where there is freedom there is also a tax', Simmel notes that workers pay a cost in the form of price fluctuations for the freedoms made possible by the introduction of money wages (p. 338). The instabilities engendered by the money economy are by no means only fiscal, moreover. Simmel goes on to describe some of the negative moral consequences of the liberations produced by money. Peasants who have been 'liberated' by cash payments may experience that 'emptiness and instability that allows one to give full rein to every accidental, whimsical and tempting impulse', just as a tradesman who sells his entire business for cash often 'experiences that typical boredom, lack of purpose in life and inner restlessness of the rentier which drives him to the oddest and most contradictory attempts to keep busy' (p. 402). In other passages Simmel discusses the significance of money as an unfettered 'pure means' and the impetus this gives to an overwhelmingly instrumentalist attitude towards life. The resulting preoccupation with instrumental calculations substantially diminishes the salience of ends and norms. In consequence, we feel

> as if the whole meaning of our existence [is] so remote that we are unable to locate it and are constantly in danger of moving away from rather than closer to it . . . The lack of something definite at the center of the soul impels us to search for momentary satisfaction in ever-new stimulations, sensations and external activities. Thus it is that we become entangled in the instability and helplessness that manifests itself as the tumult of the metropolis, as the mania for travelling, as the wild pursuit of competition and as the typically modern disloyalty with regard to taste, style, opinions and personal relationships. (1978, p. 484).

Beyond noting the negative effects of social differentiation and the modern money economy in the form of the perilous byproducts of excessive freedom, *The Philosophy of Money* identifies other effects which are manifest in the form of *new kinds of unfreedom*. Simmel makes a number of points of this nature which may be thus drawn together as comprising a third line of interpretation of modern society. He fully incorporates the frequently made point that the personalities of workers in the capitalist system of production become stunted because of the extreme specialization of industrial activity and the alienation of workers from the production process (p. 454). Just as we have become 'slaves of the production process', he adds, so 'we have become slaves of the products'. Partly this is because 'the thread by which technology weaves the energies and materials of nature into our life are just as easily to be seen as fetters that tie us down and make many things indispensable which could and even ought to be dispensed with as far as the essence of life is concerned' (p. 483). In addition, it is because of the creation of cultural products which stand over and dominate man because they are no longer relatable to palpable human concern; man has become distanced (*entfernt*) from his own being.

A number of these and other lines of interpretation of modern society are woven together in Simmel's remarkable essay 'The metropolis and mental life.' Although this is one of the most widely read of Simmel's writings it has rarely been understood thoroughly, since each of its tightly packed pages embodies a rich texture of thought elaborated in the other writings mentioned above. For this reason, however, the essay remains an appropriate place to look for ways to formulate Simmel's unified view of modernity.

Ostensibly about urbanism, this essay is primarily about the numerous contradictions which permeate social and cultural life in the modern world. It is an inquiry, Simmel announces at the outset, into the specifically modern aspects of contemporary life which bear on the struggle of individuals to maintain their autonomy and individuality in the face of the overwhelming supra-individual forces of social organization, technology and cultural tradition. To grasp the 'inner meaning', the existential significance of life, in the modern metropolis requires us to lay bare the vectors of this life-and-death struggle.

The argument focuses on three pairs of opposing vectors. First, Simmel discusses the forces which *threaten and promote the modern ideal of individual autonomy* in the metropolis. The individual's freedom of action is seriously curtailed by the pressures for adhering to precise social arrangements, punctuality and impersonal kinds of transactions which are demanded by the rationalistic ethos of the big city and its money economy. These same factors, however, promote a psychic defense of reserve and aversion behind which individuals gain a new kind of freedom of response. This facade forms the protective covering for 'a type and degree of personal freedom to which there is no analogy in other circumstances' (1971, p. 332). The freedom in question is that gained by the enlargement of the sphere of social association and the corresponding diminution of those smothering social controls exerted over dwellers in small towns and villages.

Secondly, the essay discusses the forces which *threaten and promote the modern ideal of individuality*, the freedom to develop a unique self. Cities promote this individuality by supporting an extreme degree of specialization. At the same time, the division of labor threatens individuality, not only by exacting a one-sided kind of performance which permits the personality as a whole to deteriorate, but also, through its relentless productivity, by engulfing the individual in a world of cultural objects. These reduce him to a 'mere cog' in 'the vast overwhelming organization of things and forces which gradually take out of his hands everything connected with progress, spirituality and value' (p. 337). In response to *this* oppressive situation, however, the conditions of modern urban life make possible a new source of individuality, that which arises in *protest* against the mass of depersonalized cultural accomplishment and expresses itself in the form of accentuated idiosyncratic traits and eccentric personalities, and the popularization of culture heroes like Nietzsche who preach doctrines of extreme individuality.

Finally, there is the opposition between those two ideals of individualism themselves – between the ideal of autonomy, which Simmel associates with the eighteenth-century liberalist struggle against traditional constraints, and the ideal of individuality, which Simmel associates with the nineteenth-century romantic movement and advocates of specialized vocations. Not only does the modern metropolis stimulate the development of these two ideals (as well as provide obstacles to their realization) but it is the function of the metropolis to provide an arena for the *conflict and shifting relations between these two great ideals*, a struggle which constitutes much of the 'external as well as the internal history of our time' (p. 339).

Further depth is added to Simmel's conception of modernity by his later essays on the philosophy of culture, which I shall summarize briefly. All cultural forms ultimately originate in situations where the undifferentiated unity of immediate experience is ruptured by some sort of stress. The experiencing self divides at that point into a self-conscious subject and a confronted object, one defined in whatever formal mode is appropriate to the problematic situation. This results in the creation of preliminary forms, forms whose existence is tied to the pragmatic interests and adaptive exigencies of particular situations (see Weingartner, 1960, ch. 1).

The progressive crystallization of forms is contingent on a continuing distantiation between subject and object. Pragmatically relevant forms become objectified into customary lore and tradition. They need not be invented anew each time a relevant problem erupts, but can be drawn on by any subject to satisfy some need of everyday life. A further level of distantiation between subject and object is reached when the forms become liberated from their connection with practical purposes and become objects of cultivation in their own right. For example, the rhythmic and melodic variations of sound initially formed to aid human communication become transformed into music composed and played according to intrinsic canons.

Although the attainment of this third stage of objectification of forms, which Simmel refers to as 'objective culture', is no longer directed by subjective interests, it does *relate* to the interests of subjects insofar as there is a human tendency toward self-fulfillment through 'cultivation'. What Simmel calls cultivation is a process of self-development of the psychic center of personalities that involves the assimilation of diverse cultural contents into its central core (see 1971, ch. 16).

Subjective experience and objectified cultural forms are thus appropriately differentiated, in Simmel's view, when they can be connected in one of two ways: when pragmatic forms serve to satisfy a subject's everyday needs, and when autonomous or objective cultural forms serve the subject's interest in the free development of personality. In modern society, however, the distantiation between subject and object becomes so great that two disturbing developments occur. Through the *hypertrophy of objectified forms* made possible by the division of labor and the modern money economy, forms are created at a rate which exceeds the subject's capacity to assimilate them. The development of new techniques and other cultural products proceeds limitlessly, producing the 'typically problematic situation of modern man',

> his sense of being surrounded by an innumerable number of cultural elements which are neither meaningless to him nor, in the final analysis, meaningful. In their mass they depress him, since he is not capable of assimilating them all, nor can he simply reject them, since after all they do belong potentially within the sphere of his cultural development. (1968, p. 4)

This conflict between the need for cultural forms and the creation of unassimilable cultural forms is one inherent in the nature of culture: Simmel thus refers to it as 'the tragedy of culture'. Yet it is only under the conditions of modern life as described above that the tragedy reaches its searing dénouement. The conflict exhibits a different aspect, moreover, if one regards it from the side of what might be called the *hypertrophy of subjectivity*. By this I refer to Simmel's later argument (1971 [1918], ch. 24) that the perennial struggle between contemporary forms filled with life and old, lifeless forms appears to have given way in the modern era to an antagonism of vital energies toward the very principle of form. What Simmel describes as the replacement of central organizing ideas of earlier phases of Western civilization – ideas such as being, nature, ego and society – by a modern allegiance to the idea of life may be described, in other Simmelian terms, as a retreat from the subject–object dialectic into a preoccupation with the subject's vital energies alone. This retreat is self-destructive, however. The radical opposition to forms of any sort because they constrict life energies profoundly misunderstands the nature of life. Life wishes here to obtain something impossible. 'It desires to transcend all forms and to appear in its naked immediacy', yet life can only proceed by producing and utilizing forms. The result of this extreme form of the perennial conflict be-

tween form and life process is that 'we gaze into an abyss of un-
formed life beneath our feet' (1971, p. 393).

Here we arrive at one of the central paradoxes in Simmel's view
of modernity, a matter I can do no more than formulate succinctly
at this point. In the sphere of social and economic relations, *the
maximal separation between subject and object produces the greatest
freedom*. 'If freedom means obeying the laws of one's own nature
alone', Simmel writes, 'then the distance between property and its
owner that is made possible by the money form of returns provides
to *both* a hitherto unheard-of freedom. The division of labor between
subjectivity and the norms of the object is now complete' (1978, p.
334/1958, p. 360; translation modified, emphasis added). With respect
to interpersonal relationships of superordination and subordination,
a comparably benign differentiation takes place when hierarchical
arrangements 'become merely technical forms of organization, the
purely objective character of which no longer evokes any subjective
reactions. The point is to separate the organization and the person in
such a way that the objective requirements of the organization leave
the individuality, freedom and essential life-experience of the person
completely undisturbed' (p. 336). More generally, 'it is possible to
conceive of a situation in which these casually evolving and one-
sided conditions become the form of social organization as a whole'
(p. 337); and such a conception, as one recent commentator has
suggested, may be said to constitute Simmel's social utopia (Wallisch-
Prinz, 1977, ch. 4).

On the other hand, within the cultural sphere, as we have noted,
Simmel argues that a complete distantiation between subject and the
norms of the object is *the source both of normlessness* (the revolt
against all forms) *and alienation* (the production of and oppression
by meaningless objects).

Within these few pages I have had to simplify grossly an enormously rich and evocative set of arguments. Enough has been presented, however, to suggest that Simmel may stand in a privileged
position among classic sociologists for his analysis of modernity. If
it can be said that Spencer's response to modern society was chiefly
to affirm its patterns of structural differentiation as an unfolding of
opportunities for liberty and individualism; that Durkheim's response
was to hail modern individuation but chiefly to diagnose the dangers
of excessive freedom that produced normlessness in the vanguard
spheres of modern life; and that the response of Marx and Weber
was chiefly to diagnose the problems of alienation and repression in
the central institutions of capitalist society; then it may be said that
Simmel is the only classic sociologist who offered a balanced and
penetrating account of all these phenomena – individualization, free-

dom, anomie and alienation – and did so within the framework of a coherent theoretical scheme and an expansive social-historical vision.

Simmel's extraordinarily seminal interpretation of modern society and culture thus provides another reason why his sociology stands to attract no less attention in the future that it has in the past, and why the effort to gain deeper understanding of his thought may be a meaningful quest indeed.

5

Vilfredo Pareto: Socio-Biology, System and Revolution

JOSEPH LOPREATO

Pareto's major work in sociology is the *Treatise on General Sociology* (1963 [1916]), otherwise known as *The Mind and Society*. It is a monumental work, refreshing in its rigorous approach, a bit irritating for the zeal with which it unmasks the sophistries and rationalizations that humans employ to hide their fundamental motives, and stunning in its endless procession of facts and reasonings pertaining to almost any scholarly discipline imaginable.

The reception granted to it during the third and fourth decades of the century has few parallels in the annals of sociology. Pareto became a sort of intellectual vogue touching, in addition to sociologists and political scientists, such members of the scholarly community as philosophers, *littérateurs*, historians, philologists, economists, psychologists and, what is more interesting, even entomologists, chemists, physiologists and mathematicians. The *Treatise* was until recently, in fact, one of very few sociological works to be included in such lists as 'the 100 best books ever written'.

Then came the eclipse and his influence, though still great, has been muted for some forty years. Within the modern sociological community Pareto's name evokes more the image of a distant and somewhat odd ancestor than the respect due to a genius who, like few others, penetrated sociological frontiers still unsettled today. Parsons (1968c, p. 415) explains: 'Most of the neglect of Pareto stems from the scientific limitations of subsequent generations of sociologists rather than from his irrelevance to their interests.' There is an element of truth in this verdict, but the story, as Professor Parsons no doubt recognized, is much more complex. It includes the ponderous nature of the *Treatise*;[1] the fact that a cruel ideological hoax has been successfully perpetrated against one of the freest spirits ever to grace the pages of intellectual history; and, ironically, the fact that Parsons and the other giants of sociology most influenced by Pareto's work have either failed to render explicit their debts to him or have pursued scholarly avenues with a language seemingly irrelevant to the logic and the thrust of the science contained in the *Treatise*.

Two other factors are particularly noteworthy, and they will serve to organize the present chapter. First, the heart of Pareto's sociology is what is known as 'the theory of residues' or of 'sentiments'; it is notoriously difficult theory. As Norberto Bobbio (1973, p. 21), social philosopher and sagacious scholar of Pareto's sociology, has recently stated, no critic 'has been able to say a clear word' about it. My contention in this chapter is that until recently it was not really possible to understand it fully. The reason is that, as is becoming increasingly clear, the theory was in large part an attempt to construct what in modern behavioral science has come to be known as the human 'biogram', that is, the biological endowment that interacts with environmental and socio-cultural forces to produce what evolutionists term adaptation. The biogram is the result of natural selection, but the principle of natural selection remained vague until Gregor Mendel's work had its impact at the turn of the present century. Genetics gave unequivocal meaning to 'natural selection' by establishing the unit of selection, so that today natural selection can be rather unambiguously defined as the differential contribution of genes to future generations by individuals of different genetic types belonging to the same population. Pareto's theory of the sentiments – of the human biogram – had its beginnings in the 1890s and was for all practical purposes completed by 1908, when talk of genetics was still rare. His theory thus suffers from the same vagueness that characterized Darwin's (1859) theory of evolution. It is my contention, however, that now that we have a fuller understanding of evolution we are in a position to clarify, and in part formulate, Pareto's theory by taking developments and facts of socio-biology into account. That is the first aim of this chapter.

The other factor concerns Pareto's system-equilibrium analysis, which was even further ahead of its time than the theory of sentiments. Unfortunately this aspect of Pareto's work has had little or no influence in social science because, ironically, subsequent scholars have been excessively influenced, at least implicitly, by Newtonian physics. The problem is that the systems of classical physics are surprisingly simple and static. Time, the flow of history, is irrelevant to them. As a result, sociologists, emulating classical physics, have often conceptualized equilibrium, a fundamental property of systems, as synonymous with 'stability' or even 'immobility'. Physicists and chemists are now beginning to learn how to deal theoretically with time and complex systems. Pareto anticipated the logic of these recent developments by several decades. My second and last aim in this chapter, then, is to show that Pareto's use of system and equilibrium already exhibits a full awareness of time, immanence, change and such other system properties as function, consensus and stress or conflict. In pursuing these two goals, I shall largely avoid, without in any sense intending to belittle, various more familiar interpretations of Pareto's work.

The Human Biogram

A major task of modern evolutionary science, according to the biologist E. O. Wilson (1975, p. 548), is the search for the human biogram (Count, 1958), the set of phylogenetically selected rules that both are the foundations of the socio-cultural system and interact with it. The focus on the biogram is part of the growing awareness that the interior of the living 'black box' is simply not a *tabula rasa* (Dobzhansky, 1962; Alexander, 1971). Pareto's theory of sentiments, I submit, is precisely an amazingly well-developed theory of the human biogram.

The theory has an enemy that is deeply rooted in the history of social thought. It is the rationalistic bias, which can be formulated as 'belief (B) causes conduct (C)'. That type of mistake is sometimes committed when we say, for instance, that we obey our superiors because we believe in the legitimacy of their positions. Research on other species is replete with examples of animals who know quite well which individuals to defer to, and yet we do not resort to rational motives to explain such behavior. Thus, in attributing such exclusive causality to human belief we often commit an act of anthropocentrism that unnecessarily restricts the scope of our knowledge. Often, not always, there is no direct connection between belief (B) and conduct (C). Belief and conduct are both determined by a third factor, A. The last represents a behavioral force that, in the light of modern science, may be said to have been selected during the evolutionary history of the species. This is the source of what is termed 'non-logical' conduct. There are times, too, when the force, A, gives rise to the conduct (C), and this, in turn, produces the belief (B). Finally, there is the possibility that the conduct (C) is the result of the belief (B), which in turn is generated by the force, A (Pareto, 1963 [1916], pp. 267–9).[2] In all cases the search for A widens the scope of the analysis, renders it more historical in the broad sense of the word and, as we shall see, facilitates a parsimonious classification and explanation of human conduct without sacrificing important information.

Pareto identifies forty-odd major types of the force, A, and he terms them 'sentiments' or 'residues'. We shall deal with some of them in due course.

Methods of isolating the sentiments

Wilson (1975, pp. 550–1) has proposed that, in the absence of an anthropological genetics, there are two indirect methods useful to the search for the human biogram: (1) the intense examination of human behavior with a view to singling out uniformities in its repertoire and (2) a comparison of other species, especially the higher primates, with *Homo sapiens* in an effort to see which traits are shared across related species and which are strictly intraspecific. It is a remarkable feat for a discipline barely at the state of demarcating its subject matter that Pareto followed both of these methods very early in the twentieth century. What is of signal importance is that he combined the two with an ingenious linguistic analysis suggested to him by the presence in *Homo sapiens* of a trait that he termed (972–5) the 'hunger for logical developments'. Humans not only perform certain acts; they also have a pronounced tendency to explain those acts. These popular 'theories' are usually faulty as explanations, but they are also powerful clues to the underlying sentiments.

> Current in any given group of people are a number of propositions, descriptive, preceptive, or otherwise. For example: . . . 'Love thy neighbour as thyself'. 'Learn to save if you would not one day be in need'. Such propositions, combined by logical or pseudological nexuses and amplified with factual narrations of various sorts, constitute theories, theologies, cosmogonies, systems of metaphysics, and so on . . . all such propositions and theories are experimental facts, and . . . we are here obliged to consider them . . . for *often it is through them alone that we manage to gain some knowledge of the forces which are at work in society – that is, of the tendencies and inclinations of human beings.* (7–8; emphasis added)

Consider, for example, the Latin maxim, *Dulce et decorum est pro patria mori* – it is sweet and proper to die for one's homeland. This saying may be divided into two parts: one constitutes a moral command to die for the homeland; the other purports to be an explanation of the act itself. If we abstract the explanatory part ('it is sweet and proper'), we are left with a part – the residual – that, as moral and ethnographic history shows, appears to be fairly general in humankind. That is, the residual ('to die for the home-land') constitutes a constancy, a uniformity, in time and space (not a constant in the mathematical sense). We conclude thereby that general throughout human society is a moral rule requiring that under some circumstances individuals sacrifice their lives for their groups. Pareto terms this the 'residue' (literally, what is left when the explanation has been abstracted).

We can now introduce two other sets of facts into our reasoning. First, under some circumstances human beings at all times and places have in fact sacrificed their lives for their group – they have exhibited behavior consistent with the cultural rule. Secondly, if we survey the rest of the animal kingdom, we discover that other social animals exhibit a similar tendency (cf. Wilson, 1975; Dawkins, 1976). These facts led Pareto to hypothesize the presence in the human species of a 'sentiment', an 'instinct', which in today's parlance might be termed the 'patriotic value' but which Pareto, eager to avoid anthropomorphism, termed instead 'risking one's life' (1148). The logic of this procedure, we might add, has been found useful in more than one discipline. Chomsky (1972), for example, has found cogent evidence for the argument that the similarities in language acquisition across cultures, and shared 'deep structures' of grammar in different languages, point to an innate human language capacity that is more directive than was once believed.

Residues and sentiments
Several clarifications are necessary at this juncture. We have been using the terms 'residue', 'sentiment' and 'instinct' interchangeably. But technically Pareto classifies and discusses only the residues. The reason is that only the residues are observable. The possible action of the sentiment, and therefore its theoretical relevance, is inferred from the constancy in time and space of the nucleus termed 'residue' that is interpreted to be its cultural manifestation. Residues are 'the manifestations of sentiments ... just as the rising of mercury in a thermometer is a manifestation of the rise in tempera-ture' (875). The distinction loomed large in a scholar whose basic training was after all in the mathematical sciences. Pareto was compelled to give a certain pre-eminence of exposition to the resi-dues, but his interest was clearly in the sentiments as forces ulti-mately behind residues and other cultural facts. Indeed, so keen is the underlying focus on the sentiments that in innumerable places 'residue' and 'sentiment' are used quite interchangeably. The same license, incidentally, will be taken in the present chapter.

The point must be emphasized, moreover, that the sentiments are viewed as 'inherited' behavioral traits (1845, *passim*). It is for this reason that I have spoken of Pareto's theory as a theory of the human biogram, even though in his apparent unawareness of the emerging science of genetics Pareto did not deem it necessary to decide whether sentiments should be viewed in biological or other terms. Instead, he followed the convenient and time-honored practice in science of resorting to an inferential abstraction. 'The terms "sentiments", "residues", and so on, are convenient makeshifts in sociology, just as the term "force" has proved convenient in mechanics' (1690).

Sentiments: Instinct versus learning
A few words about 'instinct' may also be useful. Among many social scientists this term continues to evoke opposition, and we tend to exorcise it with the concept of 'learning'. In biology 'instinct' has been gaining respectability. Moreover, while modern literature bestows a certain flexibility of interpretation on the term (see, for example, Dobzhansky, 1962; Schneirla, 1972; Richards, 1974), two distinct meanings seem to be emerging (Wilson, 1975). One merely sensitizes to the presence of a genetic component in behavior without prejudging the size or permissiveness of that component. The other emphasizes the idea of an unlearned behavior pattern that is not susceptible to modification through experience. The latter is the sense in which most social scientists understand instinct. Pareto rejected this second meaning, and so do modern biologists.

Speaking in genetic terms for socio-biologists, Barash (1977, p. 41) has remarked that 'behavior is not contained somehow within a gene, waiting to leap out like Athena, fully armored, from the head of Zeus. Rather, genes are blueprints, codes for a range of potential phenotypes'. Likewise, for Pareto, sentiments or instincts do not serve as exact templates for specific topographies of behavior (828); they do not manifest themselves as particular behaviors. Rather, they are guides or predispositions toward certain kinds or classes of responses to the environment. Such responses may also be viewed as evidence that in the course of evolutionary history directed behavior has been more frequently adaptive than random behavior. Sentiments may thus be thought of as *a priori* hypotheses that make useful bets about the relative appropriateness and efficiency of behavioral responses to environmental conditions.

It is fair to note that most social scientists do not deny the biological input in human behavior. Our failure consists in our refusal to confront the analytical implications of our admission – to go a step further and deeper in our explanatory endeavors. This failure is in part a vestige of the defensive stance into which early sociologists retreated in the face of attacks by self-styled referees of the intellectual order. We need be defensive no longer. Deficiencies notwithstanding, we have earned our place in the community of scientific endeavors. I think only timidity keeps us from participating with greater resolve in what is undoubtedly one of the most promising new frontiers of the scientific enterprise.

Instinct and learning are not mutually exclusive categories, for the capacity to learn is itself a biological fact. Why this is so seems simple enough, and a part of the logic of evolution. Genes, which we assume to be in some way related to sentiments, do not, strictly speaking, control behaviors. They control protein synthesis. Ultimately, this is a powerful way of manipulating behavior, but it is an awfully slow technique. Organisms genetically endowed with the ability to learn, however, are much quicker at deriving lessons from their environment; so, they have a much better chance of survival. And those organisms which can draw inferences, predict and simulate may be better off than those that learn only by trial and error. Learning, then, is the handmaid of instinct, not its alternative. Pareto's work on the human biogram will show that the instinctual thrust underlying learning predisposes us to certain classes of behavior. It is the search for such classes that, according to Pareto, provides the basis of a scientific sociology.

Sentiments of Innovation

The residues are grouped into six classes, four of which are of special importance for current sociology. Given limitations of space, I shall therefore focus on these.[3] The first, which Pareto calls 'the instinct for combinations' and I refer to here as 'sentiments of innovation', accounts for all the ways in which we combine certain things or ideas with certain other things or ideas to bring about changes.

Figuring as a force in a vast number of facts is an inclination, 'an instinct', to combine certain things or ideas with certain other things or ideas. We join a piece of wood with a piece of steel and get thereby a hammer. The scientist combines two propositions in a given way and out comes a theorem. Examples are legion. We are dealing with a fundamental, irreducible force underlying socio-cultural change. It is the source of the inventive faculty, the ingeniousness, originality, creativity, imagination, experimentation and curiosity of the species.

Pareto divides five of the classes of residues into several more specific types (genera), and at times continues the process to even finer levels. In the case of the instinct for combinations, he discusses eleven more specific sentiments, only a few of which can be touched on here. The sentiment, *Generic Combinations,* for example, underlies a large class of phenomena, some of which are of substantial interest to the modern social scientist. People everywhere have believed that by reciting certain words, sometimes in a particular sequence, or by performing certain acts, or by joining together certain properties, and so on, certain effects can be brought about. Such combinations may be thought to cure epilepsy or impotence, to insure a safe voyage, to communicate with the dead, or, in short, to bring about any desired state of affairs. Not surprisingly, then, when the calendar for 7 July 1977 yielded the combination 7/7/77, the public media reported that the number seven was extremely popular among American bettors at the race tracks. More generally, the very phenomenon of gambling itself, a multi-billion dollar industry in the USA, may be seen as an attempt to control the environment, to challenge what Sumner called the aleatory element, the element of chance in nature.

An equally broad set of phenomena are similarly comprehended by another variety of the instinct for combinations, what Pareto calls the sentiment of *Generic Likeness or Oppositeness* (913–21) but which might also be called, at least insofar as the attraction of likeness is concerned, the *tribal instinct.* This force is very important for understanding such phenomena as prejudice, discrimination, ethnic stratification, marital choice, and so on. Accordingly, it has been suggested that racial prejudice may be an irrational generalization of this much wider tendency to identify with individuals of similar physical characterstics and to be ill-disposed toward those who are different. But the sentiment in question manifests itself in a vast range of substantive fields, and in fact accounts for the enormously important ability of people to use analogy. Consequently, it performs a capital function in the production of knowledge and of culture in general. Analogies are tools with which the human mind classifies facts and discovers or constructs order in nature. It is a truism to say that without analogies science (to say nothing of philosophy and literature) would be impossible. But, scientifically, the use of analogy is not without danger, and Pareto was keenly aware of that fact, though many a confused and careless reader has reproached him for reasoning by analogy. His knowledge of the pitfalls as well as the virtues of analogies was so acute that these are classified as sophistries ('derivations') and discussed at length. One citation illustrates his position:

If offered . . . as a means of conveying some conception of an unknown, metaphors and analogies may be used scientifically as *a way of getting from the known to the unknown. Offered as demonstration, they have not the slightest scientific value.* Because a thing, A, is in certain respects similar, analogous, to another thing, B, it in no sense follows that all the traits present in A are present also in B, or that a given trait is one of those particular traits whereby analogy arises. (1614; emphasis added)

Another exceedingly important tendency treated under the present general rubric is the sentiment of *Assimilation* (937–43), though *Ritual Consumption* is a better term. 'Human beings have often believed that by eating certain substances one may come to partake of the properties of those substances. On rare occasions such phenomena may imply belief in some form of mysterious communion between a man and his totem or divinity; but more often those are different things' (937).

Social scientists have had a lot of difficulty in explaining such practices as ritual cannibalism and other exotic dietetic practices. The problem in part lies in not recognizing that, even if the forms of the practice differ widely, and the beliefs associated with them even more so, the underlying force is probably not different from that behind the Christian communion, for instance. In all likelihood, it is also at work in the modern practice of consuming tons of drugs which, more often than not, may do more harm than good. Again, it may account for the placebo effect, or the mysterious workings of inert substances. If the need is for consumption *per se*, what is consumed may be unimportant.

This illustrates how Pareto's sentiments work in scientific explanation: 'science looks for constant elements in phenomena in order to get at uniformities' (218). What matters to the scientist is not so much the great variety of rituals practiced, nor the great number of diverse substances consumed, nor yet the plethora of popular explanations given for such acts. Those are historically too fickle and, therefore, unruly to the scientific logic. What matters more is that the ritual practice of consuming substances to partake of their properties is universal. The sentiment in question helps to put together and explain a large number of seemingly disparate social facts. It is in this sense that the hypothesized residue epitomizes a scientific uniformity. Conversely, if we seek to explain as distinct entities the behavioral forms mentioned above, and the multiplicity of like ones left out, we will fail to recognize the denominator common to them all. And that necessarily renders scientific laws chimerical. A science that does not see common denominators is a discipline that discards scientific laws as fast as it constructs them.

The *pièce de résistance* among the sentiments of combination is the *Hunger for Logical Developments* (972–5). It is perhaps the most uniquely human trait, but it is a special case of a curiosity instinct, or exploratory drive, that is a broadly adaptive trait of many species (Hardy, 1965, p. 172). It refers in part to what Dobzhansky (1962, p. 214) has termed 'the restless and ostensibly idle and pointless curiosity that is expressed in the urge to explore, to pry into the nature of things, and to enjoy forms, sounds, colors, and thoughts and ideas'. It includes the urge to solve problems and to provide reasons and explanations for observations, experiences, sensations. It is also the source of human consciousness – consciousness of self as well as of the environment – and thus of the tendency to find the explanation of events in the human will (as with the rationalistic bias mentioned above) as well as in transcendental fictions and natural forces. The human imagination is always seeking causes, and when it does not find them it invents them. This sentiment, then, plays a crucial role in the rise of all systems of knowledge, and 'if one were to assert that but for theology and metaphysics experimental science would not even exist, one could not be easily confuted. Those kinds of activity are probably manifestations of one same psychic state, on the extinction of which they would vanish simultaneously' (974).

This sentiment is especially relevant for the learning-versus-instinct controversy, for learning is what takes place when the hunger for logical developments is released. Most human behavior is the immediate consequence of learning, and the more intense the curiosity instinct the further removed is behavior from instinct pure and simple (understood as a force unmodifiable by experience). This sentiment is thus responsible for the organization of complex behavioral formations that range far from simple reflex responses. So, while itself an instinct, the sentiment is a force that encroaches as it were on other instincts, setting up various levels of derived behavioral patterns and relegating pure instinct to the status of a hidden and indirect, though no less ultimately powerful, determinant of human behavior.

Sentiments of Persistence

The sentiments of combination account to a large extent for what is known as social differentiation, one of the fundamental processes of socio-cultural evolution (Spencer, 1897, 1915; Parsons, 1966). Most new combinations are ephemeral. However, 'After a [combination] has been constituted, an instinct very often comes into play that tends with varying energy to prevent the things so combined from being disjoined . . . This instinct may be compared roughly to mechanical inertia; it tends to resist the movement imparted by other instincts' (992). The instinct in question refers to a class of ten sentiments that Pareto terms 'persistences'. Combinations and persistences may be fruitfully understood as representing two sets of forces in dynamic tension and complementarity at once.

From one perspective, they may be viewed as evolutionary adaptations working in tandem and reflecting the organismic need to deal with both change and stability in the environment. They thus reveal both the ability to cope with the new, or to bring it about, and a tendency to be attached to fixed social and behavioral forms. The capacity for the new enables us to absorb knowledge and to react to specific events arising during the course of our life histories. Stable behaviors help to cope with environmental regularities that have exerted selective pressure during the evolution of the species (Waddington, 1957, ch. 5; Dobzhansky, 1967, pp. 15–16; Lorenz and Leyhausen, 1973). Accordingly, it is in the persistences that the forces accounting for the formation and endurance of the socio-cultural institutions are located; family, religion, economy, social stratification, law, education – in short, the entire institutional framework.

From another perspective, combinations and persistences are in a relationship of dynamic tension. That is due to the fact that innovation, in addition to adding to the existing socio-cultural repertoire, substitutes new patterns for existing ones. It is the function of the persistences to regulate this substitution, to check the pace and the scope of transformation. In being the judges in the final instance of what shall be added to, or abstracted from, the social order, the persistences are for socio-cultural systems what natural selection is for the rest of the animal kingdom. Specifically, the persistences perform a role analogous to the reproductive system in biological evolution. In an intricate interplay with the other classes of the sentiments, they determine which socio-cultural traits shall be selected for and which shall be selected against. This complex subject is being developed in a different context.

One of the especially noteworthy sentiments of persistence is *Relations with Places* (1041–2). This trait has received much attention in biology and to a lesser extent in sociology (e.g. van den Berghe, 1974) under various labels, 'territoriality' being perhaps the most familiar. It refers to a number of phenomena (Wilson, 1975, ch. 12; Barash, 1977, ch. 9), although it is most commonly employed in the sense of 'defended area' or defense of a relatively fixed space (e.g. van den Berghe, 1974, p. 780; Barash, 1977, p. 254).

Pareto discusses territoriality in similar fashion but also in a sense similar to the German concept of *Ortstreue*, the tendency of individuals to return to ancestral places for a variety of 'reasons', for example, reproduction and feeding. Other examples include class reunions, the visits of immigrants to the home country, the search for roots, and so on. Evidence of such territorial behavior in many species is copious (see Stokes, 1974).

The sentiment constitutes one important factor in a variety of phenomena, among which are patriotism, love for the mother tongue and for the native land, devotion to the ancestral religion, and the like. But it is also the foundation of the 'sense of property'. It provides a sense of belonging to places and things. In an evolutionary key, therefore, property may be thought of as the reification of a sum of sentiments which attach people to places, objects, or merely symbols. These persistences are, in turn, nourished by a sentiment according to which individual integrity is somehow altered without the recognition that given objects, places and symbols are inseparable from given individuals. It follows not only that the quest for property is a primordial tendency but also that the competition that is occasioned by scarcity is often more intense among the propertyless who aim for the same scarce property than among these as a group and those whose property they want. Conversely, a class of propertied individuals is likely to possess a certain consciousness of kind: not only do they constitute a group facing a common danger, expropriation; they also share the support of the moral principle that defends the integrity of private property.

The persistence sentiments are the bases of that intensely social feeling that both Durkheim and Pareto term 'religious', with the particular sentiment *Persistence of Relations between the Living and the Dead* (1052–5) playing a central role. 'The sum of relations between an individual and other individuals persists, by abstraction, in the absence of that individual or after his death' (1052). The ancient Semites had a proverb according to which to speak the names of the dead was to make them alive again. The present residue states something analogous to that: to honor the dead is to continue relating to them meaningfully as individuals.

Variation in the intensity of this sentiment is responsible for some interesting facts. When, for example, the sentiment is intense, the dead may actually materialize in the minds of the living. Hence, ghosts and other apparitions are 'real' enough; they are the tangible forms assumed by the present sentiment. By extension, the same may be said of apparitions of deities, fairies, and the like. Little wonder that, according to a Gallup poll, 54 percent of all Americans believe in angels, and about 40 percent believe in devils. One in nine believes in ghosts, and about eight out of a hundred say that they have even seen one (*Newsweek*, 1978).

When conversely the sentiment is weak, numbers of phenomena indicating a dread of death make their appearance. Mortality becomes an obsession, for the end of earthly life offers annihilation rather than the continuance of meaningful relationships. Modern people suffer from this affliction. The skyrocketing rates of suicide may in part attest to that. As Durkheim (1951) noted, the intense fear of death makes life unbearable: an endless vigil to the dreaded hour. Many cannot bear the wait. They get it over with quickly.

Sentiments of Egoism

The remaining two sets of sentiments selected for discussion may be termed 'egoism' and 'sociality' respectively. They too, like the combinations and persistences, may be viewed as sets of forces that are complementary and in a relation of dialectical tension at the same time. Social life entails a certain compromise between a purely selfish pursuit of goals and what social thinkers have severally termed 'the common good', 'the collective utility', 'the common weal', and so forth. As W. I. Thomas (1923, p. 42) put it in a strikingly Hobbesian key: 'The individual tends to a hedonistic selection of activity, pleasure first; and society to a utilitarian selection, safety first. Society wishes its members to be laborious, dependable, regular, sober, orderly, self-sacrificing; while the individual wishes less of this and more of new experience.'

Center stage among the selfish sentiments, seven or eight in number, are 'interests', namely, impulses 'to acquire possession of material goods that are useful – or merely pleasurable – for purposes of living, as well as to seek consideration and honours' (2009). They are of great intrinsic importance, but because Pareto dedicates practically his entire economics to them (e.g. Pareto 1896-7, 1906), they do not figure to any large extent in his sociology. Nevertheless, and with gross simplification, we may say that their basic message is much in keeping with the logic of natural selection. From the perspective of this principle, the basic tendency is the maximization of ego's own 'utility' as the ultimate 'design for living'. In biological perspective, according to a recent publication, the individual may be viewed as a 'survival machine behaving as if it has the [main] "purpose" of preserving its genes' (Dawkins, 1976, p. 140). In social perspective, interests impel toward the accumulation of wealth, power and influence.

Partial support for this thesis of the selfish tendency may be found in Pareto's discussion of the *Sentiments of Equality in Inferiors* (1220–8). Individuals who are motivated by these sentiments are generally convinced that they seek equality, or at least a fair deal, for all. Thus, in their public activities they harp on the sophistry (derivation) termed 'accord with collective interest' (1498–1500). Scratch a collectivist, however, and behold the most shameless self-seeker. The sentiment of equality in inferiors is really a mechanism whereby we often lift ourselves from a lower position to a higher one. If individuals talk of the interests of their social class as a whole instead of personal interest, it is because that is the acceptable mode of expression and because they are often unaware of the difference between real and apparent motivations. The class struggle is real enough, but upon close examination it is really an *individual* struggle.

The sentiments of equality in inferiors are thus really sentiments of privilege. They provide the impetus to scale the walls of inequality in order to improve one's own condition. During this stage, the individual is full of talk about equality, justice, fairness, classlessness, and the like. Once success has been achieved, however, the need for protection against the less fortunate takes over. 'People agitate for equality to get equality in general, and then go on to make countless numbers of distinctions to deny it in the particular' (1222). It follows that the 'sentiment of equality' is, paradoxically, one of the fundamental causes of enduring inequality. Yet, without it, given distributions of power and influence would remain undisturbed. Social mobility would be greatly impeded. Even the worthiest and most competent might be content to live in a state of quiescent behavior. Worse still, from an evolutionary perspective, ruling classes would deteriorate to levels that invite extinction. We shall return to this context in our later discussion of the social system.

Sentiments of Sociality

Life in society necessarily rests on a certain reciprocal goodwill between individual and individual. The sentiment may be weak or strong, but it cannot be entirely wanting. It is manifested in both animals and human beings in acts of mutual assistance and common defense. (1145).

Pareto isolates thirteen sentiments of sociality. They are forces whose ultimate function is to maintain the collective existence. They are thus forces of social order and as such are rich in theoretical significance for sociology.

We may begin by noting that, as the above quotation indicates, the sentiments of sociality suggest the presence in human society of genuinely altruistic behavior, a problem that is intensely debated nowadays among socio-biologists. His evidence led Pareto (1145–52) to speak of a tendency toward *Self-Sacrifice for the Good of Others,* but socio-biologists are strongly inclined to discount such evidence as proof of genuinely altruistic behavior. They do so in part on logical grounds: genes – those pieces of molecules that may be viewed as 'instructions' for anatomic and behavioral developments – replicate themselves as cells divide. In so doing they behave as if their main 'goal' were self-transmission to future generations. In part, socio-biologists incline toward this selfish hypothesis on the basis of some compelling facts. Many apparent acts of altruism – usually defined as action that tends to favor the survival of the recipient's genes while lowering that of the actor's genes – turn out to be quite selfish. The moment of triumph for the hypothesis of selfishness came with Hamilton's (1964; see also Trivers and Hare, 1976) discovery that the non-reproductive 'workers' among the insects of the Hymenoptera group, including ants, bees and wasps, are genetically closer to their sisters than they would be to their own offspring, should they have any. This peculiar circumstance is due to the odd, haplodiploid, form of sex determination among these insects. The important point, of course, is that sterility would, on the surface of it, suggest an extreme case of altruism. In fact, however, it is genetically extremely self-serving.

For Pareto, too, although he did hypothesize a sentiment of self-sacrifice for the good of others, the evidence of genuine altruism did not seem overwhelming. Indeed, his position explicitly states that others tend to benefit from our actions either through the unintended consequences of these or through intended effects that have served us first (Vol. 4, *passim*).

We must, therefore, search for other facts and sentiments if we must have a glimpse of genuine altruism in *Homo sapiens*. One of the most important sentiments of sociality is the *Need for Conformity* (1115–32). Recognition of this social force is extremely timely. It concerns, on the one hand, the issue of selfishness versus altruism and, on the other, the famous and still unresolved controversy between consensus and conflict theories in sociology. 'If a person departs from the uniform rule, his conduct seems to jar, and produces, quite apart from any reasoning, a sense of discomfort in the persons associated with him. An effort is made to eliminate the jar, now by persuasion, more often by censure, more often still by force' (1126). This is *Enforced Conformity*. Generally, the more strongly held a rule or value is, the greater is the tendency to defend it by resort to force. Herein lies the danger of the true believer and the ethically pure.

The association between the use of force and the intensity of belief explains the frequent association found in history between religion and force. Many a Christian has been at a loss to explain how the church of the humble Nazarene, who allegedly ordered his followers to turn the other cheek, could have produced the Crusades, the Inquisition and in general that violent spirit that has meted out countless and cruel punishments. More astonishing still is the fact that the cruelest punishment has often been reserved for the most pious, the Savanarolas and the Campanellas. But from a non-logical, an evolutionary, perspective there is no mystery to such apparent inconsistency. Religion is a fundamental human institution, and so commands the instincts that preserve the existing social order. Anything that departs from the religious uniformities of the times is bound to provoke a rabid reaction, however peaceful the religious philosophy of the founders or the nominal beliefs of the followers.

Enforced conformity, however, is not the only sort of conformity. 'Human beings', socio-biologist Wilson (1975, p. 562) has remarked, 'are absurdly easy to indoctrinate – they seek it.' Wilson and Pareto are probably both on the mark when they identify a voluntary version of the need for conformity. This is a crucial aspect of social order not only because it helps us avoid punishment, but also because it is a sort of teacher built into each of us, facilitating the process of socialization. Voluntary conformity grants us a learning shortcut, quicker and more efficient than individual trial-and-error. It is probably related also to the evolution of group defense that is a characteristic of innumerable species, and that means that once group defense was evolved, conformity came to attain survival value for the individual.

For our present purposes, however, we may see voluntary conformity as an adaptation to the costs entailed in enforced conformity. We may further hypothesize that, once a social order has been evolved in a species like ours, the penalties inherent in enforced conformity give rise not only to voluntary conformity but also to what Pareto (1160–2) and several other sociologists (e.g. Thomas, 1923) have termed the *Need for Social Approval* (or recognition, etc.). 'The need that the individual feels for beings well regarded by his group, for winning its approval, is a very powerful sentiment. On it human society may be said to rest' (1160). Currently the sentiment of social approval plays a crucial role in exchange theory (Blau, 1964; Homans, 1974), and not without justification, for, as Pareto notes (p. 1161), nearly all manifestations of the sentiments of sociality are accompanied by a desire for the approval of others, or for avoiding their censure.

This need entails a cost that is readily paid by many, namely, a behavioral predisposition that Pareto (1163) terms *Asceticism*. This is a sentiment that under some circumstances prompts 'the human being to seek sufferings or abstain from pleasures without design of personal advantage, to go counter to the instinct that impels living creatures to seek pleasurable things and avoid painful things'. It gives us a glimpse of true, ascetic altruism. Examples are common. The best refer to certain types of non-reproductive behavior: for example, monastic chastity; the occasional preference to raise, through adoption, the offspring of strangers rather than one's own; and self-immolation in the trenches or on the battlefield to guard one's buddies' lives, say, from an exploding grenade.

The need for conformity, together with several other sentiments (e.g. vengeance and territoriality), casts light on that famous topic of sociological theory which is often referred to as the Hobbesian problem of order and which has given rise to the controversy between 'consensus' theory and 'conflict' theories. I have discussed this problem elsewhere (Lopreato, 1965, 1975); so I will not dwell on it here except to emphasize that the need for conformity is a two-edged sword. It produces simultaneously types of behavior that would seem to be contradictory. Voluntary conformity is clearly a force of consensus, but enforced conformity often provokes resistance or counter-reaction. The need for conformity, thus, is at one and the same time a force of consensus and a force of conflict. The long-sought synthesis of consensus and conflict theories involves, of course, multiple and complex problems of conceptualization. But the need for conformity is a good beginning for such an enterprise.

The point may be appreciated in part also through a quick glance at the *Sentiments of Social Hierarchy* (1153–62). Such sentiments, Pareto notes, are widely observable in the animal kingdom, and are very strong in human society. 'It would seem indeed that no human society at all complex could survive without them' (1153). Social hierarchies take different forms in different species and in a given species (our own, for example) at different points in time and place. But history lends considerable weight to Pareto's proposition. In recent centuries, many a utopia of social equality has been attempted, and failed; leaders have promised that the state would wither away, but instead it has grown stronger; they have promised a classless society built on collectivization and the destruction of capitalist property, but instead a new class of owners and despots, the 'political bureaucracy', has come into being (Djilas, 1957).

Hierarchies may be viewed as mechanisms that both provoke and regulate aggression. They provoke it because, in being arrangements for the maldistribution of resources, they are constantly being challenged and defended. But they also regulate conflict because many, if not most, individuals suffer quietly the maldistribution. Indeed hierarchies establish 'an order of access to, or a scale of distribution of, resources between the members of a group' (van den Berghe, 1974). In a related key, biologists have observed that initial encounters between animals are characterized by repeated threats and fighting. But one effect of this behavior is social hierarchy, which in its turn reduces the level of conflict (Alexander, 1961; Wynne-Edwards, 1962). Hence, while there is undoubtedly justification for the widespread tendency among social scientists to view dominance relations in conflictual terms, it would seem that science might be more fully served if such relations were also viewed in consensual terms.

The Theoretical Value of the Sentiments

What is the value of the classification of residues? Let us emphasize as a beginning one of Pareto's fundamental messages: 'Our aim in these volumes is to constitute a science of sociology by stopping at residues just as the philologist stops at roots, the chemist at elements (simple bodies), the student of celestial mechanics at universal attraction, and so on' (1690, n. 2). Pareto's aim, in short, was the quest for 'constancies', for the uniformities of fact that exercise the special interest of the scientist. Those uniformities are termed 'laws'. Accordingly, residues may be viewed as foci for a more formal statement of sociological laws.

Pareto's theoretical strategy may be illustrated by returning to a sentiment briefly discussed previously: asceticism. The asceticism residue may be roughly termed a law because it epitomizes a large body of facts. Consider a Christian who does penance of some sort. Shall we conclude that the cause of the penance is his alleged belief in a God who accepts self-inflicted pain as a means of self-redemption? If our focus is on the manner in which beliefs are associated with actions, the conclusion is certainly justified. But that freezes us at a level of scientific explanation that is utterly *ad hoc*. Another man at another time and place will give another explanation for his penance. Thus, if we are serious about our discipline's being a search for scientific laws, we must widen the circle and see whether the penance of the Christian falls within a larger class of phenomena. We find, for example, that the Greek Cynics were famous for their asceticism, and yet they had no religious conception of their penance. The Spartans were superb at suffering pain as a means of maintaining strict military discipline. The Buddhists have practiced asceticism in attempts to stultify their vital energies.

Illustrations are literally numberless. Perhaps the most common and durable form of asceticism is fasting, which has been a feature of many peoples on all continents. Today, in Euro-American countries at least, abstinence from food for religious 'reasons' is uncommon. But countless millions diet, allegedly for health or aesthetic reasons, and in the United States a hungrier-than-thou way of life is sweeping the land. Shall we accept uncritically the reasons given for dieting, which propose considerations of health and beauty? Obesity is surely unhealthy and by some is considered unattractive. But if we do accept popular explanations we may fall victim to one of our most unique traits: self-deception. Chances are that today's fasting is at least in part the manifestation of the same behavioral force that accounts for the dieting and other ascetic behaviors of times gone by. The fact is that for one alleged reason or another people have always fasted, and this constant fact demands scientific recourse to an abiding force. Without that force, without the sentiment of asceticism, there would probably be no fasting even for aesthetic reasons.

We may now appreciate the fact that the evolutionary perspective is useful not so much, perhaps, because it postulates genetic forces of behavior, but because it seeks causes that organize large classes of facts recurrent in time and space. I think there is no disagreement in sociology that we lack a coherent theoretical framework, a 'paradigm' in T. S. Kuhn's (1970) terminology. I am tempted to suggest that Pareto's theory of the sentiments, duly amended to take into account new developments, constitutes the basis of a sociological paradigm that takes into account the scientific revolution in behavioral science since Darwin's and Spencer's time. Certainly it represents the spadework for the much-sought human biogram.

Classifications like the one we have dealt with perform a number of functions in addition to that suggested by the notion of paradigm. Let me briefly mention two. First, they underscore the value and extend the scope of the comparative method which, in the absence of the data and the conditions required by the classical experimental methods, appears to be an essential approach to historical phenomena. The extension lies in the fact that, having done a measure of comparative work (not enough, we would all probably agree) across the socio-cultural systems of a single species (a single case), we can now accept the challenge, however circumspectly at first, of glancing curiously across the social systems of multiple species, especially those most closely related to us.

Secondly, such classifications perform an analytical function: they aid in finding the constitutive elements of phenomena. For example, there is probably no more imaginative and creative an argument in sociology than Durkheim's discussion of the relationship between religious facts and 'society'. Who does not remember with a certain sense of awe the famous statement: 'So if [the totem] is at once the symbol of the god and of the society, is that not because the god and the society are only one?' (Durkheim, 1965, p. 236). The disquisition that leads to and from this statement is a paragon of brilliance. But the sociologists of the years to come are likely to find it too general; they will want to know just what it is in the nature of the human individual that makes possible such a truly marvelous feat, the generation of a conception that simultaneously makes an abstraction of society and a personification of the totemic principle. The answer, if Durkheim's equation is correct, may lie in the selection of specific human sentiments. The search for them and the mechanisms of their emergence would greatly extend the reach and the import of Durkheim's theory. The theory of sentiments contains the elements precisely for that sort of theoretical enterprise.

The problem of reduction
By now the specter of reductionism may have raised its ugly head many times in the minds of some readers. Actually, reductionism is a lovely word, and what it stands for should be pursued with enthusiasm. The fact is that reduction is one of the chief activities of all modern science. Indeed, one of the most important activities of science is precisely the reduction of some laws to others. The laws of Newtonian physics, for example, are reducible to the Einsteinian laws. Moreover, as Peter Medawar (1974, p. 61) has shown the reducing sciences thereby become richer in their empirical content and new concepts emerge at each level which do not appear in the preceding sciences. Reductionism, then, should be shorn of its emotional connotations and viewed simply as an indispensable methodological tool. It actually enriches all the sciences, without robbing them of their relative autonomy.

To avoid reduction, then, is to inhibit science, and as a sociological case in point I would like to suggest that our 'structural' theory, despite its talk of 'dependent' and 'independent' variables, renders sociology fundamentally acausal *exactly because we are reluctant to raise explicit questions about the basic forces that energize human beings as actors.* The concept of cause, a *sine qua non* of any law-like discipline, implies a transfer of some form of energy from one variable to another (Rush, 1957, ch. 1). But terms like occupation, income, status inconsistency, and so forth do not refer to sources of energy. They are purely nominal abstractions, or at best stand for indefinite mathematical quantities or spatial loci *through which* energy may move. They are what in physical science and in Pareto's sociology are sometimes termed 'ties' rather than 'forces' properly speaking. Hence, they are acausal. They are analogous to the term 'switch' in the electrician's craft. There is nothing inherent in the switch itself that has causal relevance. If the switch is connected to a live wire, it has a function to perform; otherwise it is useless. My point is that theoretically we tend to play with 'switches', without knowledge of whether or not they are live or inert, and without knowledge of which forces may be associated with them.

'Structural' propositions, then, are at best expressions of statistical relationships. But when such relationships are stated without concern for the underlying forces that account for them, they only too often have mere *ad hoc* value specific to a particular body of data, to a particular time, to a particular place. They may or may not capture the theoretical relationships of the underlying forces. What is worse, we have no way of knowing whether they do or not. That is why we are more adept at proving one another wrong than at confirming each other's findings.

Derivations: the role of reason

An admiring Aldous Huxley (1935, p. 8) stated that the *'Treatise* is (among many other things, of course) a museum of stupidities vaster even than Flaubert's chamber of horrors [in Bouvard et Pecuchet]'. Reference here is to Pareto's 'derivations', namely, those highly variable parts that are abstracted in the search for the residues. In the illustration we have given, for instance ('it is sweet and proper to die for one's homeland'), the derivation is the statement: 'it is sweet and proper'. This part is variable in the sense that if the Romans explained self-sacrifice in this fashion, the Americans will say instead that they die for their country in defense of 'democracy' or 'freedom', while the Germans, the Japanese, the French, and so forth will offer still other justifications for the act of self-immolation.

I firmly believe that the derivations are a most significant part of Pareto's sociology, but I have chosen in this chapter to avoid a detailed treatment of these 'masqueraders' and to lay the stress instead on that which (if we are not careful) they conceal: the sentiments. I have done so in part because of space restrictions but mostly because the sentiments are little understood, and I wish to underscore the Paretean contribution to the development of modern evolutionary theory.

A few brief comments about derivations are, however, in order. Pareto was keenly aware of the role of reason and purpose in human affairs. Both are inherent in the derivations. To a large extent, however, he accepted the naturalistic (some say 'mechanistic') postulate that while the human animal is purposive and to an extent rational, the events of the world owe less to reason and purpose than most thinkers are wont to concede. It follows that from this perspective, derivations are first and foremost tools of deception, of self as well as of others.

From another perspective, they are tools of persuasion, and it is from this vantage point that they are classified and discussed (Vol. III). We are now at the heart of one of the most significant problems in Pareto's sociology. How can derivations be means of persuasion when human conduct is ultimately motivated by the sentiments? They are means of persuasion because their basic function is to appeal to the sentiments. Most basically, therefore, derivations are the cultural tools that interact with and stimulate the sentiments; they are the mechanisms that call the sentiments to action. That means that they do perform an etiological role, but their causality is dependent on the causality of the sentiments and residues. Indeed, they are the result of the sentiment termed 'the hunger for logical developments'. They are an aspect of our consciousness. Consciousness, however, is time- and culture-bound. Being a characteristic of an ontogenetic individual, it tends to provide a perspective that is unique to a given time and place, and thus tends to hide premotivational forces at work. Pareto de-emphasizes the derivations because others have treated them as basic historical forces, indeed as history itself. That is unfortunate inasmuch as from this perspective history shows neither order nor continuity. Pareto's sociology, Mannheim's (1936, pp. 134f.) absurd misreading notwithstanding, is predicated precisely on the assumption that there is order in history. The derivations are superficial and highly variable from one generation to another, sometimes from one year to another, and even more from one place to another. As Poggioli (1965, p. 301), a *littérateur*, puts it: 'In reality they are only an intellectual parallel of fashion.' Science may be able to afford the luxury of sensitivity to fashion, but it does not begin there.

System and Equilibrium

The second major focus of this chapter, after the theory of the sentiments which has largely occupied us to this point, concerns an equally fundamental and problematic area of modern sociology: Pareto's work on system and equilibrium. His contributions here are fairly generally recognized as breakthroughs in the discipline, but they have not been allowed to influence us to any perceptible degree. As a young student in mechanical engineering, Pareto had written a dissertation on the equilibrium of systems consisting of elastic solid bodies. Oddly, this experience could have handicapped his sociology, for physical systems, as we shall see, have been conceptualized until recently in a fashion that has hindered theoretical development in physics and chemistry, and through their indirect influence in sociology and most other social sciences as well. Yet, while basically a physicist, and while frequently labeled a 'physicalist', Pareto long ago transcended the theoretical limitations of the traditional Newtonian approach to systems.

Let us begin by noting that system represents one of the true conceptual breakthroughs of the modern scientific revolution, for it has replaced the old idea of isolable units acting in one-way causality with a vision of phenomena composed of parts or elements in mutual interaction. System is the tool *par excellence* whenever the scientist is faced with complex situations involving many variables in a state of mutual dependence. System, in short, has modernized the concept of cause and has greatly advanced the progress of science.

Yet in sociology system occupies an ambiguous position. Indeed, many of our theoretical frailties are attributed to it. As Friedrichs (1970, pp. 61 *et passim*) points out, some social scientists have argued that the 'structural-functional' commitment to the system concept has hindered the examination of social conflict and change. Friedrichs (1970, p. 145) himself argues, in relation to Parsons's work, that this scholar's 'predilection for stability' is rooted in his choice of 'the focal term "system" as the characteristic concern of sociology'. I would suggest, though, that such critics have mistaken various misuses of system and related concepts by particular scholars for the logical properties of the concepts themselves. The concept of system prejudges neither the nature of social relations nor their mutability. The beauty of the concept is that as a heuristic device it may be programmed to grasp the complexity of socio-cultural phenomena in all their major features.

Pareto's system

A system may be concisely defined as a methodological construct representing a set, X, of interacting parts, $a, b, c, d \ldots$, and their properties, or variables, $p, q, r, s \ldots$. Interaction means that a, b, c, d are mutually related so that their behavior in X is different from what it would be in isolation or in another set. Put otherwise, we may say that, given a number of parts and their variables in terms of which we choose to examine phenomenon X, any change in one of the parts will be followed by changes in the others. The basic idea underlying the system construct, therefore, is *interdependence*, and we may think of it as the fundamental property of systems.[4]

Pareto's ultimate aim was an analysis of 'the general form of society'. Needless to say, he fell quite short of achieving this goal, and he knew it, terming his work a 'first approximation'. To thoroughly grasp the form of society, a system would have to account for 'all the very numerous elements' that determine it. Such a study was not possible at the turn of the century, and will very likely be impossible for a long time to come. Fortunately, though, certain elements appear to have strategic systemic importance in the sense that they are most acted upon by the excluded elements, so that by taking into account these central elements we indirectly take account of the others as well. As a first approximation, this theoretical program is acceptable enough. Successive approximations – the program for entire disciplines – would show the usefulness of such an approach and hopefully improve upon it in the process.

Pareto distinguishes between three broad classes of elements. One comprises those external factors that are roughly summarized by the term ecosystem, while a second includes such other exogenous elements as the influence of other societies upon a given society, and the effects of the previous states of the given society. A third category comprises the endogenous elements. It is these internal factors that Pareto considers systemically central and programs into his system.

The working system includes: (1) social stratification and mobility, which he terms 'social heterogeneity and circulation', (2) interests, (3) residues and (4) derivations. The first accounts for social structure and process, and will be discussed below. Interests represent rational and self-interested motivation. Residues and derivations represent cultural factors, on the one hand, and phylogenetic forces, namely, the sentiments, on the other. As he notes, for example, 'the word "residues" [is used] as including the sentiments that they manifest' (1690).

The system elements are interdependent, but only in part (2061). While interdependence is a basic property of systems, the degree to which the elements composing a system reciprocally affect each other is a matter of empirical discovery (see also Gouldner, 1959; Lopreato and Alston, 1970, p. 91; Sztompka, 1974). Indeed, it is precisely this sort of problem that a system perspective, if properly employed, is partly intended to solve. It follows that whether or not all the parts of a system contribute equally to the attainment of a given system state – to system change – is itself an empirical question. In Pareto's system, for example, the residues have more etiological force than the derivations. Sztompka (1974, pp. 87–8) refers to this form of systemic asymmetry as 'differential functionality'. It has a troubled history in whatever system theory we may have. The root of the problem is not too difficult to divine. On the one hand, the hypothesis of systemic asymmetry requires purely quantitative data and the use of a mathematical logic that have been slow in obliging us; merely to postulate interdependence, with the connotation of symmetry that it encourages, is a less demanding feat. On the other hand, and very possibly as a consequence of this first problem, there is an unfortunate tendency in social science to use ideal types not as heuristic devices but as substantive conclusions (Parsons, 1937, pp. 601–10). Nevertheless, sooner or later we must cope with the necessity of specifying the differential, and varying, contributions made by the different system elements to its changing states (see Gouldner, 1959, p. 265; Buckley, 1967, p. 67).

Interdependence does not describe merely the relationships existing among the elements of the system. It also describes their interaction with the system taken as a representation of a historically specific reality *sui generis*. That is, the form of society is determined by all the elements acting upon it; but when a society is organized in a certain way under the action of given forces, 'it acts in its turn upon them, and they, in that sense, are to be considered as in a state of interdependence with it' (2060–1). This is Pareto's concept of *emergence* and is another fundamental property of systems. It refers specifically to that force of systemic change that is residual when the action deriving from all the particular elements has been accounted for.

The fact that social structure, in this special systemic sense, emerges as a force in its own right is, in turn, responsible for another important fact: the events taking place within a society – that is, the forces acting upon it – can no longer be altogether arbitrary or random (2088–9). Emergence, in short, leads to the principle of immanence (Sorokin, 1957).

Equilibrium
Immanence is the logical basis of the concept of equilibrium, and

we may think of it, or of equilibrium, as the third basic property (along with interdependence and emergence) of systems. This property is reinforced by interdependence. The latter has equilibrating effects by virtue of the fact that a given effect introduced into a system must cycle through the interdependence of the system parts, which will *tend* to slow down, and *sometimes* possibly annul, the introduced effect. Such action in effect frees the emergent phenomenon to pursue its inner dynamics, what Sztompka (1974, p. 140) terms 'a sort of inner program' orienting the system toward 'a preferred goal state'. That is, cycles of interdependence are mechanisms through which systemic self-regulation is enhanced.

Equilibrium is one of the fundamental tools of modern science. As employed usually in physical science, it states approximately that if, for instance, an attempt is made to modify any of the variables (for example, temperature) that influence a physico-chemical system, then a reaction will take place in the system in such a way as to reduce the magnitude of the alteration that would otherwise take place in that variable.

There are, however, various kinds of systemically relevant phenomena in nature; therefore, the concept of equilibrium, to be useful, must be applied with a certain degree of flexibility. There is one type, for example, in which, barring minor perturbations, the interdependences may be cyclical in the sense that certain positions or relationships are taken by the system with recurring regularity. Such is the case, for instance, with our solar system. Another type, characteristic of our social world, is such that, while some cycles (in the above sense) may be observed in the system, the system itself is constantly changing form or position.

From our point of view, therefore, there are at least two major problems with the traditional definition of equilibrium in physical science. One might be termed the postulate of excessive system determination. The problem is suggested by the fact that socio-cultural systems are less rigidly determined; they only *tend* to react in such a way as to reduce the influence of extra-systemic factors. The degree to which they succeed in effecting such reduction varies greatly. The second problem consists of the fact that the definition does not explicitly account for *normal* change in the system, that is, for change that is unrelated to external factors and is inherent in the very organization – the immanence – of the system itself. These two problems lie at the root of much of the controversy surrounding system-equilibrium applications in sociology and sister disciplines. Many, not all, practitioners have basically followed an unmodified physical strategy. Many critics, not all, have argued, sometimes without foundation, as if those whom they criticize had followed such an approach. Still other social scientists reason as if that were the only approach available to us.

The first major systematic effort to apply the equilibrium concept to the study of society was made by Vilfredo Pareto. It is to the immense credit of this scholar that he managed to avoid both of the above problems and many others associated with them as well. He begins by pointing out that the system is 'constantly changing in form' and defines equilibrium as follows: 'the state X [equilibrium] is such that if it is artificially subjected to some modification different from the modification it undergoes normally, a reaction at once takes place *tending* to restore it to its real, its *normal*, state' (2068; emphases added).[5] What is the normal state? It is the 'original state as modified by *normal change*' (2067). Change *of* the system, as well as *in* the system, to use Parsons's (1961) useful distinction, is then normal. Moreover, the reaction to extra-systemic forces is only in the form of a *tendency* to restore the normal system state; the degree to which the tendency succeeds is a matter of empirical specification.

What kind of equilibrium is Pareto referring to? We have long recognized a variety of equilibria (see Perry *et al.*, 1963; Russett, 1966; Lopreato, 1971). Two types, however, are of fundamental importance, and they concern us here. They are the *static* and *moving* (sometimes equivocally termed 'dynamic') equilibria. In the static equilibrium, time is irrelevant, and the values of the variables at which the system elements are in equilibrium are constant. I do not see the relevance of this type of equilibrium in social science. The moving equilibrium, on the other hand, concerns systems that go through processes of continuing structural change. In such systems, the values at which the parameters are in equilibrium are likely to be continuously changing (Hagen, 1961, p. 147). This type, which reflects the fact of immanence, is the major type of equilibrium relevant to systems like those we encounter in social science.

Now, if the system is 'constantly changing in form', and if the effect of the equilibrating reaction to external forces is a tendency to return the system to the 'original state as modified by normal change', then the socio-cultural system, as Pareto views it, tends toward a *moving* equilibrium. That means that the system assumes successive states $X_1, X_2, X_3 \ldots$ of equilibrium through time. To say, then, that a system is in moving equilibrium is to say that the system is a historical phenomenon tending to trace a line of development that may be viewed as a series of preferred states. I say 'preferred' both in the sense that certain states may be attributed as goals to the people (or some of the people) represented in the system and in the imputed sense that a basic motive force of the system is its own immanent property – and consequently, system movement is always 'preferential'.

Why then, we must ask, would Friedrichs, as we have seen, and countless others associate system and equilibrium with 'stability'? Believe it or not, we have classical physics to thank for it. Fortunately, there are recent developments in physics and physical chemistry that are heartening to us social scientists as well as to physical scientists. They suggest a return to Pareto to discover developments that in a real sense parallel, and to a degree foreshadow, the recent ones in physical science.

The 1977 Nobel Prize for chemistry went to Ilya Prigogine for his work on 'dissipative structures', or structures 'far from equilibrium'. According to Prigogine (1977; see also Prigogine, 1976 and Prigogine *et al.*, 1977), in 'classical physics time plays such a minor role that future and past appear in the same way . . . in classical physics we have a kind of statical world'. Classical physics is the 'physics of being'; it deals with systems in static equilibrium. Examples are a pendulum at rest and other such things that do not have the ability to do any work. Time, however, cannot be denied. Whenever time enters the picture, we have 'dissipative structures' with 'irreversible processes', structures that are constantly generating and consuming energy. Examples of such structures are a human cell, the human body, a city and of course a society. What impressed Prigogine is the fact that these 'far-from-equilibrium' structures do have an internal order, that associated with the instabilities of such structures is a systemic tendency to 'act as a whole'.

Let us come to the main point. Dissipative structures – our own kinds of structures – are characterized as being 'far from' equilibrium as a matter of historical bias: because, that is, they are indeed quite far from the equilibrium of the static systems in classical physics. But insofar as they are capable of converting potential 'chaos' into 'order', there is really no logical reason why Prigogine could not have termed them structures in, say, moving, perhaps precarious, equilibrium. Indeed, there is a certain irony in Prigogine's language. At the same time that he is endeavoring to theoretically place physics in the flow of time, he is stuck with a terminology ('far from equilibrium') that grants to the inadequacies of classical physics the power of conceptual arbitration over the needs of both modern physical and modern social science. Prigogine is really speaking of structures far from *absolute* equilibrium. Yet, in discovering 'order out of chaos' – order in structures of such extremely complex energetic processes that from the perspective of classical physics they represent chaos – he is really implying a concept of equilibrium that transcends the logic of the 'physics of being' in favor of the logic of the 'physics of becoming'. In sociology, through Pareto, this concept of moving or energetic equilibrium goes back to 1916.

So the Paretean concept of equilibrium has long been, potentially at least, a tool with which to study social change as well as social order. What is more, there is nothing in the logic of the moving equilibrium which states, as some critics of equilibrium models have claimed, that reaction to extra-systemic change is always adjustive. The degree (and kind) of systemic change due to external forces depends on such facts as degree of immanence, interdependence and the magnitude of the external forces impinging on the system.

Perhaps the best way to answer the previously noted criticisms of equilibrium, which from the perspective of the logic of classical physics are indeed justifiable, is to observe, however briefly, Pareto's own application of what we have termed the moving or energetic system-equilibrium model.

The theory of revolution: a précis
The argument goes something as follows. Suppose we divide a society into a governing class and a governed class. Let us suppose, further, that it is in principle possible to give individuals in each class a score indicating their capacity to perform in positions of political administration (to be in the governing class). Dividing the population into the more competent and the less competent, we come up with two idealized categories which Pareto, with surprising looseness of language, terms 'classes'. The more competent category consists of 'elites'; the less competent, of 'non-elites'. Looking now at the distribution of elite and non-elite individuals, we find in the typical case that not all those in the governing class are elites, while many in the governed class are in fact elites. Accordingly, we may speak of a four-item typology, as follows:

A *Governing Class* (consisting of)
  1 *Governing Elite*
  2 *Governing Non-Elite*
B *Governed Class* (consisting of)
  3 *Non-Governing Elite*
  4 *Non-Governing Non-Elite*

This, of course, is a static representation. In fact, the distribution of the elites and non-elites between the two classes changes through time, so that sometimes the governing class consists almost exclusively of elite individuals, while at other times very few elite (that is, *competent*) individuals are in the governing class. This situation is the source of a fundamental system stress or contradiction, for Pareto conceptualized a meritocracy, a free circulation of talent and skill, as a prerequisite for equilibrium, namely, social movement with gently undulating perturbations indicating minor conflicts in society. The acme of social disorder is reached when those most competent to occupy governmental positions are found in the subject class (these are the non-governing elites), whereas the governing class consists of individuals who should instead be in the subject class (that is, they are governing non-elites).

Revolutions come about through accumulations in the higher strata of society [the governing class] – either because of a slowing down in class-circulation [mobility] or from other causes – of decadent elements no longer possessing the residues suitable for keeping them in power, and shrinking from the use of force; while meantime in the lower strata of society [the governed class] elements of superior quality are coming to the fore, possessing residues suitable for exercising the functions of government and willing enough to use force. (2057)

We shall return to the question of force in a later context. For the moment, the central point is that revolution is an expression of extreme incompetence in the governing class. The incompetence, in the typical case, is assessable in terms of the growing disparity in the distribution of sentiments between the governing class and the governed class, the latter being rich in persistences, the former becoming excessively endowed with combinations. This intensification of the sentiments of combination is most directly reflected in the governing class's growing reliance on cunning and deceit, and its accompanying avoidance of force.

The growth of incompetence in the governing class is due to several factors, for example, the inheritance of wealth or power, which most importantly hinders free mobility. Mobility is a great force for equilibrium, for it transports across class-lines the required mixtures of sentiments. With its reduction, and with the increase in sentiments of combination among the governing class, cunning and deception increase, with the associated inability to use force. Cunning, corruption and softness (or alternatively, capricious and random violence) represent for Pareto what he, rather sarcastically, terms 'humanitarianism'. The humanitarian is incapable of recognizing conflict as an inevitable aspect of the social existence, indeed as a phenomenon that in some respects is quite functional. As Busino (1975, p. 305) notes in his discussion of Pareto's work on the class struggle, the struggle is both a constant fact of life and a 'positive element, for it insures the vitality of societies'. The humanitarian is an actor who, intent on denying the undeniable reality of the ugly face of the social life, ends up by making matters worse. Within the context of the classification of sentiments, humanitarianism is represented by the sentiment termed 'instinctive repugnance to suffering' (1142–3) of any sort. The sentiment is prevalent in 'decadent ruling classes. In fact it may serve as an adequate diagnosis of such decadence' (1143).

This sentiment, therefore, represents a crucial adaptation in the evolution of human society. Its function is to counteract the self-interest that motivates governing classes to restrict mobility and remain in the saddle indefinitely. In short, instinctive repugnance to suffering on the part of a governing class is an evolved mechanism of self-destruction which works by weakening the resolve for self-defense and rendering the incompetent rulers susceptible to aggression from below.

The irony is that this softening of the rulers bears with it a myopic and self-interested posture. More precisely, perhaps, it shows the real nature of what, with a touch of paradox, was termed 'the sentiment of equality in inferiors'. The underlying quest for privilege now manifests itself in full bloom.

> The individual comes to prevail, and by far, over family, community, nation. Material interests and interests of the present or a near future come to prevail over the ideal interests of community or nation and interests of the distant future. The impulse is to enjoy the present without too much thought for the morrow. (2178)

The softer the governing class becomes, the greater its rapacity and greed for the goods of others. The more humane are its pronouncements, the greater its unlawful appropriations and usurpations of the national patrimony (1901, p. 59). Malcolm X would have loved Pareto.

It has sometimes been noted that revolts often take place when economic conditions in the subject class are relatively good (e.g. Brinton, 1938, pp. 43–4; but cf. Davies, 1962). This is Pareto's own diagnosis. The reason for such a conjunction is that the predominance of self-interest in a decadent governing class leads it to recruit individuals who specialize in economic and financial pursuits – the 'speculators'. The activities of these producers of wealth often benefit the country, but in the long run 'they prove to be borers from within' (2227). The production of wealth becomes an end above all others, with the result that many of the moral traditions of society are sacrificed to its sovereign grip.

Thus it follows that as the wealth of a nation increases, its moral degradation likewise grows. But people, Pareto seems to argue, tolerate poverty more readily than they endure moral disorder and cynicism. Hence the conjunction of revolution and relatively good economic conditions. It is not, of course, that the masses have no interests. It is rather that they are the bearers of the persistences, which are the very foundations of society. When, therefore, the moral order threatens to disintegrate – when the system moves too far from equilibrium – the masses come to its aid. In this sense, popular aggression is fundamentally *moral* conduct.

This question of the use of force in society is truly crucial to an understanding of Pareto's theory; it is a disservice to approach it in an ideological key. It is sometimes forgotten that Pareto's beloved Switzerland has long been one of the most peaceful societies in the world. Pareto loved his freedom, his books, his wine and his cats – in that order. He loathed any sort of violence. But of all the great sociologists, barring none, he was unique in his profound grasp of the role of force in society, whatever the form, time and place. Within his theoretical scheme, the failure to use force on the part of the governing class may be a fact to be ideologically applauded, but it is also an evolutionary symptom (*not a cause*) that the class no longer has the capacity to hold the reins of government. Conversely, the ability to use force on the part of the subject class is society's way of selecting against incompetent leadership. That – no more nor less. Personal predilection is irrelevant. Note that the masses, which according to many an ideologically misguided account of Pareto's work (e.g. Mannheim, 1936) were assigned no role in history, are on the contrary viewed as the repository of the forces that hold society together. They are at once the judge and the savior of last resort: when a society risks extinction through the ineptness of its rulers, the populace typically rises to the occasion and saves it from ruin (2191). This action is mediated, of course, by the leadership of the non-governing elite, who, once in the governing class, will typically make the same end. But they are in every way the evolutionary product of mass movements.

One necessarily wonders, therefore, about some interpretations of Pareto's work on revolution. One of the most respected writers has this to say: 'The great revolutions had been no more than the struggle of a new elite to displace an old one – with the "people" serving as its humble soldiers' (Hughes, 1958, p. 81). On the contrary, for Pareto revolutions perform a survival function, 'something like ridding the country of a baneful animal pest' (2191), and the masses are the repository of the residues required to bring it about. By virtue of revolution a society often avoids total dissolution and predation. But society is in a continuous process of transformation. It flows like a river. From time to time, there is a flood: violent disturbances occur. The existing governing class is replaced in large part or *in toto* by the rising elites. The flood subsides, and the river again flows in its normal bed, in equilibrium. The new governing class now begins its slow transformation leading to its own downfall. And so it goes. From a political perspective, these are the basic elements of socio-cultural evolution.

Notes: Chapter 5

This essay has profited from the comments of Moyra Byrnes, Annette Weiner and, most generously, Buford Rhea. I am enormously grateful to them.

1 Fortunately, the University of Minnesota Press and Phillip E. Allen, president of the Pareto Fund, will soon publish an abridged edition that should facilitate Paretean studies.

2 References to the *Treatise* will be to the 1963 Dover publication. The figures after the year of publication refer, as per convention, to numbered sections. Hereafter, for convenience sake, references to the *Treatise* will be shown without the publication year.

3 The other two are Sex (1324–96) and the Need for Activity – or Self-expression – (1089–1112). A case could, of course, be made in favor of the great significance of these two classes, too.

4 This is intended as a minimal definition. The execution of system analysis entails, of course, complexities that we cannot treat here.

5 The term 'artificial' is here roughly synonymous with extraneous, out-of-the-ordinary. Somewhat similar to artificial changes are short wars waged by rich countries, epidemics, floods and similar disturbances. Such changes tend to effect a slight disturbance in the state of equilibrium and then pass away (2068).

6

Durkheim's 'Elementary Forms' as 'Revelation'

EDWARD A. TIRYAKIAN

To say something original and stimulating about Emile Durkheim is
no easy matter. If the audience is one of college students, Durkheim may be hard to sell because what he writes about seems dated
and his style is rather stuffy, matter-of-fact. Moreover, the social
context of the French Third Republic is quite unfamiliar to most
Americans, yet is a key background to much of his professional
activities, and some of his essential presuppositions go very much
against the grain of contemporary hedonistic individualism, which
would undoubtedly have caused him much anguish. If the audience
is one of professional sociologists, the challenge is differently threefold. First, so much of the profession reflects Durkheim's project for
establishing sociology as a distinct academic discipline that to go
over this is tedious and unexciting precisely because the project has
been so well institutionalized. Secondly, Durkheim's sociological
realism has manifestly more of an elective affinity with a continental
'conservative' tradition than with the utilitarian liberal or radical
traditions that are the ideological mainstays of most sociologists.
This may have to be qualified, however, since the political climate
of the 1970s and 1980s is more in consonance with what may be
termed a 'new conservatism' than was the 1960s, a decade imbued
with romanticism and radicalism. Thirdly, there has been such a
spate of excellent sociological studies about Durkheim during the
past ten years, and apparently so few stones left unturned, that unless one resorts to writing critiques of earlier studies (which some
budding authors have resorted to doing) on Durkheim, one must
honestly ask oneself 'are you saying anything new'? [1]
Yet, as ought to be the case with any and all major classics, some-

thing original can always be said about them, and the present symposium affords an opportunity to do this. Consequently, the main thrust of this chapter will be to turn the spotlight on Durkheim's last major work which, in my judgement, is to the corpus of socio-logical writings what Beethoven's Opus 125 is to orchestral music – the 'peak experience.' Recognizing the perennial relevance of any classic, I would propose that different times bring out not only new mores but also new relevancies. Hence, in this chapter we shall con-sider the actuality of his *magnum opus* as well as Durkheim himself as an inspiring figure for those beginning to study sociology. As the title of this chapter suggests, I wish to couple Durkheim's seminal study with another great 'classic' of Western civilization. Although this will be done partly for heuristic purposes, it is also because I consider both works highly relevant guides for our time of radical social and cultural transformations.

Durkheim as Exemplar

Since Professor Rhea, in calling for this series of lectures, was initially stimulated by students' questions about the purpose of study-ing sociological classics and classical figures, a few words about Emile Durkheim as a role model may not be out of place.

One thing that immediately stands out about Durkheim is that from the beginning he took sociology seriously as his vocation; his paramount mission in life was to make the academic community heed this new discipline as a rigorous scientific discipline. Durkheim was in close contact with all sorts of persons – both academics and non-academics – but furthering the development and autonomy of sociology remained his salient preoccupation. Of course, Durkheim was politically 'engaged', as were his close associates (Marcel Mauss, Henri Hubert, Maurice Halwachs, Georges Davy, Celestin Bougle and others) – they were practically all 'progressives' – but Durk-heim did not allow sociology to engage in political polemics. Very much like Max Weber, he stressed the 'objectivity' of the discipline as a prerequisite for probing and examining the most sensitive and delicate social issues. And very much like Weber, Durkheim's orientation was one of social responsibility – sociology and its prac-titioners should be seen as a vehicle and as its agents for upgrading the quality of social life through increased knowledge concerning underlying conditions, processes and trends. One may disagree with this mode, but in Durkheim one finds an exemplary expression of the responsible scientist and educator.[2]

The second respect in which Durkheim can serve us as an exemp-lar is his ingenuity in indicating the sociological relevance of phenomena that others would gloss over. His first major work was the well-known *Division of Labor.* Durkheim was obviously not the first to draw attention to this ubiquitous phenomenon of complex living organisms, nor even to its importance for industrial society – Adam Smith, Karl Marx and Herbert Spencer were just some of his predecessors in this area. But what I find so imaginative about Durkheim's approach is his taking as objective indicators of change in intersubjective ties (from mechanical to organic solidarity) changes in the respective ratios of civil and criminal law to the total legal code. Using these indicators enabled him to test out a hypothesis about forms of solidarity. Durkheim was not the first to write about solidarity (which was an essential aspect of the ideology of the Third Republic), but to study it scientifically by taking the legal code as a social indicator which can be quantitatively measured was a demonstration of his powerful sociological imagination.

The Division of Labor became overnight a landmark of sociological writing and has remained a standard reference work ever since its publication as a doctoral dissertation in 1893 – which I suspect is an unmatched record of longevity in sociology. When I was a graduate student a quarter of a century ago I think it was this work of Durkheim that received the greatest attention. That may have been because in the 1950s the problems of an industrial order, labor–management cleavages and the centrality of the meaning of the work situation seemed to be at the core of Western society; alienation as an existential aspect of American society was treated as a function of the social organization of work. Only later did alienation become talked about in political terms and nobody in the 1950s was talking about (or getting attention on the theme of) 'post-industrial' society. Hence, Durkheim's *Division of Labor* was much more 'in' then than for a later generation of sociologists. However, the underlying question of the structural basis of solidarity in modern society that is at the core of Durkheim's inquiry will remain with us for the foreseeable future. Moreover, this work contains major features of modernization theory, which almost attained paradigmatic status in the 1960s in relating the transformations of Western society in the nineteenth century to the complex process of development in the non-Western or Third World in our own day. One of the things not anticipated by Durkheim, nor by most sociologists who looked at modernization as an irreversible process, was what might broadly be called the 'rediscovery of ethnicity' (TeSelle, 1974), on the one hand, and the rise of regionally based autonomist movements within established nation-states (e.g. Quebec, Scotland, Catalonia) on the other (Mayo, 1974; Link and Feld, 1979). Both of these sets of phenomena go counter to the general historical trend analyzed by Durkheim of social solidarity becoming more and more 'organic' through the ramifications of economic organization and less and less 'mechanical' (of which ethnicity and regionalism are derivative instances). Are we seeing a major transformation of the modernization process analyzed by Durkheim, or is the renewal of 'mechanical solidarity' a secondary reaction within the major trend? Obviously, the eclipse of *The Division of Labor* can only be partial.

The second major study by Durkheim, *Suicide*, is the one which stole the spotlight in the 1960s and which demonstrates even more his genius at finding sociological patterns in areas of behavior that others would dismiss as idiosyncratic. There is something very audacious in Durkheim's taking the phenomenon of suicide as a socially grounded one. For suicide in Romantic and post-Romantic Europe, stretching from Goethe's Werther to Dostoyevsky's Kirillov, was seen as *par excellence* an individual action, an assertion of the freedom and autonomy of the self over and against 'objective reality'. When one reads Durkheim's analysis, one can only marvel at his incisive demolition of non-sociological standpoints. The genius of Durkheim was to find in suicide statistics (ironically, they were provided him by his chief *bête-noire*, Gabriel Tarde) readily available data which force us to take seriously the reality of the social *sui generis*. It was as much of a coup for the nascent sociology as Freud's coup of finding dreams and slips of the tongue relevant for studying the unconscious was for the nascent psychoanalysis. Of course, once you view these phenomena as sociologically (or clinically) germane they become 'obvious', but someone has to indicate their relevance initially, and Durkheim's example may provide the inspiration today for new explorers of the social domain to find or establish certain overlooked 'data banks' as highly pertinent.

Suicide reached its zenith of popularity in the 1960s, and I think this is partly because of the climate of that decade. In the 1960s changing lifestyles, the breakdown of traditional normative standards, the cult of the anti-establishment that became 'chic' – all of these had something to do with the rapid rise of interest in the sociology of 'deviance', which replaced an earlier emphasis on 'social disorganization'. The latter was taken as an establishment perspective, whereas 'deviance' studies in their orientation are most likely to either extol non-conformity (for example, by indicating how human are the deviants), or to stress that deviant behavior is a relational phenomenon rather than an intrinsic moral attribute or even that it is the moral establishment which is culpable because it stigmatizes the doer for an act which in itself is morally neutral. Durkheim's *Suicide* is hardly a panegyric for the glorification of deviance, but in this study and also in two other works, *The Rules of Sociological Method* (1938) and 'Two rules of penal evolution' (1973), you will find the elements of a sociological theory of 'crime and punishment' which integrates deviance into general sociological concerns. Durkheim quite clearly saw that the problem of order and conformity is intrinsically related to the problems of disorder (anomie) and deviance, that deviance is socially defined and a 'normal' aspect of every society just as punishment is. It is unfortunate that the sociology of deviance and the sociology of institutionalized behavior have as a rule attracted different sets of practitioners, with Talcott Parsons and Robert Merton being notable exceptions. A better recognition of Durkheim's contribution to the problem of deviance would be very beneficial in bridging these two basic orientations.

There is one remaining aspect of *Suicide* which bears consideration, above and beyond the amazing number of new studies (e.g. Atkinson, 1978) which continue to be written by sociologists in response to this octogenarian classic. It is that Durkheim sensitizes us to watching out for changes in the rates of given phenomena as social indicators. When there is a marked change in the rate of a phenomenon, one must pay attention to the group in question and its societal context, for that may be indicative of some important deep dislocations. One aspect of suicide rates worthy of attention is that in recent years there has been a substantial increase in the suicide rate of those at the lower end of the age spectrum. Absolute numbers may be very small, but one should take seriously the increase in suicides in the USA among those aged 15–19 which have gone from 2·4 to 7·0 per 100,000 during the period 1954–73, while the rate for children between the ages of 10 and 14 rose 33 per cent between 1968 and 1975.

What accounts for this? What does it tell us about the present conditions of adolescence? What does it reveal about broader aspects of social structure? What does it portend? These are the sorts of questions which I would pose to students who might be assigned *Suicide* to read as a sociological classic.

Having suggested that Durkheim merits our sustained attention, let me turn to the work which has had increasing attention in the 1970s, which demonstrates the acme of his genius, and which may gain even greater sociological attention in years to come: *The Elementary Forms of the Religious Life* (Durkheim, 1961; hereafter abbr. *The Forms*).

Early and Recent Perspectives on 'The Forms'

The Forms was the first work of Durkheim to be translated into

English, only three years after its original publication; ironically, it suffered a period of relative benign neglect by the American sociological profession which lasted until well after the Second World War. Yet it was of great importance to social anthropology, notably in British circles (particularly that headed by E. Evans-Pritchard at Oxford University), and in a related manner in French ethnology, with such figures as Marcel Mauss, Marcel Griaule and Roger Caillois. Griaule's studies of the Dogon and Evans-Pritchard's studies of the Nuer, both highly influential in stimulating further monographs analyzing belief-systems and collective representations as symbolic expressions of social organization, have as their 'totemic ancestor' Durkheim's landmark study. If his *Suicide* is regarded as a paradigmatic research monograph relating data to theory, then *The Forms* may also be considered as seminal in the even more complex task of sociological hermeneutics, taken as seeking to decipher or decode the symbolic structures of social organization.

Before proceeding further, let me pause to observe that by a remarkable coincidence Durkheim was preparing his great study of symbolic structures of social organization at just about the same time as Freud (two years his senior) was starting depth psychology with his explorations of the symbolic nature of personality organization. Further, the year of the publication of *The Forms* was the year that Carl Jung, who had just broken with Freud,[3] published his momentous *Symbols of Transformation*. In effect, then, it might be said that depth sociology and depth psychology began at the same time. As a last prefatory observation, within a year of publication of *The Forms*, Freud published an equally radical interpretation of religion with his *Totem and Taboo*. Though there is a world of difference between the two approaches, there is a structural similarity in that the former accounts for the religious life in terms of 'primitive' social organization, while the latter accounts for it in terms of 'primitive' neurotic behavior.

The meaning that *The Forms* has had for its readers over the past seven decades has been very varied, which is probably a characteristic of any great classic. Speaking from personal experience, each new reading of the work at different stages of my academic career has brought out new layers of significance. But before I communicate what my most recent encounter with this work has suggested, let me retrace some other accounts. I will be selective in mentioning only the earliest and the latest perspectives.

Early Perspectives
Social scientists who reviewed *The Forms* shortly after its publication were not sociologists working on contemporary society but rather

anthropologists dealing with pre-industrial society. Among the group of early reviewers may be mentioned Van Gennep (Pickering, 1975), Goldenweiser (Pickering, 1975) and Malinowski (1913). Their evaluations were fairly negative. Durkheim was criticized for over-generalizing his theory of the origin of religion from a single case, and one where the quality of the ethnographic materials serving as a data base was rather uncertain at that; he was taken to task for negating the place of the individual or the subjective aspects of religion, and he was criticized for grossly simplifying epistemology in his stress on the social basis of mental categories. Further, Malinowski (1913, p. 530) noted a contradiction between Durkheim's methodological dictum announced in *The Rules of Sociological Method* to treat social facts as things and yet resorting in *The Forms* to psychological interpretations of the origins of the 'religious'.[4] There is one further early review which merits even greater attention, and that is one jointly prepared by Marcel Mauss *and* Emile Durkheim himself, which first appeared in the *Année sociologique* in the last volume published under Durkheim's editorship ([1913], translated in Pickering, 1975).[5] What did Durkheim himself see as major features of his recently published study?

Durkheim (and Mauss) begin by contrasting the methodology and conclusions of *The Forms* with James George Frazer's *Totemism and Exogamy*, published just before the former. Whereas for Frazer totemism is to be extensively studied everywhere it appears, for Durkheim it will be dealt with intensely in just a few societies; whereas Frazer approaches totemism as a loose bundle of magical beliefs, for Durkheim totemism takes us to the heart of the religious phenomenon, characterized by the distinction between the sacred and the profane. The totem is surrounded by prescriptive and proscriptive regulations, and totemism has all the essential elements of every religion.

Durkheim *qua* reviewer goes on to castigate Frazer for failure to recognize the social character of totemism, which is precisely the focus of his own study. It is not the concrete totemic animal which is sacred for its believers but the emblem which represents it. The symbol of the group is sacred to its members because the sentiments or feelings evoked by the group in its members are 'identical in nature with religious sentiments' (Pickering, 1975, p. 179). What the faithful worship is, at bottom, the moral force (i.e. ideas and beliefs and sentiments) which is that of the collectivity. Yet, to mitigate this impersonal aspect, the reviewers note that this moral force becomes individually differentiated in every person, reflecting biological and psychological variations. From this differentiation stems the notion of soul, which is a parcel of the totality of ideas (or normative structures) we have internalized from the collectivity; the soul is both the particularized form of the totemic force and the morally superior part of ourselves. With the idea of the soul there developed the idea of the personality, leading to further differentiation into spirits and civilizing heroes, which in the popular imagination are seen as heads of great social or religious institutions (on the Durkheim treatment of heroes, see Hubert, 1915, and Czarnowski, 1919). From initiation rites, which are not specific to a clan but which are tribal or even inter-tribal, the popular imagination derived the notion of a personality considered as the creator of humanity, the 'maker of men', in brief, the high god, father of mankind.[6]

Finally, state the reviewers, *The Forms* takes up the study of the cult, which is the complement of the study of religious beliefs. The cult has two sides. In its negative dimension it is made up of abstentions, of observing what is forbidden or prohibited.[7] Various rites are attached to this, including ascetic ones (such as fasting). On the other hand, various rites pertain to the positive dimension of the cult, including those of sacrifice, mimetical rites [8] and expiatory rites. For all these, *The Forms* seeks to uncover what collective feelings are expressed, maintained, or renewed in ritual action and thereby in the most essential aspects of social life.

Durkheim (and Mauss) then make the observation that the study of the religious cult and its various rituals endeavors 'to demonstrate the extent to which the details of ritual action are bound up in the most essential aspects of social life' (Pickering, 1975, p. 180). This statement, I would suggest in passing, may be thought of as like the riddle of the Sphinx; it is the key not only to an understanding of *The Forms* but also to comprehending the relevance of this classic for understanding what underlies features of the modern complex social world which seem otherwise 'irrational'.

In closing their review, Durkheim and Mauss state that the interpretation of religion which unfolds in *The Forms* treats it as a system of actions having as an end the continuous fashioning and refashioning of the spirit (*l'âme*) of the collectivity and of the individual. And, they add, although religion plays a speculative role (that is, it is a basic avenue of man's cognitive/theoretical orientation towards the world about and beyond him), 'its major function is *dynamogenic*' (1975, p. 180, emphasis added). The latter is a term which I find most suggestive, even pregnant with meaning, and which as far as I can recollect does not appear elsewhere in the writings of Durkheim and Mauss. It demonstrates that the functionalist approach to religion, so much today associated with the Durkheim position, is by no means limited to a 'static' or 'status quo' orientation; Durkheim viewed his magnum opus as a study of the dynamics of social structures as much as of their mechanics. It is the religious factor, itself activated and reactivated by the assembling of the collectivity in certain periods, which then acts as a positive feedback in giving the collectivity focus and direction in crystallizing its ideals. We shall come back to this all-important notion in a later section, but for the present let me indicate that the review closes in reaffirming that religious forces – which do exert a real moral influence on individuals – are social in that they arise from the interaction of individuals, not from isolated individuals directly. This, then, is how Durkheim, at least in reviewing his own work, saw its major outline and contributions.

Recent Perspectives

It is in recent years that *The Forms* may be said to have come into its own as a major stimulus for the sociological mind, concerned with making sense of the contemporary social world. For one, Robert Bellah, a prominent sociologist of religion, has been influenced by Durkheim in evolving his stance of 'symbolic realism', which has both ontological and epistemological dimensions (Bellah, 1970, pp. 236–59). Bellah has elsewhere (1973) pointed to two aspects of Durkheim's last work that until then had been glossed over in the sociology of religion: (1) its contribution to the development of the study of civil religion, and (2) the significance of periodic collective rituals and new movements of collective enthusiasm. Extrapolating from these observations, Bellah's interpretation of Durkheim is reflected in his own position, which coincides with that of the present writer:

> My conclusion, then, runs about as contrary to so-called secularization theory as is humanly possible. It is my feeling that religion, instead of becoming increasingly peripheral and vestigial, is again moving into the center of our cultural preoccupations. (Bellah, 1970, p. 246)

Another recent reflection on *The Forms* deserving mention is Phillip Hammond's essay on religious pluralism (1974). Much of the field of the sociology of religion has been implicitly framed by an early reading of *The Forms* drawn by social anthropologists going back to Radcliffe-Brown and Malinowski, dealing with the central place of religion in relatively small-scale and relatively isolated societies: namely, religion serves a key social function in providing the normative and cognitive bases of integration. Hammond, working from a civil religion approach, suggests that *The Forms* raises the problem of the nature and function of religion in contemporary society but does not offer a satisfactory answer; we need to pursue further the religious significance of societal integration in complex, modern society, he asserts. What catches his attention in particular is the presence of multiple meaning systems or religious pluralism, such that any church becomes less sacred. The problem that spills over from this is a reintroduction of the question of anomie, in the sense of asking what structure outside the traditional one of religious institutions comes to be the agency for redefining the encompassing reality in cognitive and moral terms. Because of its heterogeneity and cleavages, modern society cannot dispense with a generalized symbolic medium which expresses ultimate reality; yet, religious pluralism precludes any one religious organization having this role. Hammond's answer – that current legal institutions come to express in the USA an emergent 'new moral architecture' – may be debatable, but at least it shows the fruitfulness of taking seriously the problems posed in *The Forms* as leaven for coming to grips with religion and society in contemporary Western society.

There are still other recent evaluations of *The Forms* which attest to the intellectual vigor of this classic for contemporary sociologists. One is provided by Robert Alun Jones in an essay (1977) announced as a preparation for a later full-length study of *The Forms*. Jones offers a major methodological critique of the problem of how a classic in the history of sociology – taking *The Forms* as prototypical – is interpreted and understood by later writers. Reviewing multiple interpretations of what Durkheim meant to do in this work, Jones argues in so many words that later writers ignore Durkheim's real intentions and have judged or evaluated this work in terms of later sociological development rather than sought an understanding of what Durkheim himself was doing. Jones then seeks to recover Durkheim's intentions in writing *The Forms* (although curiously enough he makes no reference to the Durkheim and Mauss review). He means for this process of recuperation to illustrate a more rigorous methodology for the writing of the history of sociological theory than has prevailed, as indicated in the exegetical literature on *The Forms* (and presumably of other 'classics').[9]

Jones's approach bears much affinity with the phenomenological approach of Edmund Husserl, typified in the dictum of going 'to the things themselves', that is, of holding aside or 'bracketing' the presuppositions which interfere with viewing the phenomenon as it manifests itself. In this instance, whereas *The Forms* have been interpreted in the light of either subsequent or anterior developments, Jones seeks, if I understand him correctly, to bracket these perspectives and go directly to an understanding of what the author was seeking to do while writing his work. Incidentally, although 'positivism' associated with Durkheim and 'phenomenology' associated with Husserl are taken as perhaps the two major antagonistic methodological orientations on the current scene (the former taken to be the main 'hard' approach, the latter the main 'soft' approach to investigating social reality), two recent essays have sought to indicate some important common ground between phenomenology and Durkheimian sociology (Coenen, 1978; Tiryakian, 1978b), one of them in terms of a comparison between *The Forms* and Husserl's last major work, *The Crisis of European Sciences* (1970).

From the perspective of general theory, the most important recent reappraisal of *The Forms* is that provided by Talcott Parsons (1978), who already had helped to familiarize American sociologists with this work in a previous chapter (1968a, pp. 409–50) originally written as far back as 1937. In reading anew Durkheim's text, Parsons notes that now he sees the work not primarily as a study in the sociology of religion (undoubtedly its most frequent image) but rather as a theory of evolution of the human condition generally. Parsons cogently proposes that Durkheim was dealing with more than the religious factor in society (taking the latter in the analytical sense of social systems); he was dealing with religion as a fundamental structure of the general system of action. It is the interdependence and interrelationships of social systems, cultural systems, personality systems and biological systems which underlie what we designate as 'the human condition'; the sacred provides the essential symbols of the grounding of human existence.[10] A further substantiation of Parsons's intriguing perspective is that one of Durkheim's last essays (1960), written shortly after *The Forms*, has as its focus the social conditions of human nature.

This then is a brief and hurried look at some recent perspectives on Durkheim's last great work. Originally the province of anthropologists it is only during the past two decades that sociologists have given it proper recognition. The cask will continue to yield rich wine, since writers such as R. A. Jones and W. S. F. Pickering, among others, are preparing additional studies based on *The Forms*. In brief, we may note that this classic has already been a seminal work for two disciplines, first for anthropology and more recently for sociology.

The Elementary Forms as Revelation

To return to the challenge of introducing novelty in the reading of Durkheim, I would like to propose that *The Forms* might be considered in relation to another remarkable piece of inspiration literature, *The Book of Revelation*. If I do so, it is not only because of some structural similarities between these two 'classics', but also because I think they are most appropriate as preparation for understanding the dynamics of change before us.

Let me begin by some gross comparisons of the two. Just as *The Forms* is the last major work of Durkheim, so *Revelation* brings to a close the Bible. It completes the accounting of the world begun in *Genesis*, symmetrically opposite to it in that *Genesis* is cosmological, while *Revelation* is eschatological. That is, the former gives us a religious understanding of the beginning of the world, the latter of how the world will end. *The Forms* has both cosmological and eschatological elements: cosmological in accounting for the genesis of the categories of the mind, of religion and ultimately of the foundations of the social world; eschatological in the sense that Durkheim clearly anticipates a new collective effervescence, a new set of ideals which will generate new normative structures to a new form of societal organization (Desroche, 1974, pp. 43f.).

One may also point out that *The Forms* and *Revelation* stand out from their respective antecedents in terms of what they stress. Obviously in terms of style *Revelation* contrasts with the rest of the New Testament by its language of violence, cataclysms, bloody upheavals and physical destruction. What the two share on this point is the extremely varied and complex symbolism presented. The symbolism of *Revelation* is far more complex than any other work in the Bible; it involves colors, allegories and numbers (e.g. 666, 1260) in a plethora infinitely more complex than those studied by anthropologists in examining symbolic aspects of a concrete human society (e.g. Turner, 1967).

Certainly part of the repeated appeal of *Revelation* has been endeavors to decipher its symbolism in the light of one's contemporary situation. What upon first reading might be taken as a piece of weird science fiction writing – with strange creatures from below as well as from above clashing together in a cosmic combat – has also become in various actual historical settings the codebook and blueprint guide to making sense out of the world. *Revelation* has even functioned before the term was actually used as 'liberation theology'. I have in mind a host of millennial movements which have drawn heavily upon *Revelation*, seeing it as the key to praxis (Cohn, 1961; Thrupp, 1970; Hill, 1973; Wilson, 1973). One should bear in mind that *Revelation* is more complex as an inspirational source than just a 'myth' of a final end. It can also be interpreted as the promise or expectation of a radical new beginning, characterized by the purification and shedding of the old order (*Revelation* 21).

Everything in our present horizon points to the renewed relevance of *Revelation* in coming years. Increasingly in the next two decades of 'countdown' before the next millennium we should witness an accentuation of a *fin de siècle* mentality which will find *Revelation* apposite to decipher the meaning of our age. Rapid acceleration of moral decay, the dissolution of 'civic culture', the economic erosion and spiritual demoralization of much of the working class and middle class, the increased potential for the political control of total populations by means of genetic programming, computer technology and government bureaucratic controls, all these are some of the features propitious for a generalized feeling that the world is coming to an end. It may also be that Western society in the next century will have such a different economic, political, cultural, ecological and normative base of integration from the mass, democratic, urban, industrial and secularized Christian society which has constituted the 'modern' period that in effect we shall have a new global society that will appear as a discontinuous 'new heaven' and 'new earth'. It could be viewed as as much of a radical improvement over our present social organization as the liberal industrial society of the nineteenth century saw itself as a 'new earth' in comparison to the society of the *ancien régime*. In brief, whether as a codebook for deciphering the events associated with the termination of an old social order which has lost its 'spirit' or else as a code-book for a new age, *Revelation* should become once more a centerpiece for the collective imagination.

Durkheim's *Forms* is a sociological complement to *Revelation*. It may be taken as both the culmination of positivistic sociology and also as marking a new beginning. First let us consider how it may be viewed as the *terminus ad quo* of positivistic sociology. I have in an earlier section discussed how audacious Durkheim was in treating suicide as a social phenomenon. Just as bold is his seeking to complete scientific knowledge by taking the religious dimension as fathomable in terms of a sociological accounting. *The Forms* closes the gap between two seemingly opposite standpoints of human understanding – the scientific and the religious – by treating religion as real, but as an aspect of reality which can be understood objectively, that is, by the scientific method. There is thus achieved the positivistic ideal of the unity of knowledge expressed scientifically. And Durkheim goes back to his sociological predecessors, Auguste Comte and Henri de Saint-Simon, for his source of positivistic inspiration: it is knowledge of the social which completes the spheres of human knowledge, and knowledge of the social is the key to understanding the nature and functioning of religion. In turn, a new social order will require a new religion; ultimately, then, the sociology of religion, a synthesis of scientific knowledge and the religious verities of social structures, fulfills positivism by empirically establishing the appropriate ends and normative structures of the social order.

Related to this, *The Forms* provides a grand finale for positivistic sociology by making sense of collective expressions of the irrational, at least of what appear to be illogical, non-rational if not irrational sorts of attitudes and comportment: penitential rites, food taboos, ascetic practices, and the like. In brief, by exploring the fundamental forms of the religious life, Durkheim has pried open the lid from a vast source of irrational behavior. He has found an ingress into the study of collective behavior, which has been kept on the periphery of sociological attention rather than being a prime area of sociological concern. Durkheim in *The Forms* has laid the foundations of a dynamic social psychology, one that was further developed by his associate Maurice Halbwachs, but the significance of Durkheim's insight concerning the contagiousness of the sacred as an underlying factor in collective behavior has not been adequately exploited in later studies.

Like *Revelation, The Forms* may also be viewed as heralding a new beginning. In its very complex analysis of the fundamental symbolic nature of social reality, of the depth structures of society in which the sentiments of the sacred and of social solidarity are generated and regenerated in their manifold interaction, Durkheim has gone beyond sociology, in a way paralleled by Rank for psychology (1958). There is an unwitting return in Durkheim's analysis to the image of an *axis mundi*, studied by Eliade (1959). It is the religious life which is capable of acting as a lever against the institutionalized normative order. To understand the effect of the religious life on social actors, Durkheim completes or goes beyond a delimited positivistic sociology. He does this by probing the collective sentiments, such as ritual attitudes and enthusiasm, evoked respectively in institutionalized and non-institutionalized religious situations of great intensity, which are released in the general assembly of the collectivity. One may say that Durkheim takes us from positivistic sociology (which views the social world as a field of objects) into a depth sociology that must come to grips with the intersubjectivity of social life. It is here that Durkheim encounters two great attitudinal poles of the religious life: on the one hand, the attitudes of the religious *law* (which both proscribes and prescribes) and, on the other, the attitude of the *spirit*. This polarity recurs in all the major religions and typically is viewed as a pair of antagonistic orientations. Sociologically viewed, however, they are both necessary for social life: the former to maintain the level of institutionalization necessary for social existence to continue in a more or less orderly fashion, the latter to renovate the system of ideals which underlies institutionalization. Together their creative conflict gives viability to social solidarity.

How does this relate to the theme of a new beginning and to a new sociology? Let me broach this by a further reference to *Revelation*, namely, to one of its key features in the successive opening of the seals of the scroll of the universe, which God holds in his right hand (*Revelation* 4). We have here the ultimate mysteries of the universe, the cosmic forces which structure the universe and the earthly condition of men. As they are successively wrenched open by the Lamb, the apocalyptic process leading to the final establishment of the New Jerusalem takes place (*Revelation* 6–21). I do not wish to propose that Durkheim had *Revelation* in mind when he wrote *The Forms*, but for a final juxtaposition of these two works, let me suggest that Durkheim has in this ostensible study of Australian primitive religion opened up the seals of the fundamental factors of social existence!

The first seal is that of *social change*. The dynamics of society are to be found in the dialectic between the sacred and the profane. Economic life is taken as the embodiment of profane activity, which tends to prevail in the everyday world. Although the reference is explicitly to Australian ethnographic materials, we infer that Durkheim's analysis is intended to be more general in scope. Economic activity, characterized by 'a very mediocre intensity', provides little enhancement of social solidarity: 'The dispersed conditions in which the society finds itself results in making its life uniform, languishing and dull' (1961, p. 246).[11] This is the first phase of social life, one marked by the social distance between actors. The second phase, in sharp contrast, is marked by effervescence, a social gathering of the collectivity which lifts actors out of the profane and into the realm of the sacred, of the extraordinary. The analysis may take the Australian corroboree as a point of departure, but this genesis of transcendence, of collective 'peak experiences' is meant by Durkheim as a general feature of the human social condition. He makes this very explicit:

This is why all parties political, economic or confessional, are careful to have periodical reunions where their members may revivify their common faith by manifesting it in common. To strengthen those sentiments which, if left to themselves, would soon weaken, it is sufficient to bring those who hold them together and to put them into closer and more active relations with one another. (1961, pp. 240f.)

So, we might say, social change for Durkheim reflects the centrifugal forces of economic activity and the centripetal forces of social solidarity, the latter being set in motion by socio-political gatherings where the social group assembles from all corners to affirm and re-affirm the bases of the collectivity.

Durkheim's differential evaluation may appear out of kilter with our image of what activates modern society. Economic activity in the advanced industrial era of this century seems more exciting and influential than Sunday church-going; the stock market and corporate, multinational deals involving billions of dollars are surely more glamorous and important than religious life, are they not? However, it must be borne in mind that Durkheim is not really talking about ordinary, routinized religious activity but rather about these existentially crucial (or critical) moments in a social group when there is a gathering from all corners to affirm and reaffirm the fundamental value bases of the collectivity. Moreover, in the past ten years or so we have been witnessing an important grassroots renewal of religious consciousness, particularly within Christianity, with the spread of what may be termed the charismatic renewal. It is an unexpected consequence of the 'counter-culture' movement of the 1960s, with its emphasis on altered states of consciousness and consciousness-raising. What is involved and what will be the consequences of this general 'new religious consciousness' (Glock and Bellah, 1976) is hard to foretell, but in the light of earlier religious renewals and their cultural consequences (Tiryakian, 1979) we should recognize that religious effervescence is the harbinger of major socio-cultural change.

The eminent sociologist of religion Milton Yinger spoke for many when he declared in a recent presidential address to the American Sociological Association: 'In my judgement we are in the midst of a major civilization transformation' (Yinger, 1977). This would not be the first transformation of Western civilization. In other instances (for example, around the second, eleventh, sixteenth and early nineteenth centuries) socio-economic changes were attended by equally significant redrawings of the ties of *community*, and the renewal of community was framed in terms of religious renewals or new forms of religious consciousness. Durkheim's analysis, then, sensitizes us to the dynamics of communitarian movements, to the renovating and developing of collectivity orientation which crosscuts customary lines of social stratification, the latter being attendant on economic development. A most dramatic instance which illustrates the contemporary relevance of Durkheim's insights in *The Forms* is taking place as I write this, namely, the religious-inspired revolution in Iran led by the Ayatollah Ruhollah Khomeini. No matter what its outcome, the situation in Iran in the first months of 1979 at least demonstrates the strength of the regeneration of the sacred in popular assemblies seeking to re-establish the societal community that had languished during the preceding regime devoted to economic development. But the communitarian movement is manifest in various other political movements of autonomy in Western societies (e.g. in Wales, Quebec, Scotland, Catalonia), and there, too, there are profound interchanges of religion and polity which manifest a search for the 'roots of identity' (Mayo, 1974). Durkheim had a keen sense that the religious life held the key to the question of identity; identity is implicitly in Durkheim's treatment a complex interplay between our social existence and our representations of this existence, and it is at the subjective and intersubjective level of religious phenomenon. As he expressed it in the conclusion of *The Forms*: '. . . the collective consciousness is the highest form of the psychic life, since it is the consciousness of the consciousness' (Durkheim, 1961, p. 492). It is religious consciousness which expresses collective consciousness, and new forms of religious consciousness may be taken as expressing a nascent societal community, or a renovated one.

This, then, is what is opened up in the first seal lifted by Durkheim. The second seal is that of *knowledge*, its source and foundation. The cognitive dimension of the human condition is one that frames the basic epistemological problems of any theory of knowledge. Durkheim makes quite clear in the very introduction to *The Forms* that he seeks to renovate epistemology, whose foundation had been severely shaken by the secularization of theology into modern philosophy, and particularly as this culminated in the radical skepticism of Hume. Durkheim seeks to reconcile the polar positions of *a priori*sm and empiricism by establishing that the categories of human understanding, without which there is no accumulated knowledge, are collective representations. Stated differently, the sociological unveiling of the source of knowledge discloses that the elementary structures of knowledge – the categories and fundamental concepts such as space, time, causality, and so forth – are reflections or expressions of the fundamental parameters of social existence. They are articulations of the human social condition, *a priori* in the sense that new members of society are socialized by means of the categories of knowledge, yet empirically grounded in the reality of human society.

If knowledge both reflects and frames the structures of social organization, then in opening up this seal, Durkheim's sociology of knowledge also relates to the first seal, that of social change. For we can say that not only does an understanding of the categorizations of a society provide us with its basic rules of organization, but also that changes in the basic categorizations (e.g. those of measurement of space and time, of social titles, etc.) are intrinsically related to the dynamics of change. Changes in form of collective consciousness, in cognitive and moral boundaries, are part and parcel of changes in social organization.

The third seal is that of *power*. Knowledge and power are complementary bases of ordering social existence (Balandier, 1971). In discussing the ground of the principle of causality, which underlies our pre-scientific and scientific ordering of events, Durkheim (1961, pp. 405ff.) establishes a nexus between causality and the idea of *force*. Whence our awareness of forces? It is from the experience of moral forces that are part of our inner life. Yet these are experienced as external, for example, as sacred things and in the relation of these to profane things. For Durkheim, the idea of force makes clear that it is not an individual, personal attribute but a collective, impersonal one. This is particularly demonstrated in the characteristic of the sacred as contagious – that is, a thing which is experienced as sacred can render something that comes into contact with it sacred, while not having any reduction or loss in its own potency (for example, in the case of Christianity, the principle of apostolic succession, or in other instances, the clothing of a holy person partakes of his sacredness, even after he no longer wears it). Power, then, is a collective product, and if power or *mana* 'rubs off', if we are aware of force which can be shared without being diluted, it is because we participate in and feel the strength of collective action.[12] The French saying 'l'union fait la force' (in unity there is strength) is a pre-sociological testimony to Durkheim's reasoning.

Moreover, the idea of *force* is correlative with that of *power*, and this takes us into a host of interrelated ideas and concepts, such as ascendancy, mastership, domination, dependency. All these basic relational categories with which we classify and order the beings of the universe, states Durkheim, are derivatives of social relations: 'It is society which classifies beings into superiors and inferiors, into commanding masters and obeying servants; it is society which confers upon the former the singular property which makes the common efficacious and which makes power' (1961, p. 409).

Earlier in his study, discussing the fact that symbols of the totem are more efficacious than the totemic object itself, Durkheim has already provided an extensive discussion of the basis of power in the collectivity. The extraordinary gathering of the collectivity is 'dynamogenic', to use his own term. Heightened interaction is a direct factor in providing what we might term today 'positive feedback' in a situation of general effervescence. The one who addresses the assembly and who is in resonance with its sentiments and aspirations comes to feel a special increase of force within him, which in turn he redirects to its very source, the collectivity. The power of the pulpit and the power of the tribune are one in the sense that they tap the same feedback process. Here is Durkheim's description of the feedback:

> The sentiments provoked by his words come back to him, but enlarged and amplified, and to this degree they strengthen his own sentiment. The passionate energies he arouses re-echo within him and quicken his vital tone. It is no longer a simple individual who speaks; it is a group incarnate and personified. (1961, p. 241)

Since he precedes this discussion with reference to the night of 4 August 1789, Durkheim may well have had in mind such French revolutionary orators as Danton, Desmoulins and Robespierre. He undoubtedly would have no difficulty recognizing in our century Marcus Garvey, Sékou Touré, Nasser, Nkrumah, Castro, de Gaulle, Churchill and others who at critical moments in the existence of their respective collectivities were able to express and channel the diffuse sentiments into a common endeavor; by so doing, these persons were viewed as extraordinary, as saviors or redeemers of their nation. He who succeeds in being the 'man of the hour' does have the power, whose ultimate source is the collectivity but which the latter projects, so to speak, on to him inasmuch as he acts as their collective representation.[13]

In prying open the seal of power, Durkheim also shows us the equivocal aspects of power, that is, the fact that this force generated by the collectivity in the increased interaction of its members on special occasions is morally ambiguous. He credits Robertson Smith with having pointed out the ambiguity of sacredness (1961, p. 455). Religious forces are morally differentiated in how people experience them: those which are beneficent, upholders of the moral order, and those which are malevolent, impure, destructive. They stand in dialectical relationship to one another, and both are differentiated from profane matters (1961, pp. 456ff.). Durkheim's analysis on this score treats in a new sociological light the Hebraic image of Yahweh as having two sides, good and evil, the benevolent creator and giver of life but at the same time the wrathful destroyer of life. The biblical covenant may be seen as an endeavor of the collectivity to regulate which aspect of power it will be the object of, while utilizing the power of destruction against antagonistic collectivities. In the modern, secular age the problem or power remains: unchained or divested from an ultimate, transcendental authority, power generated by and solely from the collectivity, harnessed by the charismatic leader, may have no boundaries to limit it. The greatest demonic as well as the greatest divine collective enterprises are set in motion by Prometheus unbound.

A fourth seal opens up the dimensions of aesthetics, of mirth, of the ludic element of life – in brief, of various *leisure* activities which reinvigorate us. This pertains to what the Greeks termed 'catharis' and to that sector of social systems which Parsons termed in an earlier usage 'tension-management'. In *The Forms* Durkheim notes how ritual attitudes manifested in solemn occasions often turn to merry-making activities as an integral aspect of commemorative rites. We can further note the close ties between holy days and holidays, fasts and feasts; moreover, one very important feature of secularization is for holy days to become mere holidays. There is here an important dialectic between *asceticism* and *hedonism* which is opened up by Durkheim's observation that would well repay our attention. Thus, feasts and games derive from religious occasions. The religious gathering of the collectivity is not only a most serious matter since it is necessary for the regeneration of collective forces and collective identity; it is also a matter of great enjoyment, and one can sum up this complementarity by saying that *re-creation* of the social is interrelated with its *recreation*. Durkheim considers recreation as essential to social life and because this is a basic function of the rite, religion has a charm and attraction quite apart from its formal aims (1961, pp. 425ff.).

To do justice to the theme of *The Forms* taken in conjunction with *Revelation*, we would need to unveil three more seals; however, I will limit myself to the above quaternity. I hope this exposition will leave the reader with the desire to unveil other parameters of the social world which may be nestled in passages of *The Forms*. As the etymology of the word discloses, *religion* opens men to the ultimate bonds of the world. Durkheim's classic takes us into an encounter with the religious factor as the very center of social action and social interaction. To go beyond this classic we will need to study how –even for the period of modernity and perhaps 'post-modernity' – the historical process discloses the fundamental conditions of intergroup conflict as well as intragroup solidarity to be a religious phenomenon even more than any other social factor, including class. Perhaps it will require an effort of mind for the neophyte to read *The Elementary Forms of the Religious Life* as a document which discloses the infrastructures of our own social world and not just that of the Arunta. But once he or she sees it as the glasses necessary for a proper vision of social life, then what follows will be a revelation.

Notes: Chapter 6

1   I have elsewhere (1978a) provided an extensive overview of Durkheim, including a brief bibliographical discussion of recent other major Durkheimian studies.

2   While preparing this chapter I came across a recent volume reappraising John Dewey, who was born just a year later than Durkheim. Reading the lead essay by Charles Frankel, I was struck by how applicable this is to Durkheim, whose appointment at the Sorbonne was also in education. Thus, Frankel indicates that Dewey (like Durkheim) felt that science has to justify itself more fully than in a technical or instrumental sense by reconstructing the foundations of moral and social beliefs. Also, Dewey sought a détente 'between the sacred and the secular, the ideal and the practical . . . and most of all, in the classic dualisms of social philosophy and social practice – the individual versus society, values versus facts, ideals versus the practical, morals versus science' (Frankel, 1977, pp. 30–2). Durkheim also matched Frankel's evaluation of Dewey that the latter 'showed by his own example that it was possible to be liberal, self-critical, never wholly attached to any partisan cause, and yet to possess an outlook that could give an intelligent human being steadiness and a sense of dedication' (1977, p. 41).

3   To extend the parallel, at the time that Jung was breaking with Freud, Gaston Richard was breaking with Durkheim, essentially for the same basic reason of conflicting religious viewpoints (Pickering, 1979).

4   It might be noted that just as Durkheim was culminating his brilliant career with his analysis of primitive Australian society, Malinowski (1963) and Radcliffe-Brown (1913) began theirs by writing also on the Australians!

5   The original review occurs in a section of the *Année* assessing various works on totemism (recall that the subtitle of *The Forms* was 'The Totemic System in Australia'), including those of Frazer, Strehlow, Goldenweiser, Father Schmidt and Graebner. This may suggest why American sociologists were so slow in taking notice of this work. Those who read French will find in Mauss's review in the same section of works by Schmidt (who published the first volume of his famous *Der Ursprung der Gottesidee* the same year as *The Forms*) a hint of a rather bitter dispute between Durkheim and Schmidt concerning the origin of religion. Essentially, the contention was between Durkheim's immanentist position and Schmidt's transcendentalist one. However, this was more than an intellectual conflict since Schmidt saw Durkheim and his followers as propagators of an atheistic interpretation of religion, while the latter saw the former's ethnology as an apology for traditional Christian views.

6   Durkheim and Mauss indicate that this evolution of the ground of the religious leads to a religion that goes beyond totemism. The evolutionary perspective of Durkheim and Mauss on the religious idea is diametrically opposite to Schmidt who saw the notion of a high god as anterior to totemism, which he took to be a degenerative aspect of religious evolution.

7   What is forbidden is what renders unclean, what defiles and ultimately what disorders (Douglas, 1966).

8   In case some may have difficulty in seeing the relevance of this analysis for our contemporary setting, I would propose that one expression of mimetic rites – which eons ago may have been functional in preparing

the group for a hunting expedition – may be found today in such practices as a crowd burning a hated figure in effigy, or on a more pleasant tone, one college group capturing the mascot of another on the eve of a football game.

9 There is a similarity in Jones's effort to dust off the original Durkheim with Louis Althusser's effort to recover an understanding of what Marx intended to do, particularly in his *magnum opus, Capital* (Althusser and Balibar, 1970). It may be worth a passing mention to note that after a relatively long neglect by Western Marxists, *Capital* seems to be returning as the central source of Marxist reflection; the vogue of the 'early manuscripts' pertaining to alienation may have been related to the underlying neo-romantic current of the 1960s. *Capital* and *The Forms,* the culminating and most difficult works of their respective authors, may well turn out to be the two great poles of sociological reflection for the 1980s, at least in terms of the 'classics'.

10 Parsons's new understanding of *The Forms* and indeed Parsons's formulation of what he views as the general system of action indicate a high degree of congruence with the *Existenzphilosophie* of Karl Jaspers. At the time I proposed a complementarity between Durkheimian sociology and existential thought (1962), I had not anticipated this line of development. However, it now seems even clearer than when I first suggested congruence between the pattern variables as existential dilemmas and general existential philosophy, that existential phenomenology (particularly that of Merleau-Ponty and Jaspers) and the theory of action basically interface in essential features. A greater awareness of their complementarity in that each grounds the other would be immensely fruitful in renovating the ties between philosophy and social science.

11 It is interesting to note the complete turnabout of the image of economic activity from *Division of Labor* to *The Forms.* In his early study, it was economic activity which brought men together in terms of the solidarity generated by the division of labor.

12 William Foote Whyte's well-known account of the bowling match episode in *Street Corner Society* (1955) is an apt illustration. Though Whyte's objective bowling skills were limited, he bowled a top score because of his standing in the hierarchy of the street-corner gang; physical performance is augmented by living up to the expectations of significant others.

13 What is worth noting in this context is the important tie-in between Durkheim and Max Weber concerning the nature of power. A major source or generator of power for Weber is *charisma.* Weber, although much more individualistic than Durkheim, does stress that charismatic authority is relational inasmuch as its validity depends upon it being recognized by those in contact with the charismatic figure (Weber, 1964, p. 359). Durkheim does not use the term 'charisma'. I would suggest that 'sacredness' or 'sacred', on the one hand, and 'charisma', on the other, as used by Durkheim and Weber respectively are for all practical purposes interchangeable concepts.

7

George Herbert Mead

HERBERT BLUMER

The decision to include a presentation of the thought of George Herbert Mead in a volume devoted to the future of sociological classics is both generous and foresightful. It is generous in that Mead's thought cannot be said to have yet gained acceptance comparable with that of such figures as Comte, Durkheim, Weber, or Simmel. Mead's thought, at best, has been lodged at the periphery of sociological concern. While a relatively small number of sociologists have sustained and fostered his views with vigor, the majority have given his thought a merely courteous nod of distant acquaintance. As happens so frequently in such circumstances remote acquaintance leads to inadequate comprehension, which here takes the form of a few stereotyped characterizations, such as that Mead's thought is philosophical and not scientific, or that it deals only with the individual and not the group, or that it is 'microsociological' and not 'macrosociological', or that it is a form of social psychology and not a form of sociology, or that it is merely a variant of phenomenology, or that it shortsightedly rejects the idea of social structure, or that it lacks any devices for the study of group life. It is not surprising that in being characterized in these ways Mead's scheme of thought has been slighted by most sociologists as not worthy of serious consideration. For many sociologists Mead is a remote figure. For many other sociologists, especially non-American sociologists, Mead is an unknown figure. To include him among the present set of classical sociological figures might thus be seen as a charitable act.

Yet, in my opinion, the decision to include Mead's scheme of thought in the present volume is foresightful. There are strong prospects that his thought will attract increasing interest and adherence because of the distinctive way in which it ties together individual action and group life. Mead's scheme centers on a picture of the human being which is quite different from that at the basis of the classical sociological approaches. Further, his picture of the human being as a participant in group life stands up exceptionally well when subjected to the rigors of empirical testing. This combination of uniqueness of perspective and of empirical validation appears to be bringing about increasingly serious consideration of Mead's approach. With a better understanding of that approach there is good reason to expect that Mead's scheme will come to occupy a recognized place in the standard body of sociological thought.[1]

It may be also pointed out in these introductory remarks that the future of Mead's scheme of thought is almost certain to be different from the future of the more classical sociological perspectives dealt with in the present symposium. The difference lies in the fact that the premises and implications of the classical sociological approaches have been pretty well identified. Accordingly, the future of these approaches lies chiefly along lines of their theoretical appraisal and of their application as explanatory schemes. The situation is somewhat different in the case of Mead's scheme of thought. There has not been much development of the implications of his basic premises. I think that we may confidently expect in the future a considerable amount of scholarly treatment designed to fill in gaps in Mead's theory and to give greater form to his picture of human society.

My plan of presentation will be to first outline the major components of Mead's scheme of thought and subsequently to consider the areas that call for the theoretical development that Mead did not supply.

The gateway to understanding Mead's scheme of sociological thought is provided by the following statement of his fundamental position: 'Human society as we know it could not exist without minds and selves, since all of its most characteristic features presuppose the possession of minds and selves by its individual members' (1934, p. 227). The quotation calls immediate attention to the nature of 'minds' and 'selves'. These two concepts are basic in Mead's scheme of thought. It becomes necessary, accordingly, to identify clearly what they refer to. They are given a character by Mead that is quite different from the way in which they are usually seen in traditional and contemporary social and psychological science. The difference, we will come to note, is what sets Mead's scheme of human group life apart from the dominant approaches.

Let me begin with a consideration of the concept of 'self'. Mead used this term to mean basically that the human being becomes an object to himself. The human being can come to see himself or herself in a large variety of ways, each one of which leads to an object of himself or herself. Thus, individuals may see themselves as being male or female, children or adults, members of this or that ethnic or nationality group, as being sick or well, as belonging to this occupation or profession, as having an encouraging or a dismal future, and so on in innumerable ways. The human being may come to be many different objects to himself, and in being an object to himself the human being stands over against himself, can approach and talk to himself, and thus is put in the position of interacting with himself. He stands over against himself in no mysterious way but only in the sense that he can designate himself to himself as being a male, a student, and so forth. In being able to make such designations to himself about himself, the human being is put in the position of being able to interact with himself, that is to say, he can make a designation to himself and respond to that designation by making a new designation to himself.

This double character of standing over against oneself and of interacting with oneself gives a meaning to the concept of the 'self' in Mead's thought that is fundamentally different from the meanings that this term traditionally has in psychology and social science. Traditionally, the term is used to refer either to the sheer existence of something or to the particular kind of existence that is true of living organisms. Thus, in the first case, we can speak of a given stone as having 'in itself' a greater density than another type of stone, or of a given cloud as carrying 'in itself' a greater amount of moisture; in these cases a 'self' is imputed to the stone or the cloud merely because the stone or cloud exists. In the second case, we speak of a living organism as having a 'self' to refer to the fact that it has a dynamic or vital make-up, well illustrated by the use of the term 'ego' in human psychology. Both of these conventional uses of the term 'self' are very different from what Mead has in mind. For Mead a 'self' does not refer to the mere existence of a given thing or to the fact that a living organism may have a vital, dynamic character. Instead, a 'self' exists only if the given thing can stand over against itself (by designating itself to itself) and thereby put itself in the position of interacting with itself. In this sense, the stone would possess a self only if it were able to recognize itself as a stone and thereby be able to interact with itself on the basis of that recognition. Similarly, a living organism (a bird, a tiger, a chimpanzee) would have a self only if it were able to make objects of itself and be able to interact with itself on the basis of the objects that it makes of itself. As we can begin to recognize from these few remarks, a self comes into being under Mead's thought only when the organism that is alleged to have a self is put into the position of engaging in a particular form of interaction with itself – an interaction in the form of making designations of objects to itself. As we shall observe later, this form of interaction is seen by Mead as being thoroughly social in nature, as being a form of communication or conversation.

Alongside of this initial and sketchy picture of the self as seen by Mead we can put a similar simple and sketchy picture of the way in which Mead viewed the concept of 'mind'. Mead saw the mind as a form of behavior – a form of behavior in which the human being points out things to himself and uses what he points out to himself to organize and direct his conduct. This conception of 'mind' as a form of social behavior in which the individual is engaging in communication with himself is, of course, quite different from the traditional and conventional ways in which the mind is seen. By and large, traditional and conventional usages treat the mind as different from behavior, as composed of psychic or mental stuff, such as sensations, feelings, ideas, and images and as subject to the play of processes such as perception, cognition, imagination and ideation. The 'mind', in terms of both content and operation, is seen as having its basis in the organic make-up of the individual and as developing from that organic make-up through experience and biological maturation. Mead's idea that the mind consists of internal communication which the individual carries on with himself gives us a different picture. For example, a pain or a sensation is not a mental element unless it is designated by the individual. In indicating a pain to himself in contrast to merely having a pain of which he is unaware, the individual enters into a very different relation to the pain – he can work out a plan of action with regard to it in place of responding to it unwittingly. As this illustration suggests, the mind comes into existence for Mead when the individual indicates things to himself and converses with himself about what he so indicates.

For Mead, then, both the self and the mind are clearly social in nature – the self in enabling the human being to carry on a process of communication with himself and the mind as being the behavior that takes place in this inner communication. I assume that no serious objection would be taken to the simple points that I have made so far – that human beings make objects of themselves, that they communicate with themselves, and that there is a difference between having an experience and indicating to oneself that one is having the experience. The obvious question then arises as to whether these points have any particular importance. For Mead these points are of the greatest importance. The possession of a self and a mind in Mead's sense makes the human being into a special kind of acting organism; it gives rise to a particular way of acting; it leads to a distinctive kind of social interaction between human beings; and it imparts a distinctive character to the group life of human beings. These are the matters that have to be made clear in order to understand Mead's sociological thought.

Clarification can begin with an explanation of the way in which Mead saw how the self and the mind come into existence. Contrary to the usual view which regards the self and the mind as already present or given in the original or biological nature of human beings, Mead's view is that the self and the mind are products of participation in group life. They emerge in the process of interaction which the young child carries on with other human beings. Since the genesis of the self lies in that process of interaction it is necessary to analyze that process in order to grasp the nature of the self. The scholarly task becomes that of explaining how the young child comes to be an object to itself. It is quite erroneous to assume that becoming an object to oneself is a mere matter of maturation and hence calls for no explanation. On the contrary, the way in which the human being becomes an object to himself sets a problem of profound difficulty.

To become an object to oneself one has logically and psychologically to see oneself from the outside. One has to get outside of oneself and approach oneself from the outside. How is this possible at all? Conventional schemes in the psychological and social sciences do not even see the problem, much less address it. Mead proposes an ingenious answer to the question. He declares that one gets outside of oneself by taking the role of another human being or set of human beings, by imaginatively placing oneself in the shoes of others, thus putting oneself in the position of approaching oneself or addressing oneself from the standpoint of that role. Simple examples are to be seen in childhood play as when a little girl 'plays mother' and in doing so, talks to herself and acts toward herself like her mother does. The child may call herself by her name, reprimand herself as her mother has done, and order herself to do such and such a thing. In taking the role or part of the mother the child has put herself in a position to approach or address herself from the outside and thus to form of herself the kind of object that is represented by that approach.

For Mead, childhood play is a primary medium in the formation and development of a self; he speaks of it as the first major stage in the genesis of the self. However, it leads to a second stage in the formation of the self, the stage that Mead spoke of as the 'game stage'. What is characteristic of the game stage is that the child takes a collective role or the organized role of a group. Thus, to take Mead's favorite illustration, a member of a baseball team has to take the role of his teammates when he guides himself in executing a given play. He has to combine together a knowledge of what to anticipate in the way of behavior of the other members of his team in order to carry out his own part of the play. In Mead's language he takes the role of the group that is implicated in his action. He has to address himself from the standpoint of that organized or collective patterning of behavior into which he has to fit his own ongoing act. In taking this organized or collective role the human being is putting himself again in an outside position from which he can see himself and approach himself. Mead spoke of this as taking the role of the 'generalized other'.

For Mead, then, the human being forms his self or makes objects out of himself by seeing and addressing himself through the individual and collective roles which he is led to take in his association with others. If a young child had no opportunity of taking the roles of others, the child would not develop a self and would not make objects of itself; this is the sort of happening that takes place in the case of genuine instances of feral children or in the case of congenitally deaf children who do not learn a language.

Among the many implications of possessing a self I wish to single out three for brief discussion. These implications are, first, that the possession of a self changes in a very fundamental sense the relation of the organism to its environment; secondly, that having a self provides the means for an inner life experience; and, thirdly, that the presence of a self transforms the nature of action or behavior.

In the case of the first implication we need to note that the existence of a self leads to the formation of a new type of environment for the organism. The concept of 'environment' refers in its ordinary usage to the presence of objects which surround an organism. These surrounding objects are regarded as having an already constituted make-up that exists apart from the organism and is independent of the organism. These objects are thought of as playing upon the organism through their stimulating qualities and thereby calling forth the responses that are provided by the make-up of the organism. The responses, however complicated they may be in terms of neuro-muscular involvement, are seen as the reply of the sensitive organization of the organism. Thus, the identification of the stimulating objects, the sensitive make-up of the organism and the resulting responses constitute the three components in the study of behavior, whether of animals or human beings. These components are to be identified as they appear to the objective observer.

The possession of a self in Mead's sense of the term gives us a different picture of the relation of human beings to their surrounding world or environment. In having a self a human being is put in a position of *indicating* or pointing out to himself objects in his surroundings. To *indicate* an object is to give it a different status than that of being merely an object to which one responds. To indicate an object is essentially to identify it, to classify it, to say that it is such and such a kind of thing, in short to give the object a 'meaning'. By having a self the human being is able to make meaningful objects of things, and in becoming meaningful, objects take on a character that is different from what might be spoken of as their 'natural' or 'intrinsic' make-up. The meaning of the object for the human being is not intrinsic in the object but is brought to the object by the human being. Thus, a given so-called natural object may have significantly different meanings for human beings who approach it from different social backgrounds: a tree, for instance, may have a very different meaning for a botanist, a landscape gardener, a lumberman and a poet. If one adds the observation that human beings are prepared to act toward objects in terms of the meanings which such objects have for them, one may appreciate the importance of the difference between objects with meaning and objects conceived as independent of human beings. The possession of a self thus enables the human organism to bring into being a new environment, to convert a so-called natural world into a world of objects with meaning. To study human beings it is necessary, according to Mead, to respect the fact that they live in a world of meaningful objects and that they act toward these objects in terms of the meanings which the objects have for them.

A second implication of possessing a self is that it enables the person to have an inner life in which he may communicate with himself, without others having immediate access to that inner world. In being able to make indications to himself as he might make them to others, but without making them to others, the human being is in a position to fashion an inner social world of his own. This inner world is one of genuine social experience for him, in which he may cultivate his impulses, develop his emotions and sentiments, form and revise objects of others and himself, brood or exult over his memories, develop and restrain his inclinations, cultivate his intentions and nurture and shape plans of conduct. This inner world of social experience which enters so profoundly into the formation of personal make-up and social conduct is obviously tied into the overt behavior of individuals in their association with each other. This inner world, which comes into being by virtue of the fact that the individual engages in a process of making indications to himself, is a world of ongoing and hence developing self-interaction. It cannot be caught, consequently, by reducing it to fixed elements of organization, such as attitudes, motives, feelings and ideas; instead, it must be seen as a process in which such elements are brought into play and are subject to what happens in such play. The inner world must be seen as inner process and not as fixed inner psychical composition.

The third implication of possessing a self refers to the formation and shaping of human behavior. As I have already pointed out, to have a self means that the human being confronts his world as an organism that is interacting with it instead of as an organism that is merely responding to the play of a 'natural' environment. In having a self, the person is put in the position of indicating to himself his own action as well as pointing out to himself features of the arena in which the action is taking place. He may pick out different items of his ongoing action and different items of the situation with which he is faced, analyze these items, discuss them with himself and by virtue of this process of interaction shape a line of conduct to fit his situation. This is equivalent to saying that by virtue of having a self the human being comes to construct his action instead of merely releasing a response to stimuli. For instance, he may note an impulse such as being hungry, think about different kinds of food, look at his watch to see if it is time to eat, decide to eat, give thought to whether he should eat at this or that restaurant, examine his supply of money and, after reminding himself that he is on a diet, decide to postpone eating entirely. It is through such a process of self-interaction that the human being builds his action in his situations. This formation of action through self-interaction is not merely something that is made possible by virtue of having a self; in having a self, it is something that cannot be avoided. The human actor is forced to be a participant in his own action – a participant in no mysterious sense but in the sense of indicating to himself his action in the course of its formation and using what he notes to guide that formation. This is the kind of acting organism that results from the possession of a self.

Let me come back now to Mead's simple statement that a human society consists of people who have selves. If the possession of a self has the three kinds of results which I have just indicated, there is good reason to believe that a society made up of organisms who have selves is going to be fundamentally different from a society that is made up of organisms without selves. What is the nature of this difference? What kind of a society comes into existence when members have 'selves' in Mead's meaning of that term? This is the central question that has to be addressed in order to understand Mead's sociological thought.

The consideration of this question should begin with a statement of what Mead picked out as the fundamental nature of societies in general, that is to say, societies irrespective of whether their members had selves. What is it that makes a society a society, whether it be an insect society, an animal society, or a human society? Mead saw the fundamental nature of a society to exist in the fact that the organisms making up the society come to fit their actions to one another. The association of the organisms puts them in the position of having to adjust their activities to one another – to enter into the various coordinated arrangements of behavior that constitute the life of the society. Mead spoke of these coordinated arrangements of behavior as 'social acts', meaning thereby that the ongoing acts of the participating organisms come together to constitute organized or collective forms of action. Such social acts are illustrated by the division of function among ants as they carry on their social lives, by the coordination of the actions of separate wolves as the pack attacks its prey, or by human beings in their conversations – conversations which necessarily require an adjustment of the remarks of one participant to the remarks of another participant. Mead saw a society as made up of social acts.

Let me indicate briefly the more important implications of this simple view that a society exists in the form of social or joint acts. First, a society should be seen in terms of *action* – in terms of the ongoing interlinking activities – rather than as the mere association of organisms. Secondly, the relationship between the members of a society is relevant or significant only as it affects or enters into the ongoing activity that makes up the social or joint act; indeed, whether a relationship exists between members in a society can be ascertained only by observing their joint or social acts and inferring the relationship from these joint acts. Thirdly, a society is involved in a ceaseless process of forming social acts, that is, each social act has a limited existence, replacing and being replaced by others; the life of a society is an ongoing affair. Fourth, a society exists properly not in the form of common or similar lines of behavior but instead in the form of differentiated lines of behavior which are articulated or fit together.

To see society as existing in the social or joint acts engaged in by its members raises the question of how such joint acts are formed. How do the members of a society fit their ongoing lines of behavior to one another to form the joint acts that make up the life of their society? To consider this question one is required to study the *interaction* that takes place between the members, to see how the participants meet and respond to each other's ongoing actions as they come to fit their respective acts to one another.

It is in his analysis of social interaction that Mead has made the most important of his distinctive contributions to the study of human society. It is thus very important to identify as clearly as brief space will allow the nature of social interaction as seen by Mead. Mead saw social interaction as taking two forms, which he spoke of respectively as a 'conversation of gestures' and the 'use of significant symbols or significant gestures'. (It has become customary among many students of Mead to label these forms as 'non-symbolic interaction' and 'symbolic interaction'.) By a 'gesture' Mead meant the portion of an ongoing act that is perceived by a responding organism. A non-significant gesture is one that is responded to immediately or directly; a significant gesture is one that is interpreted or given meaning before a response is made to it. Thus a 'conversation of gestures' or non-symbolic interaction occurs when an organism responds to the perceived part of the act of another organism without noting the meaning of that gesture. One of Mead's favorite examples was the interaction between two dogs, as in the maneuvering preceding a fight between them. Each dog may approach the other, sniff the other, walk tensely around the other, growl and bare its teeth. Each of these portions of the ongoing act is a gesture which calls forth a response. Thus, the interaction of the dogs takes the form of an interplay back and forth of gestures. In this interplay each gesture is called forth by the gesture of the other dog. For example, the bristling of one dog's hair is a gesture which may lead the other dog to growl, which gesture in turn may lead the first dog to bare its teeth. In the conversation of gestures, the gesture is not made intentionally to induce a given response from the other dog but is, itself, just called forth as an unpremeditated response. Each organism responds directly and immediately to the gesture of the other without basing that response on either an interpretation of what the other organism is seeking to do or on an intention to use one's gestural response as a means of inducing the other organism to respond in a given way.

In contrast, symbolic interaction, or interaction using significant gestures, has a fundamentally different character. In it the participants are responding to each other's gestures as they confront the ongoing activity of each other but the gesture has a different character. The gesture is now picked out by the responding organism and given a meaning, with the response being based on that meaning. Thus, the shaking of a fist by a human being, instead of calling forth an immediate act of flight by another human being, may be *interpreted* as a sign of anger and of intention to inflict harm on one. The responder bases his response on how he interprets the gesture. Further, in symbolic interaction one may use one's gesture purposely to call forth a given response; thus, one may shake one's fist not merely as an outburst of anger but as a *designed* effort to get the other person to flee. In symbolic interaction, the gesture of the other person is not responded to immediately and directly but is first picked out for interpretation before response is made to it; correspondingly, one's own gesture is not just automatically called forth but is purposely designed to induce a given response from the other participant.

This brief account of the 'significant gesture' – the gesture which is the mark of symbolic interaction – also clarifies what Mead meant in saying that in using the significant symbol one is responding to one's gesture as the other person is responding to it. Mead had in mind that a significant gesture has the same meaning for the person who uses it as it has for the person to whom it is directed. Thus, to shake one's fist to scare away another person would mean that one gave to that shaking of the fist the same meaning that it would have for the person to whom that gesture was directed. Significant gestures or symbols carry, then, a common meaning, or in Mead's terms they evoke a common response on the part of the person who uses the gesture and on the part of the person to whom the gesture is directed. It is this feature which allows significant gestures to be used to control action: knowing the common meaning which is given to the shaking of the fist allows one to use that gesture to indicate to another person what he should do and similarly allows that person to understand what the person using that gesture expects him to do. This is communication in the true sense of the term, that is, the user of the gesture knows what he wishes the other person to understand and, in turn, the other person understands what the user of the gesture has in mind.

Social interaction on the level of the significant gesture, of symbolic interaction, is clearly dependent on the possession and play of the self. In contrast, non-symbolic interaction does not involve the presence or play of selves. In non-symbolic interaction the participating organism does not indicate to itself what the other organism 'has in mind' or is trying to do; nor does the organism indicate to itself what it wants the other organism to do. Instead, each organism responds directly to the gesture of the other, with its own response serving in turn to call forth immediately a response from the other organism. Non-symbolic interaction thus fits the conventional model of the environment–organism relationship spoken of earlier, wherein the environment has an intrinsic make-up that plays as a stimulus upon the organism, calling forth from the organism a response that is set by the sensitivity or organization of the organism. With this conventional model there is no need or place for a self, since the organism does not have to work out an understanding of what the happenings in the environment mean before it responds to them.

Mead, of course, recognized that human beings engaged in both non-symbolic and symbolic interaction. In their interaction with one another, human beings may respond to many aspects of the actions of each other without being aware of those aspects, that is, without indicating those aspects to themselves. But Mead recognized that the distinctive and predominantly important form of interaction in human society is in the use of significant symbols.

The import of the foregoing brief discussion is that self-interaction must be seen as an inescapable component of social interaction in human society. The study of social interaction in human societies cannot be covered effectively without including the study of the self-interaction that is involved in responding to others and in acting toward others. Thus, if the life of a human society consists of what the people in that society do, and if what they do depends on how they interact, and if that interaction involves self-interaction, the essentially redundant question is 'what effect does self-interaction have on human group life'? Mead's scheme of sociological thought is shaped to deal with this question.

An initial clue is given by the interesting observations made by Mead in comparing insect, animal and human societies. Group life in the case of insect and animal societies is remarkably fixed in structure. The modes of living scarcely differ from one group to another group within the same species and remain the same through time. In contrast, human group life varies enormously from society to society and is capable of undergoing vast transformation from generation to generation in the same society. This difference has its basis in the biological make-up of the respective species. The sizable complexity of structure in the usual insect society is due to the fact that the individual members are biologically differentiated from each other, with each member doing that kind of activity for which it is biologically or physiologically specialized. The picture is startlingly different in the case of human societies. Human beings are essentially biologically or physiologically alike, aside from sex and age differences, so to explain group life in human societies one obviously has to proceed along a very different line. Animal societies are similar to human societies in that their members are biologically alike, yet they are very simple in structure and, like insect societies, fixed in structure. Mead regards the differences that have been mentioned between insect societies and human societies, and between animal societies and human societies, as due to the absence and presence of self-interaction. Not having selves, insect societies develop complex social structures only through biological specialization of their members. Not having selves, animal societies are able to develop only simple social structures, which remain fixed. Having selves, human societies can come to develop very complex structures – structures which may vary enormously from society to society and in the same society from time to time. These observations raise, again, the question of how the possession of selves enters into the formation of a society.

In his analysis of *social acts* Mead sketched the dependency of human societies on self-interaction. I have explained earlier that Mead regarded the distinctive mark of all societies, human or otherwise, to be the formation of social acts by their members. A social act is a collective or joint action constituted by the alignment or fitting together of the lines of activity of the separate organisms. The life of a society is made up of social acts. The interlinkage of social acts constitutes the structure of a society. At the heart of our discussion is the question of how social acts are formed and how these social acts come to fit together in larger forms or patterns. Social acts in animal and insect societies are to be explained essentially in terms of the biological make-up of the separate organisms which leads the animals to respond to each other, through conversations of gesture, in fixed ways. But these biological explanations cannot account for the social acts in human societies. The large variety of such acts in human societies and their shifting character demand a different kind of explanation.

Human social acts range from simple cooperative acts in face-to-face situations, for example, eating together, to huge structures of coordinated activities in large organizations and institutions, for example, the interlinked activities of the diverse sets of persons involved in upholding the institution of private property – police, prosecuting attorneys, courts, legislators, registrars, accountants, and so on.

Whether the social act be small or large, simple or complex, it involves the fitting together of the diverse actions of the participants. As the given social act moves along, each participant is called on to fit his, her, or its (in the case of group or corporate actors) activity at appropriate points to the activities of the other participants in the social act. The question that we have to consider is 'how do the participants come to fit acts to one another in human societies?'

I wish to approach this question by pointing out what takes place in a simple social act – one involving, let us say, just two individuals, as in the case of the purchase of an article in a store. One person, as a customer, asks the store clerk the sales price of the given item; before he asks the clerk, he has to indicate to himself that he wants to find out the sales price; the clerk has to indicate to himself and understand the question that is being asked of him; he, further, has to indicate to himself the appropriate response before he replies; his reply, in turn, is interpreted and evaluated by the customer. We see in this brief account the play back and forth of meaningful gestures – the symbolic interaction about which we have spoken previously. This joint act is built up, as it proceeds, by each participant noting the other's action, interpreting that action, figuring out what he is to do, deciding on a line of behavior, being ready to change his behavior if conditions demand or allow, and so forth. The joint act in human society is formed in this fashion through the indications that the participants make, each to the other and each to himself. Interaction with oneself is interwoven with interaction with others.

The same process of interaction – interpreting the actions of others and having one's own actions interpreted by others – takes place between the participants in large, complex social acts. The participants in such acts are likely to be many, carrying on different actions, entering into the joint act at different points, and having contact with only a few of the participants at these points. Yet their actions, even though spread out in networks and chains of association, constitute a social act in Mead's sense of the term. At each of the points of the network or chain-like arrangement where different sets of participants meet, the participants have to interpret one another's activity and adjust their own activity on the basis of the interpretation. We have such an arrangement in the case of a highly diversified labor force in a large factory. Or we can see it in the many diverse sets of people involved in the maintenance of property rights. In both cases, the involved participants who meet one another at this or that point in the operation of the factory or in the transactions concerning property have to interpret each other's actions and adjust to them. Large social acts could not possibly take place in human society without such interpretation by the participants as they deal with one another's actions. There are, to be true, differences between the alignment of participant actions in large, complex social acts and the alignment of participant actions in small, simple social acts. In the large social acts the participants are likely to be organized groups of some sort; also, the participants may engage in only a part of the social act, and thus meet only a portion of the other participants. However, these differences, which I will discuss later, do not alter the fact that large and complex social acts in human society take place only through an interpretive process at all points in the concatenated arrangement.

The centrality of the interpretive process in the formation of the social or joint acts that make up the social life of a human society invites a deeper analysis. Most sociological schemes either deny the operation of an interpretive process or else relegate it to the position of mere servant or instrument of some larger transcending process.

The larger transcending process thereby becomes important, and the interpretive process becomes inconsequential. Accordingly, in order to avoid misunderstanding of the interpretive process it is advisable to explain it further, particularly in relation to social acts. There are several points to be made in this explanation, so for purposes of convenience I will number them.

(1)　It is necessary to recognize that social acts may range from those which are unchanging and repetitive to those which are different from instance to instance, or which are being formed for the first time. Fixed and repetitive social acts are abundantly familiar to us, and the social life of any human society, certainly of one in a settled state, is made up predominantly of such routines and rituals. In their case the participants know what they are to do; their interpretation of each other's acts and the guidance of their own respective acts are laid out, so to speak, in advance. Alongside of such regularized social acts there are new joint acts that have to be formed in every society, especially in changing societies. In such matters as meeting strained personal relations, in the creation of new organizations, in meeting crises and problems, and so on, the participants are confronted with new situations which require new arrangements or new joint acts. The participants in such situations lack in varying measure the shared understandings that would enable them to fit their individual actions together smoothly as a matter of course. Instead, in order to reach an alignment of actions they have to engage in such processes as analyzing their situations, feeling out each other's intentions, assessing the possibilities of different kinds of action, improving or creating a new mode of conduct, and revising or discarding a mode of behavior if it proves to be unsuitable. To sum up the first point, the social or joint acts that constitute group life in human societies vary between those which are already patterned by previous understanding and those that have to be newly formed in differing degree.

(2)　It should be recognized that the interpretive process is in play in all social acts, whether they be heavily routinized or markedly novel. In the case of routinized or ritualized social acts, the interpretive process becomes a matter of noticing and adhering to common understandings as to how to act. Even though the participants know what they are to do, they have to observe each other, identify each other's actions and anticipated actions, and indicate to themselves and to each other what is to be done. The interpretive process is different in the case of social acts in which the participants have to work out new relations or alignments of their actions. Instead of merely guiding themselves by already established common understandings the participants have to make

new interpretations as to how to act. The formation of new interpretations may be simple in some situations and exceedingly complex and uncertain in others. The unravelling, analysis and comprehension of what takes place in the interpretive process as human
beings form their social acts becomes in Mead's scheme the central
task of social science.

(3) The analysis which Mead has made of the interpretive process through which social acts are formed in human society, while
basic, is sketchy and general. He did not seek in his writings to spell
out the variety of ways, inside of his basic framework, by which
social acts, especially new social acts, are formed. The basic framework with which we are left consists of (a) taking the role of the
'generalized other', (b) taking the role of other participants in the
given social act and (c) responding to this role-taking by forming a
prospective line of action. To take the role of the 'generalized
other' means that the participant is indicating to himself the way
in which his 'community' views the situation in which he has to
act. Such interpretations using the community definitions or symbols
are made at the very beginning of a social act in order to identify
the social act and thus get one's bearings. The participant will
identify in some way the social act into which he has to enter, for
example, a trading transaction, a quarrel, a game, friendly discussion, a church service. Further, the participant will continue to
apply community definitions throughout the social act as a means
of understanding it and adjusting to it. As suggested above, the
dependency of the interpretive process on taking the role of the
generalized other is particularly pronounced in the case of routinized
and ritualized behavior. In addition to taking the role of the
generalized other the participant in a social act has to take, also,
the roles of the other participants to whose behavior he has to
adjust in the immediate situation. To adjust, he has to form some
idea of what the other persons are doing or what they are about to
do. This close attention to what other participants are going to do
becomes more pronounced in new and unestablished social acts.
In Mead's scheme the participant in a social act forms his interpretation by taking the role of the community and the roles of
other participants, and then responding to these roles by discourse
with himself in which he maps out what he intends to do. The
interpretations which lay the basis for his action in the social act
arise out of the process of taking community roles, taking the roles
of other participants and judging his own intentions and prospective
action.

(4) The interpretive process is not only the means by which
each participant forms his own action so that it fits the acts of

others. It is also the means by which each participant contributes
to the creation of the situation which has to be faced by the other
participants in the developing social act. This observation rests on
the fact that the participants are making indications to one another
as they interact. These indications made to others are defining
devices to them, confronting them with matters they have to take
into account in forming their own behavior. In this very important
way, indications made to others serve to form the situation to
which they have to adjust. The interpretive process which leads to
the making of indications to others thus operates to form the
situation that comes into being as the social act is being developed.

(5) In the social acts which are being formed, the participants
may come to meet one another, see one another and act toward
one another in many different ways. The joint acts that are formed
may be the result of clear-cut understandings as to how people are
to act, but they may also come into being through many other
forms of adjustment. The participants in a social act may fit their
behavior to one another through a process of negotiation in which
they make concessions and modify positions; or they may make
adjustments of their actions through coercion; or through a common enthusiasm which propels them along; or by following the
declarations of a charismatic person; or by realizing that their
situation requires them to collaborate peacefully in the development
of a new joint act; or as a result of effective persuasion by some of
the participants. In short, there are many ways in which joint acts
in a human society may be formed – all of them legitimate and
genuine parts of what is generally spoken of as the process that
constitutes the 'social order'. While these observations may seem
obvious, indeed trite, they are largely rejected or ignored by the
dominant schemes in social science today. I will address this matter
later.

(6) The possession of a self enables a person to interact with
himself while he is interacting with others. Such self-interaction
enables a participant in the social act to act in an unexpected or
unique way. In being able to indicate to himself what other participants are doing, or in evaluating his own situation, or by assessing
his own action, a participant can take an unexpected or deviant
stance. Self-interaction has the potential of placing an individual in
opposition to his associates and to his society.

The foregoing discussion permits us now to identify more clearly
the significant ways in which Mead's perspective of human society
differs from other perspectives that are dominant today in the
social and psychological sciences. The distinctiveness of Mead's

perspectives comes from four basic premises which we have now considered: (1) a human being comes to form a self which enables him to interact with himself in large measure as he interacts with others; (2) such self-interaction is interwoven with social inter-action and influences that social interaction; (3) such interaction with others (symbolic interaction) is the means by which human beings are able to form social or joint acts; (4) the formation of joint acts constitutes the social life of a human society. These premises depict a human society as made up of living and acting people, meeting each other in many kinds of situations and having to fit behavior to one another in those situations. A society exists in the joint or social acts which are formed and carried out by the members.

The major points of view which I wish to compare with Mead's perspective are that human society is (1) an organization of culture, (2) a social structure, (3) a social system, (4) a process of social exchange, (5) a conflict process, (6) a power arrangement, (7) a class conflict in the Marxist sense and (8) a mere composite of indi-viduals with differing psychological make-up. While these perspec-tives are usually merged together in different combinations in scholarly writings, they can and should be singled out for separate treatment. My treatment of each of these perspectives will be restricted to basic essentials.

(1) The cultural perspective, taken by itself, assumes that a human society consists of an organization of ways of living that have been developed historically, that is passed on from one generation to another, and that determines and explains (a) how the members of a society interact with each other, (b) how they come to act together as they carry on the life of the society and (c) how they are respectively shaped into given kinds of individuals. In taking this position, the cultural perspective differs at funda-mental points from Mead's picture of human society. Without doubt, there are many instances of joint or collective action which are culturally prescribed (as in the case of routinized and ritualized behavior) or which, in Mead's language, are under the sole control of the generalized other. However, to attempt to bring all instances of social interaction under the play of community prescriptions ignores (a) the process of self-interaction which Mead makes so central in his analysis and (b) the need of participants in the social act to give attention not merely to common community definitions but to the ongoing activities of one another. Self-interaction and taking the roles of other participants in the social act opens the doors to the possibilities of directing one's own action along new lines. The cultural perspective does not catch this matter. Mead's

view is that social or joint acts, whether regularized or novel, are constructed through a process of symbolic interaction. Accordingly, human group life must be seen as arising from, and being carried on by, that process. The cultural perspective fails to do this.

(2) The structural perspective sees human society as a structure of differentiated parts. There is incredible difference among 'structuralists' as to what these parts are, but the basic assumption is that a society exists as a differentiated arrangement of parts or units connected with one another to form a 'structure'. In a status structure, for example, the modes of behavior associated with status positions are seen as 'social roles', and human society appears as a structure of differentiated roles. A structural scheme extends its explanation in two directions: (*a*) the structural unit (e.g. status position) is used to explain the behavior of the individuals who belong to that unit and (*b*) the arrangement of structured units is used to explain group life in its collective character.

Such a view elevates social structure to the determining factor in human group life. As in the case of the cultural perspective, though, the structural perspective ignores the process of self-interaction and the ways in which this process enters into and affects the formation of the social or joint acts that make up social life. To assume that interaction and adjustment of behavior is set by and explained by social structure is to drop a curtain over what Mead has taken such pains to identify and analyze. The structural approach fails to see human society as a moving, ongoing process of living in which individual and collective participants have to work out their alignments of behavior to one another. The approach does not single out for scrutiny or study the process in which human beings find it necessary to interpret the actions of one another, to judge those actions in the light of the developing social act and to figure out their own response. In lodging causation and explanation in a social structure, the structural perspective presupposes that self-interaction and interpretive social interaction do not occur, or are inconsequential, or are mere servants of the structure.

(3) The view of human society as a 'social system' is similar in many respects to structural views. It adds, however, the premiss that the parts are bound together in an interdependent arrangement, forming thereby a system. This interdependent arrangement is treated as an entity or a whole in its own right, with the parts deriving their character from the whole. But the system approach ignores or explains away the matters which are central to Mead's picture of human society. It denies or belittles social interaction in the form of significant symbols. In the system scheme, the interaction is between whatever is chosen as the parts. The parts

are rarely human beings but are such 'systematic' elements as status positions, social roles, points in social networks, and so on. Further, social interaction is set by the system and not by the participating individuals. Thus, there is no need to study social interaction as an adjustive process in which the human participants are taking account for one another, or to view human group life as being a process in which participants are forming joint or social acts. Instead, group life is treated as the satisfaction of systemic requirements. And just as there is no need to see group life as the action of participants who are interpreting each other's acts, there is no need to introduce the self-interaction that is involved in such interpretation. The system approach does not see human society as made up of individuals with selves, whereas Mead sees human society in precisely this way.[2]

(4) The 'exchange' perspective of human society approximates Mead's perspective in that it recognizes human group life to exist in the interaction of the individuals who comprise the group. However, it does not see this interaction in the way that was seen by Mead. The exchange view rests on the premiss that in interaction with others each human being guides his action by a rough calculation of the relative benefits and costs that the action will yield, much as in classical utilitarian economics. In current sociological theory it has come to incorporate the idea of positive and negative rewards (gratification and punishment), especially as developed in the 'operant conditioning' theory of B. F. Skinner.

This account of social interaction falls far short of Mead's, missing, among other things, the process of self-interaction. In Mead's analysis, moreover, the interpretations which the individual makes of others and of his situation cover much more than an assessment of his possible gains and penalties. The interpretations may, for instance, lead the person to abide by community standards, thus undertaking onerous and disliked action at the expense of what the participant would prefer to do on an exchange basis. The defining process which is involved in constructing and maintaining social or joint acts is far more complex and variable than a mere exchange in terms of benefits and costs. The picture of human group life presented by exchange theory thus fails to catch the variety of joint acts in group life and, similarly, does not reflect adequately the interaction involved in the formation of such joint acts.

(5) Mead's picture of social interaction in human society is also fundamentally different from that of conflict theory. The major differences are along two lines: first, Mead recognized that social interaction covers far more than conflict relations and, secondly,

he brought conflict inside of the interpretive process. That social interaction between human beings extends far beyond conflct, in even the broadest meaning of the term, should be apparent from casual observation. We observe countless social acts in which the fitting together of lines of behavior is not a conflict process. This is true of most routinized and ritualized social acts, for example, or of 'team play' and in organized collective action generally. Mead's theory of social interaction covers the full range of social acts in human societies; conflict theory, at best, is confined to relatively few social acts. Mead's theory, moreover, brings conflict relations inside the interpretive process. A conflict arises when parties see themselves in conflict; it is under this condition that they see each other as opponents or enemies and take stances against one another. If the participants do not interpret their relations as being in conflict, their views of one another, their stances and their actions toward one another are markedly different. In a genuine sense, in the sense of social acts, conflict relations and conflict behavior are dependent on the interpretive process. This point has important implications. It means that the recognition by the parties that they are in a conflict relation is as important as the conditions that are alleged to cause their conflict. It means, further, that instead of thinking that 'contradictions' in group life are the basic causes and explanations of conflict (as conflict theory frequently does) it is necessary to see how so-called contradictions come to be seen and defined. What are identified by scholars as social contradictions in a society may never be perceived as contradictions by the people of that society; this leads to a profoundly different social process.

(6) Only a few words are required to distinguish Mead's picture of human society from theories that see human society in terms of the exercise of power, for power theory is a variant of both structural and conflict theories. Power theories assume that what individuals or groups do in their actions in the society is dependent on the power of their position. Those with great power can control others and achieve the satisfaction of their interests; correspondingly, those with little power are under the control of those with greater power and are, accordingly, limited in what they are able to do. Group life is to be seen as basically a struggle between power contestants; the accommodation of such contestants to one another gives rise to a 'power structure'.

It should be obvious, first of all, that the struggle for power or the exercise of power takes place or is required in only a portion of social acts, namely, in those acts in which participants have to vie with one another in the deliberate control of a developing social act. There are multitudes of social acs in which this does not take place, as in the case (again) of routinized and ritualized social acts, or in deliberate cooperative acts, or in acts of expressive behavior. A further difference between Mead's perspective and the power perspective arises in the explanation of power struggles or the exercise of power when these occur. Power theory places the power in the participant or in his position; it is the location of power that leads the power theorist to speak of a power structure. In Mead's perspective, however, where a power contest is in play the respective power of the participants depends on how the participants define each other in the given situations in which the participants meet. Even though the participants may be the same in different situations and may be recognized as retaining their respective status positions, the varying nature of the situations as interpreted by the participants may lead to a shifting of power among them; in one situation a given participant may assess available resources as giving him control over the developing social act, whereas in another situation involving the same participants he may interpret his position as weak.

(7) Because of the affinity of the Marxist theory to the structural, social system, conflict and power perspectives of human society, the distinctions that have already been made between Mead's scheme and the structural, system, conflict and power schemes apply also to the Marxist scheme. Yet, it may be helpful if the basic differences are put more precisely. Briefly, Mead's view and the Marxist view differ with regard to (a) the source of social acts and (b) the play of interpretation in the formation of social acts. The Marxist view is logically committed to the premiss that social acts (as defined by Mead) have their origin in the given class structure and are to be accounted for by that structure. Mead's view is that social acts arise whenever human beings meet and find it necessary to adjust their ongoing behavior to one another. Thus, there are multitudes of social acts in a capitalist society – in families, neighborhoods, communities and institutions – which cannot be traced by even the most strained reasoning to the class structure.

The other major difference centers on the interpretive process. The Marxist scheme, in terms of its logic, presupposes that the ways in which human beings see and interpret their experience and their world is determined by the class structure; the only exception to this, if it is an exception, is the condition of 'false consciousness' which blinds members of an exploited class (the proletariat) to their real situation. Mead's scheme, in contrast, sees the interpretive process as having much more flexibility and variability than this. Thus, to limit ourselves to a single point of the Marxist scheme, 'social contradictions' may or may not be seen as such by people in a society; further, if so seen, the interpretive process may lead people in different directions as to what, if anything, is to be done with regard to the social contradiction. Mead's scheme, in short, allows for a variability in defining situations that the Marxist scheme does not permit.

(8) The remaining view of human society that needs to be compared with Mead's perspective is the view that is characteristic of psychological approaches generally, regardless of how these approaches differ from one another. Psychological schemes seek to explain the action of people in a society in terms of factors lodged in the psychological make-up of the individual members of that society. These psychological factors vary enormously, ranging from sheer neuro-muscular responses to sets of ego-needs, with all kinds of intermediate factors, such as attitudes, feelings, cognitive elements, conscious motives, unconscious motives, and so on; but psychological approaches are essentially alike in viewing human society as a mere collection of individuals and in seeing group life as a combination of individual activities, regardless of how much the individuals influence one another in their association. Accordingly, the scholar explains group life by going back to the psychological make-up of the participating individuals.

Mead's view differs markedly from this widespread psychological perspective. First, the psychological perspective does not recognize the presence of social acts in Mead's sense of that term. For Mead, the joint or aligned social act is not a mere combination of the acts of separate individuals; the social act has a character of its own which has to be recognized in order to understand the actions of the separate individuals. A trading transaction, for instance, is a joint act: buying cannot take place without selling, nor selling without buying. But it is not the addition of the actions of the buyer to the actions of the seller that make up the trading transaction. The study of the formation of the trading transaction requires that one focus attention on what is happening to the joint act, not by forgetting it in favor of studying the separate actions of the buyer and of the seller. It may be necessary for other reasons to give attention to the actions of the buyer and the seller, separately from each other; but to confine one's attention to these separate actions does not catch the 'jointedness' of their engaged act. This observation applies to all social acts as viewed by Mead: the *joint* act is the unit of human societies.

The second major difference between Mead's scheme and the common view held by psychologists is that for Mead the human being interacts *socially* with himself, he can carry on discourse with himself as he does with others. Psychological schemes, if they make room for a self, rarely see the self in this way. Those psychological schemes that identify the 'self' with an ego fail to catch the reflexive character that Mead has made central to his picture of the self, namely, that the human being becomes an object to himself and thus can interact with himself. The same difference exists in the case of the psychological schemes which see the 'self' as a socially formed part or aspect of the psychological organization of the individual, for example, as an importation of the values, rules, understandings and beliefs of the group into the individual. These views of the self fail to catch what Mead stresses as the importance of possessing a self, namely, the ability to indicate objects to oneself and to others and to use these indications to forge one's behavior and to guide the behavior of others. This picture of the human being as one who acts toward others by interacting with himself is alien to the general psychological perspective.

The foregoing sketchy comparison of Mead's perspective with other major perspectives of human society should help to identify more clearly the distinctive features of Mead's scheme. The more important of these distinctive features are, first, that a human society exists in ongoing action instead of in settled relations or structure; a society should be studied in terms of social acts in progress and not in terms of acts already formed. Secondly, since the formation of social acts occurs through an interpreting and defining process, ongoing group life has to be seen in terms of that process; group activity is not mere response evoked by stimuli but is fashioned by participants as they interpret their situations. Thirdly, by virtue of self-interaction which forces each participant to indicate and appraise his situation, the participant is brought as an active agent into the formation of the social act; the participation is not a mere channel for the play and expression of forces lodged outside of him. He has to guide his own action inside of a limiting framework.

These three distinctive features yield a picture of human society that is noticeably different from the ways in which human society is seen in conventional theories. And this picture of human society has given rise, predictably, to several important yet unwarranted criticisms of Mead's approach. It is appropriate to consider these criticisms in order to be sure that Mead's scheme is seen correctly.

One criticism of Mead's approach is that it presupposes that human beings act on the basis of 'free will', thereby removing their behavior from the domain of scientific study. The critics assert that under Mead's scheme the human participant is depicted as being free to do whatever he wishes, regardless of his social relation to others. This criticism is shallow and without warrant. Without entering into the useless metaphysical argument as to what is meant by 'free will' it is sufficient to point out that for Mead the participant forms his conduct in a social situation through a process of self-interaction. Two matters are to be noted here. First, this process of self-interaction is thoroughly empirical and therefore open to scientific inquiry and observation. Secondly, the acting participant has to fit his action into the ongoing social act and is thus both directed by and bound by the character of the social act. Social acts would be impossible if people in association could do anything they wished.

A second frequent criticism is that Mead's scheme converts human society into mere subjective imagery, the objective environment is transformed into a world of subjective meanings which are themselves subject to revision *ad infinitum*, and hence the world of objective reality is obliterated. This criticism is false. Mead was a pragmatist in philosophical belief. He clearly recognized a world of objective things which were lodged not in a person's head but in an outside world. He called attention, of course, to the fact that for human beings the outside world was *unavoidably* seen in terms of how it was indicated or defined by such human beings. However, such indications or definitions are subject to validation by examining the objects that are indicated or defined to see whether they bear out the content of the indication or definition. Thus, to illustrate, an assertion that a given ethnic group acts toward another ethnic group in a specified way because of the manner in which it views that ethnic group is an assertion that is open to empirical investigation. One can test the assertion by making appropriate inquiry into the way in which the members of the first ethnic group view the second ethnic group and then by seeing whether this view is borne out in the actions of the first ethnic group. These two lines of inquiry require observations of an objective world, not portrayals of streams of consciousness. Mead was not a phenomenologist.

Another criticism that is made of Mead's perspective of human society is that the perspective applies only to the area of 'microsociety' and not to 'macrosociety'. The critics holding this view acknowledge that Mead's scheme fits instances of small and close human association, but they contend that it does not fit those areas of group life in which the participants stand in remote and indirect relations to one another, as is the case in the complex division of labor in modern society, or in large governmental bureaucracies. In such instances, the critics contend, participants cannot be said to be engaged in either a conversation of gestures or symbolic interaction with each other, since for the most part they do not meet or even know of one another. In reply to this criticism, it should be pointed out that complex social acts consist necessarily of the activities of human beings at innumerable points in which they must meet each other and adjust to one another as the operation is being carried out. At each of these points (which in total constitute the operation) the participants necessarily have to interpret one another's actions. In this indisputable sense the entire operation, however complex and proliferated it may be, requires symbolic interaction throughout its entire career. There is more to be said on this topic, though, and I shall return to it in a moment after reviewing a final, and related, criticism.

The remaining major criticism of Mead's scheme is that it makes no provision for the place and role of social structure. The critics contend that in focusing its attention on participants who are engaging in interaction Mead's scheme overlooks the social structure inside of which such interaction takes place. Such a structure, at a minimum, is said to be a framework inside of which interaction has to fit, and beyond this minimum the social structure is a positive factor that determines the nature of social interaction. But the charge that Mead's scheme either denies or misrepresents the influence of social structure is not true. The charge is equivalent to claiming that the social act, as defined by Mead, comes into being and takes form free and apart from any established arrangement or relation in the given society. This is not the case, though, for the social act, as we have seen, is formed through a process in which the participants almost always apply community definitions to the situation in which the social act is being formed. These definitions (which come from the generalized other) bring the social act into connection with, and in line with, a body of expected behavior and thereby give a community shape to the social act, though of course in varying degree. This observation provides the most solid answer to the criticism that Mead's scheme makes no place for social structure.

Embedded in both the 'macrosociety' criticism and the 'social structure' criticism is a legitimate question that must be raised about Mead's treatment of these topics. In brief, how do participants adjust to each other in large and complex acts if they do not meet or even know of each other? The question refers to the role and influence of remote and unrecognized structure on the immediate social acts in which people engage; it is a question of the relation between the operation of the 'large' society on the one hand and on the other hand the formation by the participants of their respective activities. By a 'large society' I refer to a huge, highly differentiated and complex society in which members are engaged in joint or adjusted actions, largely without knowing of one another or without entering into direct symbolic interaction with each other. As I have mentioned, manifestations of such large societies are to be seen in a vast division of labor, a vast communication network, a vast bureaucratic structure, or a huge complex of institutions. Participants in the operation of any one of these forms of a large society have different spatial and temporal locations so that they encounter one another only in small numbers at very limited points. Yet they are all caught up in a vast joint societal activity. The questions that we must address are (1) how did Mead see and treat this 'large society' and (2) how did he relate this large society to the individual participant?

(1) Mead clearly recognized and dealt with the existence of the large society. This needs to be stressed since Mead's critics and most of his followers give no attention to this portion of Mead's views. In noting that the formation and possession of 'selves' is what distinguishes human societies from animal and insect societies, Mead saw that human societies could not only take different forms but would inevitably grow into more complex forms as human minds (the result of selves) played upon and developed social acts. In meeting the problems that are set by their association, human beings reconstruct their joint acts, giving rise to changes in their relations and in what they do. But in addition, their joint acts link up with one another to form larger and larger complexes. Mead saw this process, in which human group life is formed into a larger organization, as a social-evolutionary process – one which, in the long run, was bound to continue. It was bound to continue because of four factors or conditions which are in play in human society. These four factors are communication, economic exchange, religious interest and social conflict. Let me explain briefly the way in which Mead saw these four factors as leading to the formation of 'large society'.

For Mead, communication was the basic process at work in human societies. He saw communication as taking place when participants use significant symbols, that is, make indications to one another that have the same meaning for those to whom the indications are directed as they do for those who make the indications. This sharing of the meaning of an indication brings the participants into a genuine social relation, one in which their lines of behavior fit each other to form a common or transcending social act. Communication is to be seen, then, as an organizing process; as it spreads, whatever its direction, it gives rise to a wider and larger organization.

Inside of the communicative process, economic exchange may

take place as a special form of human contact and association. Mead attached a great deal of importance to economic transactions in bringing human beings into larger organized relations. He noted that the exchange of products led easily to establishing links between participants who had no direct association with each other, and this tying together of people into larger organizations through economic exchange was treated by Mead as a universal process that grows in importance with increased and diversified association.

Mead saw a similar reaching-out process in human society as a result of the religious attitude. He regarded the religious attitude as springing from an original human impulse of neighborliness. This impulse carries, so to speak, a disposition and a potentiality that leads individuals to widen their domain of association with people. Thus, the religious attitude promotes the formation of the religious cult, which in turn tends to evolve in the direction of a major religion with its premiss of universality. Mead was aware that this universalizing tendency of the religious attitude encountered checks and reversals, but insofar as members of conflicting religious groups succeed in taking each other's roles the groundwork is laid for an increased sense of a wider human community. The religious attitude lays the basis for the incorporation of outside people into a larger organization beyond the immediate structure in which given people live.

Finally, Mead included social conflict as a process which led to the formation of ever larger organized relations. For Mead, conflict is not to be thought of as merely a disintegrative process which severs and separates parties from each other. To the contrary, it may operate to require the conflicting parties to work out new adjustments to each other and thereby establish a new organization between them. Conflict is to be seen as providing the need and the incentive for the reconstruction of organized relations. As the occasions for conflict extend or increase in modern society, there is corresponding pressure toward larger organization.

Mead, then, was keenly aware of the formation of human society in the large. Communication, economic exchange, the expression of religious feeling and the process of social conflict were seen by him as universal processes at work to bring larger organized relations into being within and between human societies. Further, these four processes are to be seen as expanding and becoming more vigorous in our modern world. This ever-enlarging character of human society, especially under modern conditions of association, occupied a central position in Mead's analytical picture. For Mead, human group life as a social process included not merely the adjustments of human behavior that take place at the innumerable points of immediate contact of human beings but included also the fitting together of these adjustments into larger transcending forms of organization.

(2) We can now address the question of how Mead saw the relations between the large organization and a participant in it. How does a participant fit his action into the large organization when he has contact with only a limited number of other participants and meets them at only restricted parts of their ongoing process? Mead's answer is that the participant does this by taking the role of what we have previously spoken of as the 'generalized other' or the abstract community. The abstract community refers to the organized or integrated arrangement of activities in the community, chiefly in the form of *institutions*. An institution, such as a family system, a system of private property, or a system of public education, was defined by Mead as 'a common response of all members of a community to a particular situation'. An institution represents an arrangement of diverse activities (such as those of owners, agents, police, judges, recorders, and so on, involved in upholding private property) covered by a set of principles that reflects that organized arrangement. The set of principles constitutes the 'logic' of the institution. Now, according to Mead, in taking the role of the 'generalized other' the participant is putting himself in the position to grasp the logic of a given institution or a given complex of institutions and to use this logic to guide his behavior in a given institutional situation. In this way, his action at any given point of a large societal action is based not merely on the limited character of what he is presented with at that point but is also derived from the sense of the larger social arrangement which he grasps through the generalized other. The generalized other enables the participant in the larger society to get a sense of the larger complex into which his action is to fit.

Mead recognized that there could be a gap between the larger social act in which a person was participating and the person's picture of this social act as given by his generalized other. First, the generalized other formed by a participant could be restricted to a narrow community instead of reflecting the larger community implicated in the given social act; in this (very common) way the participant is guided by an inadequate or distorted understanding of the larger organized act in which he is involved. Secondly, human society with its universalizing tendencies toward new and larger organization is always a step ahead, so to speak, of the formation of the 'logic' of the given organization that is growing up; thus, the community's recognition of that organization may lag behind the organization itself. In either of these two circumstances the larger organized social act and the picture of it yielded by the generalized other do not match each other.

It was precisely this discrepancy between the development of the large social act and the picture of that act that Mead saw as the major problem in modern society. His answer to the problem was to declare that the participants have to develop an understanding of their larger social acts through the medium of a more accurate generalized other. This was the theoretical step necessary to bring a modern society abreast of its own development, to put it in the position to exercise intelligent control over its own development. Mead has been accused of being a romantic utopian in taking this position; yet it is in line with his basic view that human group life is fundamentally a social process of interpretation. If the members of a society are able to develop more refined and accurate role-taking, their understanding and control of what is taking place is clearly improved. This is the way, according to Mead, by which a human society is able to exercise intelligent direction over its destiny.

The perceptive reader of Mead will recognize that he leaves un-answered a number of highly significant questions about applying his scheme to the analysis of human society. I wish to identify these questions. I wish, also, to point out that the questions are unavoid-able in the study of human society, even though they are consistently ignored by the major approaches in current sociology. The better to understand these concluding matters it is desirable, once more, to keep in mind the distinctiveness of Mead's approach. Mead's analysis is distinctive in that it presumes that human societies are made up of persons who have 'selves'. The possession of selves means that the actors have to take each other's roles, interpret each other's ongoing actions, analyze and judge each other's actions and construct their own individual acts through self-interaction – with all of this taking place within the framework of ongoing social or joint acts. So far as I can see, no one of the other major current approaches to the study of human society recognizes that human beings have selves (in Mead's sense) and that human beings are engaged in constructing ongoing joint acts, which together constitute the stuff of human group life. A critical appraisal of the merits of Mead's approach versus other approaches turns on whether Mead's views of the self and of the social act are correct. The reader can and should test Mead's premises by observing himself to see whether he is, indeed, engaged in indicating to himself what other persons are doing and whether he, in turn, is interpreting and planning what to do. If it is true that human beings have selves, as Mead con-tends, and if it is further true that they are engaged in forming social or joint acts through a communicative and interpretive process, then any tenable scheme designed to study and analyze human society would have to respect these truths. Keeping these simple points in mind, we can now turn our attention to the significant problems that remain in applying Mead's scheme.

The first of these open problems refers to how one should study the processes by which the 'large' society is built. As explained above, Mead saw this enlarging process as arising from communication, economic exchange, the expansion of religious interest and the resolution of social conflict. Yet a recognition that large, complex society comes into being through these four processes does not provide us with the guides and the methods for studying these processes. Mead did essentially nothing to devise or develop methods that could be followed in studying the social processes that he identified. He was not engaged professionally in social science research and was not led to address the questions of how such research was to be carried on. Thus, one will not find in Mead's work the answers to the methodological questions as to how one probes into the tough problems set by the formation of large, complex social acts.

In these circumstances, one might perhaps say that scholars who wish to study human society are justified in turning away from Mead's view and in employing the modes of study of other approaches, such as the cultural, structural, social system, Marxist and other perspectives. Yet, as I have already explained, these approaches are basically deficient in that they fail to see and catch the fact that human beings are engaged in defining and interpreting each other's actions at all points in the formation of large, complex social acts, or at all points of their contact in large, complex social structures. Other approaches ignore or by-pass this interpretive process, which is part and parcel of the way large social acts are formed and the way large social structures function. Mead's scheme makes unavoidable the inclusion of the interpretive process in the formation and the operation of large society. How this process is to be studied in this context is one of the significant problems that is posed but not answered by Mead's approach.

A second problem of major significance left unanswered is how can one study, and thus perfect, what Mead has in mind in speaking of the 'generalized other'. Mead obviously elevated the 'generalized other' to a place of major importance in his scheme. The generalized other is the chief position from which a human participant grasps and understands the social world inside of which he has to develop his conduct. Thus questions of how the generalized other is formed and how its formation may be improved are of capital importance. Mead does not give us any help in facing these crucial questions. His assertion that one takes the role of the organized group is a profound observation, but how this is done is untouched by him. Thus, we are given no aid in tracing how people construct their 'generalized others' and, accordingly, we do not have a set of techniques which would enable people and scholars alike to improve their ability to take group roles.

The absence of information on these matters in Mead's work can easily lead to the assumption that we can and should forget what Mead has in mind in speaking of the generalized other. One could contend that such conventional sociological terms as 'social norms', 'social values', 'social beliefs', 'social understandings' and 'community definitions' are sufficient to cover what Mead was referring to. But it is a mistake to assume that this is the case. A community definition, such as a norm, a rule, an understanding, or an injunction, may identify the specific action that one is to perform; however, it does not cover the relation of that specific action to other actions to which it may be tied, nor does it convey a sense of how seriously the action is viewed by the community. In short, the meaning that is conveyed by the 'generalized other' covers the way in which the community sees and values a cluster of related matters and not merely the specification of this or that item. We have no concept in social science that even approximates the kind of empirical reference that is suggested by Mead's term of the 'generalized other', namely, an organized, diversified and interwoven sense of the orientation of a society or of a part of a society. In my judgement, this kind of empirical reference is definitely needed in the study and analysis of human society. Its vagueness in Mead's hands is no call for its abandonment or neglect, but is instead a challenge for its clarification and refinement.

Mead's picture of human group life leaves a third significant problem area to which he gives little attention. This third area of concern can be spoken of as the study of the 'social situation'. Only a little reflection is necessary to recognize that Mead's scheme introduces the social situation as an analytical element or factor of the greatest importance. The social situation is the scene of social action and enters decisively into the formation of social action. We see this immediately when we note that for Mead the social or joint act is an ongoing or developing affair. The social act is built up in the course of its own development. This occurs, as we have seen, by the participants approaching the scene of action with a preliminary definition of what confronts them. But their task is then to fit their actions to one another, and this requires them, as we have seen, to take and define each other's roles as they adjust to one another in the formation of the ongoing joint act. The situation which the participants have to face is constituted by one another's action and by the interpretation which they make of this ongoing action. The situation, in this sense, enters the social act as the social act is being formed. This is just a formal way of saying that people in association act in terms of their situation as that situation is being set by their respective actions.

There is a significant difference between the way in which Mead's theory and other theories seek to explain action in the situation in terms of what the participants bring to the situation; thus, we have explanations of the situation in terms of such factors as cultural norms and values, role prescriptions, pressures of reference groups and arrays of psychological motives. In contrast, in Mead's scheme the participant is engaged in defining the situation as the social act proceeds, guiding himself by the definition which he is making. To understand social action it is necessary to incorporate this process of the interpretation of the evolving situation in which the participants are placed as they take account of each other's ongoing actions. The analysis of the social situation is more complicated than is suggested by this brief account; a fuller account would require one to explain how the differing perspectives and definitions of the participants come to fit together, and also how situations give rise to one another in a chain-like arrangement. However, the simple observation that the participants have to guide their adjustment to one another by a running definition of their situation should suffice to emphasize the importance of the 'situation' in Mead's approach.

Mead, though, says very little about how the social situation enters into the social act or, put otherwise, how the social situation and the social act interact. His remarks on this topic are limited to observations on the role of institutional values in the formation of institutional actions, as in the upholding of property rights by police, prosecuting attorneys, judges, and so on. But these instances of institutional organization represent only a portion of the social situations facing people in forming social acts; they represent social situations which are for the most part already ritualized. The vital problem confronting the analyst of human society is how to handle the social situations in which the participants are working with, or developing, different definitions. In these undefined situations the working out of adjustments to one another cannot be explained by what the participants bring to their situation; it is necessary to include what they take into account in the formation of their social act. Mead should not be faulted for not devising an analytical account of how the developing social situation is to be brought inside of the developing social act.

No one of the other major theories of human society does this either. Mead's theory has the merit of pointing to the problem. Other theories do not even raise the problem.

In concluding the present account of Mead's view of human society it is well to re-emphasize that Mead built his view around the premiss that human beings possess 'selves'. The possession of a self makes the human being into a fundamentally different kind of actor from the human being that is depicted in the theories that dominate the social and psychological sciences. With a self, the action of the human being is no longer a mere response to factors playing on or through him; instead, the action is worked out by the human being as he handles his situations and handles himself in his situations. A society made up of such members is very different from a society made up of members who do not possess selves. This is what Mead's scheme endeavors to stress. Human societies are composed of organisms with selves.

Notes: Chapter 7

1 The writings of Mead which are particularly relevant to his sociology and therefore this paper are: 'The social self' (1913); 'A behavioristic account of the significant symbol' (1922); 'The genesis of the self and social control' (1924); *The Philosophy of the Present* (1932); *Mind, Self and Society: From the Standpoint of a Social Behaviorist* (1934); *Movements of Thought in the Nineteenth Century* (1936); *The Philosophy of the Act* (1938).

2 It is true that in many places Mead refers to human society as a 'system'. He uses the reference to call attention to the interconnection of different parts of social life. He does not use the term to mean that human group life is an entity that can be studied apart from the fashioning of action by its members.

8

The Uses of Classical Sociological Theory

LEWIS A. COSER

The uses of sociological theory for the investigation and explanation of social phenomena seem to me largely of two interrelated kinds. Theories sensitize the investigator as to what to look at and what to eschew in the quest for systematic knowledge. I shall be brief in dealing with this point. But theories are also toolkits for initiating specific inquiries. My main emphasis will be on this subject.

Theory as a Guide to Observation and Explanation

One of the major functions of theory is to order experience with the help of concepts and to select relevant aspects and data among the enormous multitude of 'facts' that confront any investigator of social phenomena. Without a theoretically derived conceptual apparatus, one would experience the world as what William James once called a 'blooming, buzzing confusion'. Without guidelines as to what to attend to and what to leave out of consideration, ordinary social actors as well as scholarly investigators would be stymied by the circumstances that it is plainly impossible to deal with all the 'facts'. Simply to record all the data about, say, a classroom of students would surely require a lifetime. And such a lifetime of study would, of course, provide only mountains of useless information. A theory is a guide to what to look at, and what to ignore, in any type of inquiry. By directing inquiry, and by focusing on a set of data relevant to the theory while deliberately neglecting others, a theory acts like a searchlight in illuminating one area while leaving another in darkness. This implies, of course, as the literary critic Kenneth Burke argued a while ago, that 'a way of seeing is always a way of not seeing' (1956, p. 70). But this is as it should be, since for scientists or laypersons not wedded to one exclusive set of concepts and theories it is always possible to use alternative sets to illuminate areas neglected by earlier investigations.

A few examples will be useful. When Sigmund Freud developed his theory of the Oedipus complex and of infantile sexuality, he sensitized researchers to areas of human behavior which they hitherto had failed to bring under scrutiny. Having previously believed that sexuality only emerged at puberty, investigators had failed to look at infants or young children for evidence of erotic activities and expressions of libidinal urges. And even though literary treatments and philosophical inquiries had for a long time focused on the evidence of strains and tensions in the relations between fathers and sons, it was only after Freud that systematic observations of Oedipal tensions between them were undertaken. The point I wish to make is not that Freud was necessarily right in his theorizing; he was probably only partly correct. What matters here is that he opened a new and fertile field of inquiry by directing subsequent generations of researchers to previously neglected facets of human behavior.

When Max Weber developed the concept of 'status situation', he, just like Freud, directed investigators to a set of phenomena hitherto neglected. Weber argued that the concept 'class situation', which had previously been in the forefront of attention of sociologists, did not suffice to illuminate the full operation of stratification systems and had to be supplemented. 'In contrast to the purely economically determined "class situation" ', he argued, 'we wish to designate as status situation every typical component of the life fate of men that is determined by a specific, positive or negative, social estimation of honor. [It] is normally expressed by the fact that above all else, a specific style of life can be expected from all those who wish to belong to the circle' (Gerth and Mills, 1948, pp. 186–7). By developing this theoretical notion, Weber directed his attention, as well as that of subsequent investigators, to those phenomena within stratification hierarchies that could not be explained by economic criteria alone. He sensitized investigators to the major role honor, life-style and related notions play in the hierarchical ordering of societies. The notion of status situation made it easier to explain the dominant position of the Prussian Junkers in Imperial Germany or the Boston Brahmins in the political and cultural life of Boston. Similarly, and on the other side of the medal, the negatively privileged position of groups whose social honor is impugned and whose life-style is devalued could be analyzed in ways that were not available through class categories. In these cases, to be sure, the phenomena themselves were known and observed before Weber, whereas many of those Freud dealt with were previously unknown; but the groups to which Weber directed attention could be fully understood and fitted into a larger pattern through Weber's novel conceptualization of status situations.

Another sociological classic, Georg Simmel's *Conflict* (1955), drew attention to the positive functions of conflict. Such functions had been neglected by previous researchers and theorists. These, following 'common sense', had perceived only the negative and dissociating consequences of conflict behavior. Stressing the group-binding functions of conflict, Simmel could argue as follows:

> There probably exists no social unit in which convergent and divergent currents among its members are not inseparably interwoven. An absolutely centripetal and harmonious group . . . not only is empirically unreal, it could not show life process. Just as the universe needs 'love and hate', that is, attractive and repulsive forces in order to have any form at all, so society, too . . . needs harmony and disharmony, . . . association and competition . . . favorable and unfavorable tendencies. (1955, p. 15)

By laying the groundwork for a theory of conflict, Simmel drew attention to hitherto largely neglected perspectives on social life that, since his day, have been explored in a variety of studies (cf. Coser, 1956).

To summarize: one of the major uses of theories and sets of theoretically derived concepts is to sensitize research to investigate data and phenomena that have hitherto remained in obscurity. Once such 'theory-soaked' sets of data have been identified and extracted from inchoate reality, it becomes possible to establish relationships between them, to discover associations or uniformities. In other words, the typical if–then propositions of science can only come into play when, through prior theoretical reflection, the researcher has been able to identify which 'if's are likely to be important and which are not.

Theory as a Kit of Tools

When a plumber is called to the house because a drainpipe needs fixing, he is likely to bring a toolkit along. He is aware that the causes of the malfunctioning may be many and that he cannot rely on just one tool to put matters right. Analogies are always somewhat misleading, but I believe, nevertheless, that one may think of the investigation of specific problems in social analysis as yielding best results when not just one tool, but a set of tools, is employed. I shall illustrate this through a specific array of phenomena that require explanation.

The rise of the Nazi movement

With the onset of the Great Depression in Germany, and especially after 1930, the Nazi movement rose rapidly in Germany, both in terms of membership and in terms of electoral success. Yet it was also apparent that the appeal of the Nazis differed in various classes, in various regions and in different religious bodies. The question I hence wish to ask is 'what tools does classical sociological theory provide to explain this differential impact of the Nazi movement on various segments of the German population?' I do not intend to provide novel explanations of the Nazi phenomenon, a task that would require years of work, but only to use the Nazi data as an example for the uses of sociological classics as tools of inquiry.

ITEM: 'The National Socialist ideology,' writes Karl Dietrich Brecher, the foremost historian of the Nazi movement, 'never got a foothold in the class-conscious working class. The Nazis were more successful to win over the unemployed' (1969, p. 171).

ITEM: Analyzing the membership lists of the Nazi movement in 1935 (which differ only slightly from the 1932 figures), Barrington Moore calculates that about 12 percent of the total male labor force were Nazi Party members. Yet only 8 percent of the workers were Nazi members and only 7 percent of the skilled metalworkers. Of the miners, the Nazis recruited only 5 percent. These figures include the unemployed. Since we know that the unemployed had a much higher rate of participation in the Nazi party than the employed, and since 42 percent of the workers were unemployed, it is to be assumed that the Nazi membership among employed workers must have been lower than 8 percent (Moore, 1978, pp. 403ff.). An earlier analyst of party membership in 1933 and 1935, Hans Gerth, comes to the same conclusion, stating that 'the non-agricultural proletariat was considerably underrepresented in the Nazi party' (1952, p. 106).

What accounts for the relative success of the Nazis to attract unemployed workers, and their relative lack of success with the employed Rummaging in our theoretical toolkit we come upon some significant clues from the writings of Karl Marx. Marx argued in *The Poverty of Philosophy* (1847, pp. 145–6; see also Bendix and

Lipset, 1966, p. 9) and elsewhere that class solidarity among workers would develop when labor struggles over economic benefits, physical concentration of masses of people and easy communication among them would lead to the development of solidarity and political organization. The communality of interests among workers, Marx stated, would *ab initio* unite workers as 'a class against capital, but not yet *for itself*'. But during the ensuing class conflicts, 'this mass becomes united and constitutes itself as a class *for itself*' (1847, pp. 145–6).

The history of the German labor movement in the later part of the nineteenth century and the early years of the twentieth readily testifies that Marx's prediction came largely to pass. The German workers did not become a revolutionary class as Marx had expected, but they developed a class-consciousness that made them a 'class for themselves'. As a consequence, the employed workers proved largely impervious to the Nazi appeal, maintaining their allegiance to the Social Democrats and, to some extent, the Communists. But why should this not have been the case among the unemployed?

Here again, recourse to Marx's theory of class-consciousness is useful. It will be recalled that Marx argued that for a working-class-consciousness to arise it was of the essence that workers be concentrated in large factories and that communication between them be easy. But unemployed workers are largely deconcentrated, isolated, privatized, and they no longer have the chance to communicate with those of their fellows who are still employed. Having no access to a workplace, they are cut off from their fellows and are transformed into social atoms.

Marx did not say anything immediately pertinent about unemployed workers, but he had something significant to say about another category of people who live in isolation and lack communicative ties with their fellows: the French peasantry around the middle of the nineteenth century. 'The small peasants', he writes, 'form a vast mass, the members of which live in similar conditions, but without entering into manifold relations with one another. Their mode of production isolates them from one another, instead of bringing them into mutual intercourse' (1852, p. 109). Lack of communication among small peasants, Marx argues, prevented them from forming common attitudes and a common class-consciousness. They were, so he says, 'like potatoes in a sack', a collection of individuals without ties among each other. Under such conditions, he suggests, they are at the mercy of demagogic leaders, in his example Napoleon III, who can exploit the misery suffered individually and in isolation.

The German unemployed workers, it would seem, were very much in the position of the small peasants in nineteenth-century France.

Cut off from communication and commerce with their fellows, having been forced to sever their bonds with their employed comrades, progressively isolated, they were much more ready than the employed to listen to the appeals of Hitler and to look at him as a savior.

Furthermore, the condition of the unemployed can be described by reference to Weber's notion of 'life-chances on the market', that is, the chances an individual has of sharing in the socially created economic or cultural goods which typically exist in a society.[1] By virtue of being unemployed, people experienced a significant loss of their lifechances since they were no longer able to sell their skills or labor power on the market. They had not only lost their jobs, but they had also lost the sense of collective strength that they had gained as long as they were employed and organized. Experiencing a sense of weakness and despair, they craved for some miracle that would make them whole again.

ITEM: The electoral appeals of the Nazi Party were more successful in the country than in the cities. 'With one exception', writes Brecher, 'in the elections of 1932, regions where the Nazis did best show a more than average agricultural character' (1960, p. 648).

At first sight it may seem that Marx's prediction that the peasantry would not react to political events with class-consciousness would be a sufficient explanation of the disproportionate inroads the Nazis made among German peasants. But a closer look at electoral statistics reveals that the Nazi impact differed between various strata of the peasantry. These statistics reveal that some strata of the peasant population seemed rather impervious to Nazi penetration, while others easily fell prey to the appeals of the Nazi movement. Following another lead from Marx's focus on the productive process, it turns out that in all of northern Germany the small peasantry indeed went over to the Nazis in large numbers and at an early date, while the rural nobility and the big farmers did not. Neither did agricultural laborers; they proved to be almost as immune to the Nazi appeal as were their counterparts in the city.

Like the unemployed in the cities, small farmers experienced a very pronounced loss of their life-chances. Well-to-do farmers, estate-owners and areas of diversified farming, to be sure, all suffered from the depression and the attendant catastrophic fall in the prices of agricultural products. But it was the small farmers, who even before the depression only managed to eke out a precarious living from their land, who suffered most. The differentiated impact of market conditions on different types of rural enterprises, a basic

Marxian notion, together with the isolation of small farms, helps explain why small peasant owners, rather than other rural categories of people, furnished so many recruits – and very early recruits to boot – to the Nazi cause.

In contrast to them, agricultural workers identified with the working class. Of these agricultural workers, only 6 percent were party members (compared to, it will be remembered, 12 percent of the total labor force; Moore, 1978, pp. 403ff.), and their unemployment rate was a low 12 percent compared to the 42 percent of urban workers.

What I have said so far pertains, however, only to the largely Protestant regions of northern Germany.

ITEM: Of the twenty electoral areas where the Nazis obtained an above-average vote in 1932, sixteen were Protestant and four were Catholic (Brecher, 1960, p. 648). Generally, even though the Nazi movement was born in Bavaria, it remained weak in Catholic Bavaria as well as in much of the rest of the Catholic south of Germany.

To explain this religious differential we must broaden Marx's concept of class-consciousness by having recourse to Durkheim's concept of social cohesion and solidarity. Durkheim suggested in *Suicide* that the lower rate of suicides among Catholics as compared to Protestants could be explained by the higher integration and solidarity in Catholic religious communities and their priestly guidance, in contrast to the emphasis on the guidance of the individual conscience among Protestants. The Catholic communities, Durkheim argued, were marked by social cohesion, while Protestant areas showed greater degrees of excessive individualism or even anomie.

Durkheim's conceptualization would seem to be useful to explain the differing religious voting patterns during the rise of the Nazi movement. In Catholic areas, the guidance of the parish priest, backed up by a whole panoply of religious organizations, provided to Catholics a sense of community which was largely absent in Protestant areas. Moreover, the Catholics had a party of their own, the *Zentrum,* which, throughout the whole Weimar period, had represented not only their religious but also their secular interests. The *Zentrum* and the church played a role among Catholics which was in many ways similiar to that of the Social Democrats among industrial workers. Religious party and church forged religious solidarities in somewhat the same manner as the Social Democrats forged class solidarities. As a result, the Nazis made as few inroads among devout Catholics as they made among class-conscious workers. Religious bonds among Catholics effectively immunized them against the demogogic appeals of the Nazis.

Durkheim's notion of excessive Protestant individualism as a source of anomie becomes even more convincing when one supplements it with Weber's analysis of *The Protestant Ethic*. Weber argued that Protestants became main carriers of the capitalist spirit because of an elective affinity between the teachings of the Protestant divines and the acquisitive this-worldly behavior required by capitalist enterprise. He argued that the inner-worldly asceticism and the methodical discipline that animated Protestants in perpetual quest for signs of salvation provided a powerful stimulus for capitalist activities. Yet Weber made these points in reference to a period of strong economic development and rapid capitalist expansion. In such periods, there did indeed exist an excellent fit between Protestant strivings and economic success. But in Germany, throughout the period of inflation, and again a few years later during the depression, the fit between aspirations and actual results disappeared. When Protestant men and women felt that the economic world had become unexplainable and irrational so that there seemed no longer any connection between methodical, disciplined and thrifty behavior and worldly success, the Protestant ethic began to lose its hold. Middle-class Protestants had saved for years to buy a house or to allow for the higher education of their children, yet all these savings had been wiped out by a catastrophic inflation. A few years later, a high proportion of them, despite living up to the rules of the game, despite following the injunctions of inner-worldly asceticism, lost their jobs, their businesses, their worldly goods. They experienced a significant loss in their life-chances. Under these conditions, and given the relative weakness of religious communal ties among them, it stands to reason that the impact of the Nazis was much stronger in the Protestant than in the Catholic areas.

Having accounted for some class differences, some rural–urban divergences and some religious differences in the appeal of the Nazis, we are still faced with regional particularities that at first glance seem impervious to a Marxian, Weberian, or Durkheimian analysis.

ITEM: Already by 1930 the region of Schleswig-Holstein had become one of the strongholds of the Hitler movement. In the elections of 1932 this region was the only one where the Nazis reached a majority of the vote (51 percent), despite the fact that in the years immediately before and after the First World War, the region had been a stronghold of the Liberal and Social-Democratic parties (Heberle, 1951, p. 223).

Schleswig-Holstein largely consisted of highly cohesive rural communities that served as empirical examples for the elaboration of Ferdinand Toennies's notion of *Gemeinschaft*. Toennies was a native of that region. The fact that this area was Nazi-dominated already at an early stage of the Nazi movement contradicts Durkheim's theory of social cohesion. This theory would lead us to expect that the communal character of the area would make it immune to the appeal of Nazism. The fact that it was not is a challenge to Durkheim's conceptualization.

Toennies built much of his sociology on the differences he perceived in his youth between the life-styles of his native region and that of the rest of Germany. Toennies is, of course, the scholar who elaborated the difference in terms of human relations between *Gemeinschaft* and *Gesellschaft*, between community and association, that has since had so large an impact on subsequent sociological theorists from Weber to Parsons and Nisbet. To put it into a nutshell, Toennies argued that in communities the 'we' had primacy over the 'I'. *Gemeinschaft* is characterized by 'intimate, private, and exclusive living together'. In community, one 'lives from birth on, bound to it in weal and woe'. *Gesellschaft,* in contrast, is characterized by individualism and the cash nexus; it is a Hobbesian world in which others are not experienced as fellow members of a community but as means toward the furtherance of one's own ends (Toennies, 1949, ch. 1).

Toennies seems largely to have arrived at this fruitful dichotomy by comparing conditions in the villages of his native region, which still lived, for the most part, according to communal standards evolved in the Middle Ages, and the surrounding wider society, which had been engaged in a frantic march toward urbanization, industrialization and modernization ever since the founding of the German Reich in 1871.

In the years of the depression, from 1929 on, these age-old communities suffered their death pangs. Rudolf Heberle, who has made a pioneering ecological study of the region and of the rise of the Nazi movement within it, writes: 'The real strongholds of the Hitler movement were on the *Geest*, the central subregion. Here were concentrated the village communities where more than eighty per cent, sometimes one-hundred per cent, of the vote was cast for the Nazis' (1951, p. 226). The *Geest* farmers, he writes, were mainly dependent on two extremely sensitive markets for young beef cattle and for hogs. Having only meager financial reserves, they were as a rule in a worse financial plight than were their wealthier neighbors. But perhaps more important, the *Geest* zone had neither a landless proletariat nor big landholders. In addition, as Heberle put it, 'The criticism of Prussian policy . . . the demand for native civil servants, the refusal to accept Berlin as the general center of culture, were all outlets for a disposition which had been formed for a long time before the war. At bottom the criticism of Prussia was merely an expression of a general antipathy against the social system of industrial capitalism' (1945, p. 49).

The small *Geest* farmers, in their plight, turned against the whole world of *Gesellschaft* that had undermined, so they felt, the very basis of their communal existence. They were experiencing a significant loss of their life-chances. They fought for their collective existence. Having been used, over the ages, to collective responses of the *Gemeinschaft*, they maintained collective reactions but, in their extraordinary predicament, now turned to a party which in its demagogic appeals not only promised to set economic conditions aright, but also stole the idea of *Gemeinschaft*, transmuting it into the slogans of a *Volksgemeinschaft* based on blood and soil which would restore Germany to its racial and ancestral roots.

Here was a case where the old solidarities of the communal village turned to the advantage of the Nazis. This seems to be in contrast to the Catholic form of solidarity which tended to maintain itself against the Nazis. Yet there is an important difference between the *Geest* and the Catholic religious community: in the former, the *Gemeinschaft* was threatened by financial plight, by Prussian centralization, by industrial capitalism. Catholics were not threatened in this way. Their church was intact, the parishes were intact, their value-system had not been put to a test. Far from being an exception to the rule, Schleswig-Holstein confirmed the rule of *Gemeinschaft* effectiveness: the *Geest* area showed a high 'degree of social solidarity which was reflected in more unanimous voting' (Heberle, 1951, p. 228) for the Nazis because these people were threatened by the *Gesellschaft* just as the Catholics showed a high degree of social solidarity which was reflected in more unanimous voting against the Nazis because they were not threatened by the *Gesellschaft*.

Let me now turn to another important stratum that turned early to the Nazi Party and brought it significant recruits, in both membership and electoral support: the urban salaried middle class and the urban self-employed.

ITEM: While the Nazi membership 'quota' of the whole male labor force was roughly 12 percent, teachers' participation was 40 percent, that of self-employed merchants 25 percent, and white-collar employees accounted for 20 percent. All the middle-class occupations were drawn to the Nazi Party from a shade over their quota to more than three times this rate (Moore, 1978, p. 403). White-collar employees, while representing roughly 12½ percent of the gainfully employed, furnished about 21 percent of the party membership (Gerth, 1952, p. 106).

An interpretation of these trends would seem to be powerfully advanced by having recourse to both Marxian and Weberian schemes of explanation. As Barrington Moore puts it:

> The resentments that . . . nourished the Nazi movement were those of 'the little man' angry at the injustices of a social order that threatened or failed to reward the virtues of hard work and self-denial as these personal efforts became crystallized in the merchant's store, the craftsman's manual skill, the white-collar job, and the technician's and journalist's gift. Here was one possible outcome of the labor theory of value. (1978, p. 406).

All these categories of people were, to one extent or another, marginal to the two key classes which, to Marx, dominated the social scene. They were ground, to use another Marxian simile, between the two major grindstones of the capitalist socio-economic dynamic: the capitalists and the working class. Marx was plainly wrong, as Edward Bernstein had been quick to point out long before the Nazi rise to power (1961 [1899]), to expect the middle class to decline numerically. But it seems correct to assert that salaried employees, being men and women in the middle, unable to develop powerful solidarities similar to those of the working class, insecure by virtue of being dependent on management for their salaries, yet trying to distance themselves in their 'clean' office positions from 'dirty' manual occupations, resented their lack of specific weight in the politics of the Weimar Republic. The self-employed among the middle class, in addition, suffered from a general sense of loss of status as well as class standing. When the depression hit they became strong supporters of a party that, in its demagogic appeal, promised to give them again the honored and respected status that modernity had seemingly denied them.

The Weberian notion of status, about which I commented earlier, as well as the Marxian notion of marginality in relation to the determining dynamics of the capitalist civilization, seems to go a long way in explaining the disproportionately high involvement of the various middle-class strata in the Nazi movement. These concepts address themselves to the conditions of anomie referred to earlier. In summary: the middle class had experienced a significant loss of their life-chances.

ITEM: 'A detailed ecological analysis of voting in German cities with 25,000 or more population in 1932, indicates that the larger the city, the smaller the Nazi vote. The Nazis secured less of their total votes in cities over 25,000 in size than did any of the other five major parties.' (Lipset, 1960, pp. 145–6)

In the explanation of this pattern it is again Weber who seems most helpful. In smaller cities, as in county seats, the moral and political entrepreneurs had in the past been largely recruited from the self-employed middle class. Local store-owners or small-town professionals such as lawyers and physicians had constituted the local elite that expected deference and honor from the rest of the population. They had a distinctive style of life and hence status situation which, so they thought, entitled them to positions of leadership. But with the increasing modernization of the country, this exceptional position was gradually eroded as national and state bureaucracies, directed from the center, pre-empted most significant decision-making, and as national economic trends tended to prevail over locally determined economic factors. As a result, these previous local elites were undermined in their status positions, and their claims for deference remained unendorsed. They had experienced a significant loss of life-chances. When, as a result of inflation and depression, their economic position was also made highly insecure, they used their remnants of power to endorse a party, the Nazis, which promised to revive the old status order. In larger cities, on the other hand, modernity had already won over the claims of tradition, and power had been passed to national elites securely tied to modern urban and industrial developments. Here, national trends prevailed over local conditions, and people (with the significant exception of white collar strata and the self-employed) voted largely in terms of their class rather than their status situation. Cosmopolitan orientations predominated over remnants of local hierarchies.

I shall resist the temptation to introduce still other sets of conceptualization that might explain further differences in the appeal of the Nazis before their coming to power. Let me say only that concepts such as 'differential rates of mobility', 'relative deprivation', 'role differentiation', advanced by a generation of sociologists that followed the generation of the classics, could be integrated with the concepts that I have examined to throw further light on the data under consideration.

I hope that enough has been said in these pages to back up my overall contention that we neglect the classics of sociology only at our peril. Were sociology as cumulative a discipline as, say, physics, it would hardly be necessary for the practicing sociologist to study the classics. Their significant findings would all have been incorporated into current textbook knowledge. There is no need for physicists to read Newton. But such cumulation has not yet occurred in sociology; moreover one may legitimately doubt that it will occur in the foreseeable future, or ever. This being so, recourse to a variety of only imperfectly coordinated theoretical schemes may turn out to be a positive virtue. A disciplined eclecticism, the uses of a variety of theories of the middle range, is likely to be the most productive strategy in the foreseeable future. As long as this is the case, and for all I know it may be the case for a long time to come, recourse to the classics will continue to be necessary. They will continue to provide major tools for kits which, I hope, we shall put to more and more sophisticated uses. It is in this connection that a beautiful phrase by Goethe gains added significance: 'What you have inherited from your fathers, you must earn in order to possess'.

Notes: Chapter 8

1 I borrowed this definition of Weber's concept from Giddens (1973. pp. 130–1).

9

Revisiting the Classics throughout a Long Career

TALCOTT PARSONS

Let me begin by burdening you with a few considerations about my early career. I am now one of the seniors in the sociological business, having first defined myself as a sociologist in some sense in the mid-1920s – a little more than fifty years ago – so I ought to have done a little reflecting about my relation to prior tradition by this time.

My first contact with a sociological classic was with the influence of Weber.[1] I spent my first graduate year at the London School of Economics, where a different tradition was in the ascendancy. L. T. Hobhouse was still active, though he had been ill. Morris Ginsberg, who succeeded him as professor of sociology, was very active. Bronislaw Malinowski, the anthropologist, became a very important influence on my intellectual development. However, I went to Heidelberg the next year, on a newly arranged German-American exchange fellowship program, with very few plans and without the slightest idea of what I was going to run into. I heard about the program, applied, was awarded a grant, and was then assigned to Heidelberg without having any personal voice in that decision at all. It was when I arrived in Heidelberg that I first heard the name of Max Weber as an important figure. The year was 1925. Weber had died in 1920 at the age of 56. Heidelberg had been Weber's home for most of his active career, though during most of his creative period he did not teach. Although a private scholar, he had become a very dominant influence in the intellectual community of Heidelberg. So I was thrown by chance – serendipity – into this particular intellectual circle.[2] It turned out to be the most important one in continental Europe, except perhaps for the Durkheim circle, and of course the Freud circle in Vienna, which we would not call sociological in the usual sense. Weber soon came to be an exceedingly important influence in my thinking. The first thing of his I read was the study *The Protestant Ethic and the Spirit of Capitalism* (Weber, 1930). You might know that I read it in German for the very good reason that there was no English translation at the time. The very fact that I later decided to translate it is an index of its impact on me. When I first went to Heidelberg I did not have in mind being a degree candidate, but I discovered that I could become one without terrible complications, and so I did. I decided on a dissertation project in which Weber's work was central. It concerned the concept of capitalism in German social science literature. It started with Karl Marx, but ended with Max Weber. So I became very thoroughly immersed in Weberian theory at a very crucial point.

Now Durkheim was another matter. After coming back from Heidelberg and settling down at Harvard, again with extremely uncertain expectations for the future, I conceived the idea of making a study of the relations – differences and articulations – between economic theory and what in a broad way I called sociological theory. I started deliberately with a study of a very prominent economic theorist of the previous generation, Alfred Marshall. Pareto was also a particularly important figure for my project, because he was both an economic theorist in his own right and a sociologist. Of course I already had Weber's theoretical work deeply involved in my thinking on these matters. The general plan of a book, which eventually came to be *The Structure of Social Action* (Parsons, 1937), rounded out when I decided to make a really intensive study of Durkheim's thinking as well. I did this entirely on my own without any contact with the 'Durkheimians'. I had had some previous acquaintance with Durkheim's work, notably in London through both Ginsberg and Malinowski, who took a very dim view of Durkheim's intellectual quality and contribution. But the more I studied Durkheim in the original the more I came to disagree with Malinowski and Ginsberg about him.[3]

At any rate, that is how *The Structure of Social Action* took shape. I approached my central problem through Marshall, an economist, who had *implicit* sociological attitudes; through Pareto who had *both* economic and sociological aspects; and through two other figures who were more sociologists than economists, but who bore powerfully on economic problems. Weber had been a professor of economics, even though his doctorate was taken in jurisprudence and most of his work was considered sociological and historical. And you must remember that Durkheim's first book, though proclaiming its sociological nature, was entitled *The Division of Labor in Society* (1933), and hence dealt with a topic of economic analysis.

Now just a word about Freud. When I finished *The Structure of Social Action*, which took a number of years, I cast about for what to do next. By this time it was the mid-1930s. I decided to make a study of the phenomenon of professional occupations and professional practice in modern society. I felt that this field had been grossly neglected in all the discussions over capitalism and socialism. The relation of the professional to his client or patient seemed, as a type, to fit neither the common conception of a self-interested, profit-maximizing capitalistic relation nor the conception of a socialistic relation devoted to the good of the social whole. I wanted to explore empirically this important category of socio-economic relation that seemed to fall entirely between the usual terms of ideological and even social scientific discussion of the time (Parsons, 1939, 1951, ch.X). Among the professions I chose medical practice. From the point of view with which I approached the analysis of medical practice, I was very early plunged into the problems associated with what medical people were at the time calling 'the psychic factor' in disease. In that connection I had a very decisive conversation with Elton Mayo, who was a psychologist doing research in the field of industrial sociology that became the Western Electric studies. I am sure many of you are familiar with *Management and the Worker* and the related publications (Roethlisberger and Dickson, 1939; Mayo, 1960). I was talking to Mayo about these problems, and he shot at me the question 'How thoroughly have you read Freud?' I had to confess that I had done only very fragmentary reading of Freud. Mayo said 'You ought *really* to read Freud'. So I did. And it was one of the most important experiences I ever had. I read a great deal of Freud.[4]

This is not to say that there were no other figures. I mentioned Marshall and Pareto. There were Simmel and Toennies and many others. But these three, Weber and Durkheim and Freud, have stuck with me in a very particularly important way. In trying to recount a little bit how they have, I have often used the word 'revisit'. That is a codeword for me. I have paid intensive 'revisits' to all three in somewhat different contexts ever since these initial introductions, and they are going on right now more than fifty years after I first came under Weber's influence. These revisits have occurred in various connections, but I should like to take one continuous theme as a framework for the present discussion, namely, the problem with which I started in the book *The Structure of Social Action*, the relation of things economic to other aspects of society, culture and personality – all three – in an interconnected set of networks.

Let us start with Weber and certain continuities with his thought. Weber was a protean figure who wrote about an enormous range of problems, facts and phenomena, as many of you, of course, are aware. My starting point was *The Protestant Ethic* – I mentioned having translated it – but it has remained a focal reference for my thinking ever since I first read it in the 1920s. Why and how did it? I would answer by saying that Weber formulated the most radical challenge to the utilitarian view of economic behavior that had been stated up to that time. That is, he saw that productive economic behavior could be interpreted to be a *calling* – Weber adapted the English word 'calling' which had been used by the seventeenth-century Puritan authors whom he studied in the text – motivated in religious terms. This view stood in the most radical contrast to the orthodox allegation that the rational pursuit of self-interest was what motivated all economic behavior; and this tradition went way back to Aristotle's distinction between natural and unnatural acquisition. Market behavior was unnatural acquisition for Aristotle, way back in the fourth century BC, and similar interpretations had been sustained ever since. Well, Weber was a man with really radical ideas, in the intellectual not the political sense, and challenged this very deep-seated tradition. The theoretical implications of Weber's conception of economic activity ramified from this challenge in a great many directions.

In my own career a lot of revisits to the classics have come by way of environmentally presented challenges. A few years later another bout with Weber arose in such a way. A draft English translation had been made of the first two chapters of Weber's enormous *Wirtschaft und Gesellschaft*, which is now available in full translation under the title *Economy and Society* (Weber, 1968). Part I of the German edition included a third important chapter and was the more theoretical part. I was asked my opinion about the quality of the draft translation, and I rendered an unfavorable opinion. I said it had to be greatly revised and should not be published without the extremely important third chapter, the treatment of types of authority. As sometimes happens when one renders that sort of opinion, I was asked to undertake the job. I gave it a great deal of thought and finally decided to do it (Weber, 1947). So the English translation of the first part I was really responsible for. The original draft translator was a Mr Henderson, a young English economist. Just about the time I undertook the work the Second World War broke out and Henderson was called into the British armed forces. He never had any connection with the translation project after that. Well, there is nothing like translating a complex and difficult work as a way of learning what it is about. One is faced with difficult problems, not only about rendering what the author said into another language, but also of determining what he really *meant* by what he wrote in his own language. I think it is a very important kind of intellectual discipline, one of the best I know and a major reason why we ought never to be content with knowledge only of our native language.

However that may be, I wrote for the translation an introduction which came to over eighty printed pages. In working on the translation and introduction, my attention was called to the importance of problems of organization theory, as we often call it. Of course Weber himself was one of the main founders of organization theory, particularly under the heading of bureaucracy. But I had come under another influence in the intervening period, that of a very remarkable American businessman named Chester I. Barnard. His name is very familiar to those who work in the field of formal organization. He wrote a notable book entitled *The Functions of the Executive* (1938). Now he was a businessman, not a social scientist. But I got to know him personally and can testify that he had a better theoretical knowledge of economics and sociology than the overwhelming majority of professionals. By the way, he was president of the New Jersey Bell Telephone Company at the time he wrote that book, but later became president of the Rockefeller Foundation and the first chairman of the board of directors of the National Science Foundation. So he had a very notable career, quite different from those of most businessmen. But, putting Barnard's and Weber's ideas together, and developing some of the implications of my dissertation on the nature of capitalistic society, proved to be another major stimulus to the development of general theory (Parsons, 1960, chs 1–5, 1969, ch. 14).

I think one might say that Weber's substantive, empirical work fell into two main categories. The theory of modern bureaucracy and capitalism along with a great deal of the comparative historical work on its background was one aspect. The other principal aspect was the sociology of religion. There is a sense in which the Protestant ethic study was a link between the two because it concerned the relation of certain religious phenomena and movements to the level of institutional order and organization. Well, another revisit came along in that, in addition to the studies of Confucianism and Taoism, of Hinduism and Buddhism, and ancient Judaism (a series he never completed), Weber wrote a compendious treatment of the sociology of religion. It was intended to be part of *Wirtschaft und Gesellschaft*, and was originally published after his death as part of that. But before the English version of the whole *Wirtschaft und Gesellschaft* was even planned, however, the sociology of religion section was translated into English (Weber, 1963). I had nothing to do with the translation – it happens to be a very good one – but I was asked to write an introduction to it. I wrote quite a long essay on Weber's whole sociology of religion, taking it as practically another primary aspect of his entire corpus. Parenthetically, let me note that I came to the conclusion, and I stated it in my remarks at the Weber Centenary held by the German Sociological Association in 1964, that the core of Weber's substantive view of societies lay in his sociology of law (Parsons, 1971). That refers in part to his original training in jurisprudence. I have a running disagreement on this topic with Reinhard Bendix, who thinks that the political sociology is the real core of Weber's substantive concern (Bendix, 1962; Bendix and Roth, 1971). Well, I stated my view in the Proceedings of the Centenary, and I have felt confirmed in it ever since, even though it has not received many echoes in the subsequent literature.

Now I am back at still another revisit today, and I shall say just a word about trying to articulate Weber and Freud. This is not a common articulation. The two are seldom mentioned in the same paragraph in any writing I have run into. However, the stimulus to the articulation is that both figures contributed much to our thinking about certain features of the nature of rational action. The problem of rational conduct was a very central theme for Weber right through his career. The fact that he was trained as a lawyer and that he was a professor of economics, in addition to doing sociology, is highly relevant to this problem orientation, because concern with what is meant by rational action has been very central to each of these fields of thought. Freud is usually thought of as the apostle of the nonrational, some would even say the irrational – the id, the instincts, the unconscious, and all the rest. But the American branch of psychoanalysis has paid a great deal of attention to what are called 'ego functions'. It suddenly struck me that Freud and Weber converged on certain features of rational action after starting from two different sides : Weber from the side of the value system, the institutional structure, the legal system as regulatory of markets, communication systems, and so forth, at the macrosocial level; Freud from the side of the individual's involvement in elementary social interaction – à la George Herbert Mead and Herbert Blumer – very much on the microsocial level. Despite differences of level of analysis, there are certain striking common features, notably stress on the potentials for instability and on the need for regulation. Thus I became convinced that there is a real theoretical parallel between Weber's conception of a value system and its institutionalization in procedures of social control and Freud's concept of the super-ego.[5] Well, the convergence goes well beyond these points, but I do not want to have to omit some more talk about Durkheim and Freud.

Durkheim originally came into my work through *The Division of Labor*, because I was concerned with the nature of capitalistic society, so called, and with the relation between a sociological analysis and an economic analysis of phenomena in modern capitalistic society. It was in acute consciousness of those problems that I seriously and thoroughly read *The Division of Labor*. When people talked about Durkheim in those days they usually did not refer to that book at all. They referred either to the essay 'Individual and collective representations' (1953, pp. 1–34), or to *The Elementary Forms of the Religious Life* (1965). Even the study of suicide (1951) was not much read in many social scientific circles. The shibboleth formula commonly applied to Durkheim was 'the group mind fallacy', with emphasis on the word 'fallacy'.[6] Durkheim was alleged to have gone astray by believing in the 'group mind'. Now this is a *very* naive interpretation of Durkheim, as I hope that those who have done some reading of Durkheim are well aware. The thing that really struck me in Durkheim's early work was his conception of the institutional framework within which interactive behavior occurs, notably the institution of contract. I have year after year assigned in my classes Book 1, Chapter 7 of *The Division of Labor*, on contractual and organic solidarity, which contains the famous, to me devastating, critique of Herbert Spencer's idea of contractual relations. Where Spencer alleged that all the terms of a contractual relation are agreed upon *ad hoc* by the contracting parties, Durkheim showed that that just is not true – indeed, not possible. There are institutions regulating conflicts, for example, with interests of third parties, which the contracting parties are *not* at liberty to alter and which are enforced by the courts and administrative agencies. It is a beautiful theoretical analysis and its implications can lead one in many, many different directions.

My concern with Weber's sociology of religion led very naturally to revisits – I had been misled by my teachers about Durkheim on religion – to *The Elementary Forms*. Only a few years ago I made such a thorough revisit that I completely reread *The Elementary Forms of the Religious Life* right straight through from cover to cover, and I am happy to say in French, because the original is always better than a translation.[7] (As an ex-translator, I would say that with emphasis. Unfortunately I never read my Aristotle in Greek.) Well, this revisit, which resulted in an article in Glock and Hammond's volume on the sociology of religion, *Beyond the Classics?* (1973), led to what to me was a very major *new* insight. And here is a methodological or procedural point I want to leave with you. If the works in question really belong in the category of great human intellectual achievements – and this is certainly true of a great deal of Weber's and Durkheim's work – you can never exhaust their meaning and their significance for your work in a single reading. If you go back to them, you *always* find something new you did not understand before. Their texture is incredibly rich.

Now, let me just try to state very succinctly the new idea I got from Durkheim in about 1970. I came to understand that by 'society' as the famous reality *sui generis* Durkheim really meant the internal environment of the system of human action. Some of you will be familiar with the concept of internal environment as it has been used in biology, particularly in physiology. The blood is the most important part of the internal environment of mammalian organisms, including human organisms. Most of the cells and tissues of the body are not in contact with the external environment at all. They do not see along with the eyes, they do not hear with the ears, or feel with the skin. Muscles make it possible to move about, but the muscles never have contact with the ground or the air and so forth. They have contact only with the internal environment; indeed, specialized organs relate to each other chiefly through the internal environment. Durkheim was himself probably not fully aware of these implications, although the introducer of that very fruitful idea, the French physiologist Claude Bernard, was an older contemporary of Durkheim, worked in the same Paris as Durkheim, and almost certainly had some influence upon him (Hirst, 1975). The notion of an internal environment is a very central idea for a scientific field. I think one of the main reasons why Durkheim is so centrally important to the history of social science is that, in various discussions of the *milieu sociale*, as he termed it, he really formulated the essentials of a view of a sociological internal environment as nobody else did. As certainly Weber did not.

I cannot further detail Durkheim's conception here. However, let me just indicate my view that this conception is a major basis of Durkheim's status as our great theorist of social integration, that is, of the problem of how societies either hold together or, as in many cases, fail to hold together and break up. I have become increasingly concerned with this aspect of Durkheim's thinking over these many years (Parsons, 1968b).

Let me say just a few further words about Freud. My own early concern with Freud was in the field that we sociologists call socialization theory, which has nothing to do with government control of the means of production, but with child development, the family environment of maturation, and so on. This interest grew directly out of my concern with medical practice and the psychic factor in disease, because it very soon became clear that there were certain analogies between the role of the physician and the role of parents in the socialization process. Of course Freud, in his theories of transference and counter-transference, had presented the makings of some of the understanding of just what was in common. Freud, after all, invented the procedure of psychoanalysis – from scratch. It was an extraordinary achievement. And psychoanalytic therapy simply could not be effective unless it linked with the socialization processes by which analysands, the people subjected to the therapeutic procedure, had in fact come to be what they were. This need for linkage underlies the psychoanalytic concern with early childhood, which I think needs some correction, yet is itself a very fundamental contribution. Freud did not develop this link to the sociological aspects of the family very far – after all, he was not a sociologist and also went somewhat astray when he ventured into related areas of anthropology, as in *Totem and Taboo* (1938) – but he did present ideas that could be worked out more thoroughly in a sociological context. Thus, Freud's discussions of socialization clearly stress the importance of *social* objects to which the child has become emotionally attached, especially the parents, as the crucial influence upon the development of the child's character or personality. Indeed, Freud argues that the basic structures of an individual's personality are formed through the internalization or introjection of the figures of his or her parents. It has seemed to me that Freud's analysis of the process of personality development amounts simply to an account of how, through many steps, a child comes to be actively engaged within a social environment or milieu. His stress on the fundamental importance of object relations is just what we might expect on the basis of a Durkheimian notion of the social milieu surrounding the child.

Now the sociology of the professions, the sociology of family and kinship and the study of the socialization process all form a complex. A recent treatment of my own contribution in this field by the French scholar Francois Bourricaud presents an excellent summary, much clearer and fuller than I have ever pulled together myself, and I very much commend it to you. Bourricaud (1977) chose a title for his book which delights me, *Institutionalized Individualism*, which is in self-conscious contrast to 'utilitarian individualism'. This line of work can be said to lead in the direction of what might be called psychoanalytic sociology. A book with that title has recently been published by Weinstein and Platt (1973) and is a fairly interesting study. Platt was my collaborator on *The American University* (1973) a few years ago, and I know him very well indeed.

However that may be, there is another pertinent aspect of Freud's contribution, namely, his thinking on the theory of symbolic systems. The field of symbolism has in our own time come to be an increasingly active and salient field. The growth of linguistics has contributed a great deal to it. Certain kinds of anthropology, notably Lévi-Strauss's well-known structuralism, have also contributed to it. I paid a recent revisit to Freud in this connection after receiving a request to write a kind of reconsideration of a major work of Freud's from the standpoint of the present period of the twentieth century (Parsons, 1974). I was permitted to choose any one of Freud's contributions, and I chose *The Interpretation of Dreams* (1965). And, as in the case of Durkheim's *Elementary Forms*, I reread *The Interpretation of Dreams* from cover to cover in the original language. It is truly a remarkable work. It was Freud's earliest mature theoretical work. It was published in 1900, when he was 44, so it was not just a bright boy, but a very mature man, who wrote it. It proceeds not from records of psychoanalytic sessions, but from a very thorough review of the literature on dreams, from taking accounts of dreams from a variety of other sources and above all from analysis of Freud's own dreams. It sets forth practically the whole major framework of psychoanalytic thinking. From my recent revisit, I came to understand that the core of the conceptual revolution it wrought was to pin down, in a way that no other of his writings did, the centrality of what Freud called the psychic point of view. That is, what he called the psychic refers to a set of motive-connected symbolic entities. I would suggest that the total group of motivationally interrelated symbolic objects can be regarded as comprising an internal environment of the whole personality. Thus, all of the main factors that enter centrally into Freud's theoretical thinking – whether conscious, unconscious, or preconscious and whether elements of the id, ego, or super-ego – are to be interpreted as being symbolic or having symbolic effects upon motivation. His definition of instinct, for example, makes the distinction of the symbolic domain with the utmost care. An instinct is not an organic entity. It is a representation (or symbolization), in the psyche, of organic processes. Now that is a very different proposition from the usual misinterpretation of Freud, which maintains that he was a biological reductionist, that he did not really believe in the independent reality of things psychic. This misinterpretation, by the way, has been greatly favored by the very use of the word 'instinct', which was not Freud's word. Remember, Freud wrote in German, and the word he used most frequently in this connection was *Trieb*, for which I think a better translation is 'impulse'. *Trieb* and instinct should not be equated. Well, this is another area in which processes of interrelation and convergence have been going on.

Now, to close, what can I say about my own continuities and about the framework I have discussed here? I think one of the most distressing features of our current intellectual situation in the social sciences has been the divorce, institutionally and to a large extent intellectually, between economics and sociology. When I was coming into the field it was quite natural to have a common interest in both disciplines, as I did, and to be interested in relating them to each other. In my early years I wrote a number of pieces, besides *The Structure of Social Action*, trying to pursue that interest.[8] But that interest has practically gone out. I bet very few students in sociology, even graduate students, have ever had any courses in economics, particularly in economic theory. Probably fewer economists have had any formal work in sociology. You find serious theoretical interrelation here and there, but very sporadically. Now this relation I think has been, looking back, the most important single thread of continuity in my own intellectual development. I mentioned that it provided the main problematic of *The Structure of Social Action*. I came back to it, on a new theoretical level, in the 1950s. The most conspicuous product of that work was a small book on which I collaborated with Neil Smelser, to which with no intention of disrespect to Max Weber we gave the title *Economy and Society* (1956). We carefully explained in the preface why we chose that title, and we dedicated the book to the memory of Alfred Marshall and Max Weber, truly not a gesture of disrespect. This work embodied a phase of theoretical thinking well beyond the state of *The Structure of Social Action*, based largely on what I and others have called the four-function paradigm. A big theme of the book was relating the classification of the factors of production in economics to the four-function paradigm in general social systems theory and, beyond that, in the general system of action. Some of you will recognize these themes. Another phase of the continuing work on the interrelation of economic and sociological theory has come to a head for me in the last couple of years, and I am now at work on a book which will bring out some new features of it.[9]

Interwoven with the economic-sociological framework have been more substantive themes such as the concern for the professions; the concern for the psychology of the individual, socialization and the institutional settings of personal and cognitive development; the theory of symbolism; and the concern for the comparative study of religion and its relations to these other subject matters. If I may express one concluding thought, it is that, without an intellectually rich tradition to revisit, I do not think that disciplines like our own, with all their difficulties and complexities, could advance. That is the basis for my plea today for our continuing to revisit the classics.

Notes: Chapter 9

Talcott Parsons died before he could revise his lecture for publication. The present chapter is a transcript of a tape recording of his talk, given at East Carolina University on 19 April 1978, and has been edited for this volume by Professor Victor Lidz of the University of Pennsylvania. Professor Lidz has also amplified several points in order to clarify the general argument. A copy of the unedited version of the lecture will be deposited with the Talcott Parsons Papers in the Harvard University Archives.

1 In April 1978 Talcott Parsons also delivered a talk on his vicarious relationship to Max Weber, and its influence on his career, at the Annual Meetings of the Eastern Sociological Association. That talk, edited by Jackson Toby, appears in a volume edited by Robert K. Merton and Matilda White Riley (Parsons, 1980).

2 See Marianne Weber, 1975, for an account of the Weber circle in Heidelberg. See also Paul Honigsheim, 1968, for reminiscences of one of the younger members of the circle.

3 Something of the flavor of their disagreements with Durkheim can be found in George E. G. Catlin's 'introduction to the translation' of Durkheim's *Rules* (1938).

4 Professor Parsons actually completed a course of non-clinical training in the Boston Psychoanalytic Institute and later even taught at the Institute. On his interpretation of Freud see Parsons, 1964, chs 1–4; Parsons and Bales, 1955; Parsons, 1959.

5 The convergence between Weber and Freud on the understanding of rationality was explored by Talcott Parsons in a talk at a meeting of the Society for Psychohistory in 1977.

6 See, for example, George E. G. Catlin, 'introduction to the translation', in Durkheim, 1938.

7 On other occasions, Professor Parsons commented on having read *The Elementary Forms of the Religious Life* many times, almost annually, since sometime in the 1930s. Although these were not complete 'cover to cover' readings, his remark here on having made an occasional thorough rereading should not lead the reader to underestimate how often and how carefully he consulted *The Elementary Forms* and other works similarly fundamental to his intellectual development.

8 For example, the first published essays were on ' "Capitalism" in recent German literature: Sombart and Weber' (Parsons, 1928, 1929).

9 A draft of this book, *The American Societal Community*, was nearly completed before Talcott Parsons's death. It will be edited and then published by The Free Press.

Bibliography

Abel, T. (1929), *Systematic Sociology in Germany* (New York: Columbia University Press).

Abel, T. (1959), 'The contribution of Georg Simmel: a reappraisal', *American Sociological Review*, vol. 24, pp. 473–9.

Alexander, R. D. (1961), 'Aggressiveness, territoriality, and sexual behaviour in field crickets', *Behaviour*, vol. 17, nos 2/3, pp. 130–223.

Alexander, R. D. (1971), 'The search for an evolutionary philosophy of man', *Proceedings of the Royal Society of Victoria*, vol. 84, pp. 99–120.

Althusser, L., and Balibar, E. (1970), *Reading 'Capital'* (London: New Left Books).

Aron, R. (1967), *Main Currents in Sociological Thought* (New York: Basic Books).

Atkinson, J. M. (1978), *Discovering Suicide: Studies in the Social Organization of Sudden Death* (Pittsburgh, Pa: University of Pittsburgh Press).

Balandier, G. (1971), *Sens et Puissance* (Paris: Presses Universitaires de France).

Barash, D. P. (1977), *Sociobiology and Behavior* (New York: Elsevier).

Barber, B. (1957), *Social Stratification* (New York: Harcourt, Brace & World).

Barnard, C. I. (1938), *The Functions of the Executive* (Cambridge, Mass.: Harvard University Press).

Bellah, R. N. (1970), *Beyond Belief* (New York: Harper & Row).

Bellah, R. N. (1973), introduction to *Emile Durkheim on Morality and Society*, ed. R. N. Bellah (Chicago: University of Chicago Press).

Bendix, R. (1962), *Max Weber: An Intellectual Portrait* (Garden City, NY: Doubleday).

Bendix, R., and Lipset, S. M. (eds) (1953), *Class, Status and Power*, 1st edn (Glencoe, Ill.: The Free Press).

Bendix, R., and Lipset, S. M. (1966), 'Marx's theory of social class', in *Class, Status, and Power,* 2nd edn, ed. R. Bendix and S. M. Lipset (New York: The Free Press).

Bendix, R., and Roth, G. (1971), *Scholarship and Partisanship: Essays on Max Weber* (Berkeley, Calif.: University of California Press).

Berger, P., and Luckmann, T. (1967), *The Social Construction of Reality* (Garden City, NY: Doubleday/Anchor).

Berlin, I. (1976), *Vico and Herder: Two Studies in the History of Ideas* (New York: Viking Press).

Bernstein, E. (1961), *Evolutionary Socialism* (New York: Schocken); 1st German edn 1899.

Blau, P. M. (1964), *Exchange and Power in Social Life* (New York: Wiley).

Bobbio, N. (ed.) (1973), *Pareto e il Sistema Sociale* (Firenze: Sansoni).

Bourricaud, F. (1977), *L'Individualism institutionnel: essai sur la sociologie de Talcott Parsons* (Paris: Presses Universitaires de France).

Braudel, F. (1966), *The Mediterranean and the Mediterranean World in the Age of Philip II*, 2 vols (New York: Harper/Colophon), English edn.

Brecher, K. D. (1960), *Die Aufloesung der Weimarer Republik* (Villingen, Schwarzwald: Ring-Verlag).

Brecher, K. D. (1969), *Die Deutsche Diktatur* (Cologne and Berlin: Kiepenheuer & Witsch).

Brinton, C. (1938), *The Anatomy of Revolution* (New York: Norton).

Brown, R. (1965), *Social Psychology* (New York: The Free Press).

Buckley, W. (1967), *Sociology and Modern Systems Theory* (Englewood Cliffs, NJ: Prentice-Hall).

Burke, K. (1956), *Permanence and Change* (New York: New Republic).

Busino, G. (1975), *Sociologia e Storia: Elementi per un Dibattito* (Napoli: Guida Editori).

Cahnman, W. J. (1973), *Ferdinand Toennies – A New Evaluation* (Leiden: Brill).

Cahnman, W. J. (1976), 'Vico and historical sociology', *Social Research*, vol. 43, pp. 826–36.

Cahnman, W. J. (1977), 'Toennies in America', *History and Theory*, vol. XVI, pp. 147–67.

Cahnman, W. J., and Boskoff, A. (1964), *Sociology and History: Theory and Research* (New York: The Free Press).

Cahnman, W. J., and Heberle, R. (1971), *Ferdinand Toennies on Sociology: Pure, Applied, and Empirical* (Chicago: University of Chicago Press).

Chomsky, N. (1972), *Language and Mind* (New York: Harcourt, Brace, Jovanovich).

Coenen, H. (1978), 'Lecture phénoménologique de l'oeuvre de Durkheim', paper presented at the 9th World Congress of Sociology, Uppsala, Sweden.

Cohn, N. (1961), *The Pursuit of the Millennium* (New York: Harper/Torchbooks).

Collins, R. (1975), *Conflict Sociology: Toward an Explanatory Science* (New York: Academic Press).

Coser, L. (1956), *The Functions of Social Conflict* (New York: The Free Press).

Coser, L. (1974), *Greedy Institutions* (New York: The Free Press).

Count, E. W. (1958), 'The biological basis of human sociality', *American Anthropologist*, vol. 60, pp. 1049–85.

Croce, B. (1964), *The Philosophy of Giambattista Vico*, trans. R. C. Collingwood (New York: Russell & Russell).

Cuber, J. F., and Kenkel, W. F. (1954), *Social Stratification in the United States* (New York: Appleton-Century-Crofts).

Czarnowski, S. (1919), *Le Culte des héros et ses conditions sociales: Saint Patrick et le culte des héros* (Paris: Felix Alcan).

Darwin, C. (1859), *The Origin of Species* (New York: New American Library/Mentor, 1958).

Davies, J. C. (1962), 'Toward a theory of revolution', *American Sociological Review*, vol. 27, pp. 5–19.

Dawkins, R. (1976), *The Selfish Gene* (New York: Oxford University Press).

Desroche, H. (1974), *Les Religions de contrebande* (Paris: Répères-Mame).

Dewey, J. (1939), *Theory of Valuation* (Chicago: University of Chicago Press).

Dilthey, W. (1957–74), *Gesammelte Schriften*, 17 vols (Stuttgart: Teubner).

Djilas, M. (1957), *The New Class: An Analysis of the Communist System* (New York: Praeger).

Dobzhansky, T. (1962), *Mankind Evolving* (New Haven, Conn.: Yale University Press).

Dobzhansky, T. (1967), 'On types, genotypes, and the genetic diversity in populations', in *Genetic Diversity and Human Behavior*, ed. J. N. Spuhler (Chicago: Aldine).

Dotson, F. (1974), 'Marx and Engels on the family: retrospect with a moral', *The American Sociologist*, vol. 9.

Dowse, R. E., and Hughes, J. A. (1972), *Political Sociology* (New York: Wiley).

Douglas, M. (1966), *Purity and Danger* (London: Routledge & Kegan Paul).

Dumont, L. (1970), *Homo Hierarchicus: An Essay on the Caste System* (Chicago: University of Chicago Press).

Durkheim, E. (1933), *The Division of Labor in Society*, trans. George Simpson (New York: Macmillan/The Free Press).

Durkheim, E. (1938), *The Rules of Sociological Method* (Chicago: University of Chicago Press).

Durkheim, E. (1951), *Suicide* (New York: The Free Press).

Durkheim, E. (1953), 'Individual and collective representations', in *Sociology and Philosophy*, trans. D. F. Pocock (New York: The Free Press).

Durkheim, E. (1961, 1965), *The Elementary Forms of the Religious Life* (New York: Collier, 1961; The Free Press, 1965).

Durkheim, E. (1960), 'The dualism of human nature and its social conditions', in *Emile Durkheim 1858–1917*, ed. Kurt H. Wolff (Columbus, Ohio: Ohio State University Press), pp. 325–40.

Durkheim, E. (1973), 'Two rules of penal evolution', trans. with an introduction by T. A. Jones and A. T. Scull, *Economy and Society*, vol. 2, pp. 285–308.

Durkheim, E., and Mauss, M. (1975), review of J. G. Frazer, *Totemism and Exogamy,* and of E. Durkheim, *Les Formes élémentaires de la vie religieuse*, in *Durkheim on Religion*, Vol. 1, ed. W. S. F. Pickering (London and Boston: Routledge & Kegan Paul), pp. 174–80.

Eliade, M. (1959), *The Sacred and the Profane* (New York: Harper/Torchbooks).

Fèbvre, L., *et al.* (eds) (1930), *Civilisation: le mot et l'idée* (Paris: La Renaissance du Livre).
Focher, F. (1977), *Vico e Hobbes* (Naples: Giannini).
Frankel, C. (1977), 'John Dewey's social philosophy', in *New Studies in the Philosophy of John Dewey,* ed. S. M. Cahn (Hanover, NH: University Press of New England), pp. 3–44.
Freud, S. (1938), 'Totem and taboo', *The Basic Writings of Sigmund Freud,* ed. and trans. A. A. Brill (New York: The Modern Library), pp. 807–930.
Freud, S. (1965), *The Interpretation of Dreams,* trans. J. Strachey (New York: Avon).
Friedrichs, R. W. (1970), *A Sociology of Sociology* (New York: The Free Press).
Funkenstein, A. (1976), 'Natural science and social theory: Hobbes, Spinoza and Vico', in *Giambattista Vico's Science of Humanity,* ed. G. Tagliacozzo and D. Verene (Baltimore, Md, and London: Johns Hopkins University Press), pp. 187–212.
Fustel de Coulanges, N. D. (1956), *The Ancient City* (Garden City, NY: Doubleday/Anchor).
Garin, E. (1962), 'Per una storia della fortuna di Hobbes nel Settecento italiano', *Rivista Critica di Storia della Filosofia,* vol. 7, pp. 514–27.
Gerth, H. (1952), 'The Nazi Party: its leadership and composition', in *Reader in Bureaucracy,* ed. R. K. Merton *et al.* (New York: The Free Press).
Gerth, H., and Mills, C. W. (eds) (1948), *From Max Weber* (New York: Oxford University Press).
Giddens, A. (1972), *Politics and Sociology in the Thought of Max Weber* (London: Macmillan).
Giddens, A. (1973), *The Class Structure of the Advanced Societies* (New York: Barnes & Noble).
Giddens, A. (1976), *New Rules of Sociological Method* (New York: Basic Books).
Giddens, A. (1977), *Studies in Social and Political Theory* (London: Hutchinson).
Glock, C. Y., and Bellah, R. N. (eds) (1976), *The New Religious Consciousness* (Berkeley, Calif.: University of California Press).
Glock, C. Y., and Hammond, P. A. (1973), *Beyond the Classics?* (New York: Harper & Row).
Goffman, E. (1974), *Frame Analysis* (New York: Harper/Colophon).
Gouldner, A. W. (1959), 'Reciprocity and autonomy in functional theory', in *Symposium on Sociological Theory,* ed. L. Gross (New York: Harper & Row).
Green, M. (1974), *The von Richthofen Sisters* (New York: Basic Books).
Guiraud, P. (1895), 'Fustel de Coulanges', in *Centenaire de l'Ecole Supérieure Normale* (Paris: Hachette), pp. 324–34.
Habermas, J. (1973), *Legitimation Crisis* (Boston, Mass.: Beacon Press).
Hagen, E. E. (1961), 'Analytical models in the study of social systems', *American Journal of Sociology,* vol. 67, pp. 144–51.

Hamilton, W. D. (1964), 'The genetical theory of social behaviour: I and II', *Journal of Theoretical Biology*, vol. 7, pp. 1–52.

Hammond, P. E. (1974), 'Religious pluralism and Durkheim's integration thesis', in *Changing Perspectives in the Scientific Study of Religion*, ed. A. W. Eister (New York: Wiley), pp. 115–42.

Hardy, A. (1965), *The Living Stream* (New York: Harper & Row).

Heberle, R. (1945), *From Democracy to Nazism* (Baton Rouge, La: Louisiana State University Press).

Heberle, R. (1951), *Social Movements* (New York: Appleton-Century-Crofts).

Henderson, L. J. (1935), *Pareto's General Sociology* (Cambridge, Mass.: Harvard University Press).

Hill, C. (1973), *The World Turned Upside Down: Radical Ideas During the English Revolution* (New York: Viking).

Hirst, P. Q. (1975), *Durkheim, Bernard and Epistemology* (London: Routledge & Kegan Paul).

Hobbes, T. (1839a), *The English Works*, 11 vols, ed. Sir W. Molesworth (London: Bohn).

Hobbes, T. (1839b), *Opera philosophica quae latine scripsit omnia*, 5 vols, ed. Sir W. Molesworth (London: Bohn).

Hobbes, T. (1968), *Leviathan*, ed. C. B. Macpherson (Harmondsworth: Penguin).

Hobbes, T. (1969a), *The Elements of Law Natural and Politic*, ed. F. Toennies (London: Frank Cass).

Hobbes, T. (1969b), *Behemoth or the Long Parliament*, ed. F. Toennies (London: Frank Cass).

Homans, G. C. (1974), *Social Behavior: Its Elementary Forms* (New York: Harcourt, Brace, Jovanovich).

Honigsheim, P. (1968), *On Max Weber* (New York: The Free Press).

Hubert, H. (1915), *Le Culte des héros et ses conditions sociales* (Paris: Felix Alcan).

Hughes, H. S. (1958), *Consciousness and Society* (New York: Knopf).

Husserl, E. (1970), *The Crisis of European Sciences and Transcendental Phenomenology* (Evanston, Ill.: Northwestern University Press).

Huxley, A. (1935), 'Review of Pareto's "The mind and society" ', *New York Herald Tribune Books*, 9 June, pp. 1–8.

Janowitz, M. (1975), 'Sociological theory and social control', *American Journal of Sociology*, vol. 81, pp. 82–108.

Janowitz, M. (1978), *The Last Half-Century: Societal Change and Politics in America* (Chicago: University of Chicago Press).

Jaspers, K. (1964), *Three Essays: Leonardo, Descartes, Max Weber* (New York: Harcourt, Brace & World).

Jones, R. A. (n.d.), 'Myth and symbol among the Nacirema Tsigoloicos: a Durkheimian ethnography', Department of Sociology, University of Illinois, Urbana, Illinois.

Jones, R. A. (1977), 'On understanding a sociological classic', *American Journal of Sociology*, vol. 83, pp. 279–319.

Kahl, J. A. (1957), *The American Class Structure* (New York: Rinehart).

Kuhn, T. S. (1970), *The Structure of Scientific Revolutions*, 2nd edn (Chicago: University of Chicago Press).

Levine, D. N. (1959), 'The structure of Simmel's social thought', in *Georg Simmel, 1858–1918*, ed. K. H. Wolff (Columbus, Ohio: Ohio State University Press).

Levine, D. N. (1971), introduction to G. Simmel, *On Individuality and Social Forms* (Chicago: University of Chicago Press).

Levine, D. N. (1975), 'Review of *The Essential Comte* and *The Crisis of Industrial Civilization: The Early Essays of Auguste Comte'*, *American Journal of Sociology*, vol. 81, pp. 654–6.

Levine, D. N. (1978), 'Review of R. K. Merton, *Sociological Ambivalence and Other Essays'*, *American Journal of Sociology*, vol. 83, pp. 1277–80.

Levine, D. N. (forthcoming), 'Rationality and freedom: Weber and beyond'.

Levine, D. N., Carter, E. B., and Gorman, E. M. (1976), 'Simmel's influence on American sociology', pts I and II, *American Journal of Sociology*, vol. 81, pp. 813–45 and 1112–32.

Link, W., and Feld, W. J. (eds) (1979), *The New Nationalism* (New York: Pergamon).

Lipset, S. M. (1960), *Political Man* (New York: Doubleday).

Lipset, S. M. (1967), 'Political sociology', in *Sociology: An Introduction*, ed. N. J. Smelser (New York: Wiley).

Lopreato, J. (1965), *Vilfredo Pareto* (New York: Crowell).

Lopreato, J. (1971), 'The concept of equilibrium: sociological tantalizer', in *Institutions and Social Exchange: The Sociologies of Talcott Parsons and George C. Homans*, ed. H. Turk and R. L. Simpson (Indianapolis: Bobbs-Merrill).

Lopreato, J. (1975), *The Sociology of Vilfredo Pareto* (Morristown: General Learning Press).

Lopreato, J., and Alston, L. (1970), 'Ideal types and the idealization strategy', *American Sociological Review*, vol. 35, pp. 88–96.

Lorenz, K., and Leyhausen, P. (1973), *Motivation of Human and Animal Behavior: An Ethological View* (New York: Van Nostrand Reinhold).

Lowenthal, R. (1976), 'Social transformation and democratic legitimacy', *Social Research*, vol. 43.

Lukes, S. (1972), *Emile Durkheim: His Life and Work* (New York: Harper & Row).

MacIntyre, A. (1966), *A Short History of Ethics* (New York: Macmillan).

Macpherson, C. B. (1962), *The Political Theory of Possessive Individualism* (Oxford: Clarendon Press).

MacRae, D. G. (1974), *Weber* (London: Fontana).

Makkreel, R. (1975), *Dilthey, Philosopher of the Human Studies* (Princeton, NJ: Princeton University Press).

Malinowski, B. (1913), 'Review of *Les Formes élémentaires de la vie religieuse'*, *Folklore*, vol. 24, pp. 525–31.

Malinowski, B. (1963), *The Family Among the Australian Aborigines: A Sociological Study* (New York: Schocken).

Mannheim, K. (1936), *Ideology and Utopia* (New York: Harcourt, Brace).

Marcuse, H. (1955), *Eros and Civilization* (New York: Vintage Books).

Marx, K. (1847), *The Poverty of Philosophy* (New York: International Publishers, n.d.).

Marx, K. (1852), *The Eighteenth Brumaire* (New York: International Publishers, n.d.).

Marx, K. (1961), *Economic and Philosophical Manuscripts of 1844* (Moscow: Foreign Languages Publishing House).

Marx, K., and Engels, F. (1951), *Selected Works*, Vol. II (Moscow: Foreign Languages Publishing House).

Marx, K., and Engels, F. (1953), *Selected Correspondence* (Moscow: Foreign Languages Publishing House).

Mayer, K. B. (1955), *Class and Society* (Garden City, NY: Doubleday).

Mayo, E. (1960), *The Human Problems of an Industrial Civilization* (New York:, Viking Press).

Mayo, P. E. (1974), *The Roots of Identity* (London: Allen Lane).

Mead, G. H. (1913), 'The social self', *Journal of Philosophy, Psychology, and Scientific Methods*, vol. X, pp. 374–80; repr. in Mead (1964).

Mead, G. H. (1922), 'A behaviorist account of the significant symbol', *The Journal of Philosophy*, vol. XIX, pp. 157–63; repr. in Mead (1964).

Mead, G. H. (1924–5), 'The genesis of the self and social control', *International Journal of Ethics*, vol. XXXV, pp. 251–77; repr. in Mead (1964).

Mead, G. H. (1932), *The Philosophy of the Present*, ed. A. E. Murphy (La Salle, Ill.: Open Court).

Mead, G. H. (1934), *Mind, Self and Society: From the Standpoint of a Social Behaviorist*, ed. C. W. Morris (Chicago: University of Chicago Press).

Mead, G. H. (1936), *Movements of Thought in the Nineteenth Century*, ed. M. H. Moore (Chicago: University of Chicago Press).

Mead, G. H. (1938), *The Philosophy of the Act*, ed. C. W. Morris (Chicago: University of Chicago Press).

Mead, G. H. (1964), *Selected Writings*, ed. A. J. Reck (Indianapolis: Bobbs-Merrill).

Medawar, P. (1974), 'A geometric model of reduction and emergence', in *Studies in the Philosophy of Biology*, ed. F. J. Ayala and T. Dobzhansky (New York: Macmillan).

Merton, R. K. (1968), *Social Theory and Social Structure*, 3rd rev. edn (New York: The Free Press).

Merton, R. K. (1976), *Sociological Ambivalence and Other Essays* (New York: The Free Press).

Merton, R. K., Gray, A. P., Hockey, B., and Selvin, H. C. (eds) (1952), *Reader in Bureaucracy* (Glencoe, Ill.: The Free Press).

Michelet, J. (1971–5), *Oeuvres complètes*, 5 vols, ed. P. Viallaneix (Paris: Flammarion).

Miller, S. (1978), 'Bureaucracy baiting', *American Scholar*, vol. 47, pp. 205–22.

Mitzman, A. (1970), *The Iron Cage: An Historical Interpretation of Max Weber* (New York: Knopf).

Mommsen, W. J. (1974), *The Age of Bureaucracy: Perspectives on the Political Sociology of Max Weber* (New York: Harper & Row).

Moore, B. (1978), *The Social Bases of Obedience and Revolt* (White Plains, NY: Sharpe).

Nelson, B. (1976), 'Vico and comparative historical civilizational sociology', *Social Research*, vol. 43, pp. 874–81.

Newsweek (1978), 'A vote for the Sasquatch', 26 June.

Nicolini, F. (1931), *Fonti e riferimenti storici della Seconda Scienza Nuova* (Bari: Laterza).

Nicolini, F. (1942), 'Vico, Hobbes e una postilla inedita alla Scienza Nuova', *Atti dell' Academia Pontaniana di Napoli*, Vol. LXI (Naples: Rapolla).

Nicolini, F. (1949a), 'Di alcuni rapporti ideali tra il Vico e lo Hobbes con qualche referimento al Machiavelli', *Atti dell' Academia Pontaniana di Napoli*, Vol. I (Napoli: Giannini), pp. 25–43.

Nicolini, F. (1949b), *La Religiosità di G. B. Vico* (Bari: Laterza).

Nisbet, R. A. (1969), *Social Change and History* (New York: Oxford University Press).

Orum, A. M. (1978), *Introduction to Political Sociology* (Englewood Cliffs, NJ: Prentice-Hall).

Pachter, H. (1978), 'Freedom, authority, participation', *Dissent*, vol. 25, pp. 304–6.

Pareto, V. (1896–7), *Cours d'économie politique*, 2 vols (Lausanne: Rouge).

Pareto, V. (1963), *A Treatise on General Sociology*, 4 vols (New York: Dover); first published 1916.

Pareto, V. (1968), *The Rise and Fall of the Elites: An Application of Theoretical Sociology* (Totowa, NJ: Bedminster Press); first published 1901.

Pareto, V. (1971), *Manual of Political Economy* (New York: Kelly); first published 1906.

Park, R. E. (1952), *The Collected Papers of Robert Ezra Park*, 3 vols, ed. E. C. Hughes *et al.* (New York: The Free Press).

Park, R. E., and Burgess, E. W. (1972), *Introduction to the Science of Society* (Chicago: University of Chicago Press); first published 1921.

Parsons, T. (1928, 1929), ' "Capitalism" in recent German literature: Sombart and Weber', *Journal of Political Economy*, vol. 36, pp. 641–61, vol. 37, pp. 31–51.

Parsons, T. (1937), *The Structure of Social Action* (New York: McGraw-Hill).

Parsons, T. (1939), 'The professions and social structure', *Social Forces*, vol. 17, pp. 457–67; repr. in Parsons (1949).

Parsons, T. (1949), *Essays in Sociological Theory* (New York: The Free Press).

Parsons, T. (1951), *The Social System* (New York: The Free Press).

Parsons, T. (1959), 'An approach to psychological theory in terms of the theory of action', in *Psychology: A Study of a Science*, ed. S. Koch (New York: McGraw-Hill).

Parsons, T. (1960), *Structure and Process in Modern Societies* (New York: The Free Press).

Parsons, T. (1961), 'An outline of the social system', in *Theories of Society*, Vol. 1, ed. T. Parsons *et al.* (New York: The Free Press).

Parsons, T. (1964), *Social Structure and Personality* (New York: The Free Press).

Parsons, T. (1966), *Societies: Evolutionary and Comparative Perspectives* (Englewood Cliffs, NJ: Prentice-Hall).

Parsons, T. (1968a), *The Structure of Social Action* (New York: The Free Press); repr. of Parsons (1937).

Parsons, T. (1968b), 'Emile Durkheim', in *International Encyclopedia of the Social Sciences*, ed. D. Sills (New York: Macmillan and The Free Press).

Parsons, T. (1968c), 'Vilfredo Pareto's contribution to sociology', in *International Encyclopedia of the Social Sciences*, ed. D. Sills (New York: Macmillan and The Free Press).

Parsons, T. (1969), *Politics and Social Structure* (New York: The Free Press).

Parsons, T. (1971), 'Value-freedom and objectivity', in *Max Weber and Sociology Today*, ed. O. Stammer (New York: Harper & Row).

Parsons, T. (1974), '*The Interpretation of Dreams*, by Sigmund Freud', *Daedalus*, vol. 103, pp. 91–6.

Parsons, T. (1978), 'Durkheim on religion revisited: another look at *The Elementary Forms of the Religious Life*', in T. Parsons, *Action Theory and the Human Condition* (New York: The Free Press), pp. 213–32.

Parsons, T. (1980), 'The circumstances of my encounter with Max Weber', in *Sociological Traditions from Generation to Generation*, ed. R. K. Merton and M. W. Riley (Norwood, NJ: Ablex).

Parsons, T., and Bales, R. F. (1955), *Family, Socialization and Interaction Process* (New York: The Free Press).

Parsons, T., and Platt, G. M. (1973), *The American University* (Cambridge, Mass.: Harvard University Press).

Parsons, T., and Smelser, N. (1956), *Economy and Society* (New York: The Free Press).

Perry, R. H., Chilton, C. H., and Kirkpatrick, S. D. (1963), *Chemical Engineer's Handbook*, 4th edn (New York: McGraw-Hill).

Peters, R. (1956), *Hobbes* (Harmondsworth: Penguin).

Pickering, W. S. F. (ed.) (1975), *Durkheim on Religion* (London and Boston: Routledge & Kegan Paul).

Pickering, W. S. F. (1979), 'Gaston Richard: collaborateur et adversaire', *Revue française de sociologie*, vol. 20, pp. 163–82.

Poggioli, R. (1965), *The Spirit of the Letter: Essays in European Literature* (Cambridge, Mass.: Harvard University Press).

Polanyi, M. (1966), *The Tacit Dimension* (Garden City, NY: Doubleday).

Pons, A. (1969), 'Vico and French thought', in *Giambattista Vico: An International Symposium*, ed. G. Tagliacozzo and H. V. White (Baltimore, Md: Johns Hopkins University Press), pp. 165–83.

Prigogine, I. (1976), 'Order through fluctuation: self-organization and social system', in *Evolution and Consciousness*, ed. E. Jantsch and C. H. Waddington (Reading, Mass.: Addison-Wesley).

Prigogine, I. (1977), 'Order out of chaos?', public lecture delivered at the University of Texas, Austin, 18 November.

Prigogine, I., Allen, P. M., and Herman, R. (1977), 'The evolution of complexity and the laws of nature', in *Goals in a Global Society*, Vol. 1, ed. E. Laszlo and J. Bierman (New York: Pergamon).

Radcliffe-Brown, A. R. (1913), 'Three tribes of Western Australia', *Journal of the Royal Anthropological Institute of Great Britain and Ireland*, vol. 43, pp. 143–94.

Rank, O. (1958), *Beyond Psychology* (New York: Dover).

Redfield, R. (1930), *Tepoztlán: A Mexican Village: A Study of Folk Life* (Chicago: University of Chicago Press).

Richards, R. J. (1974), 'The innate and the learned: the evolution of Konrad Lorenz's theory of instinct', *Philosophy of the Social Sciences*, vol. 4, pp. 111–33.

Roethlisberger, F. J., and Dickson, W. J. (1939), *Management and the Worker* (Cambridge, Mass.: Harvard University Press).

Rush, J. H. (1957), *The Dawn of Life* (New York: Doubleday).

Russett, C. E. (1966), *The Concept of Equilibrium in American Social Thought* (New Haven, Conn.: Yale University Press).

Sartre, J.-P. (1947), *Existentialism* (New York: Philosophical Library).

Schlatter, R. (ed.) (1975), *Hobbes' Thucydides* (New Brunswick, NJ: Rutgers University Press).

Schneirla, T. C. (1972), 'Interrelationship of the "innate" and the "acquired" in instinctive behavior', in *Function and Evolution of Behavior*, ed. P. H. Klopfer and J. P. Hailman (Reading, Mass.: Addison-Wesley).

Simmel, G. (1890), *Ueber sociale Differenzierung. Soziologische und psychologische Untersuchungen* ('Staats- und socialwissenschaftliche Forschungen', ed. Gustav Schmoller, vol. 10, no. 1) (Leipzig: Duncker & Humblot).

Simmel, G. (1894), 'Das Problem der Sociologie', *Jahrbuch für Gestzgebung, Verwaltung und Volkswirtschaft im Deutschen Reich*, vol. 18, pp. 271–7.

Simmel, G. (1896), 'Zur Methodik der Sozialwissenschaft', *Jahrbuch für Gesetzgebung, Verwaltung and Volkswirtschaft im Deutschen Reich*, vol. 20, pp. 575–85.

Simmel, G. (1900), *Philosophie des Geldes* (Leipzig: Duncker & Humblot).

Simmel, G. (1903), 'Die Grosstädte und das Geistesleben', *Die Grosstadt. Vorträge und Aufsätze zur Städteausstellung – Jahrbuch der Gehe-Stiftung*, vol. 9, pp. 185–206.

Simmel, G. (1908a), *Soziologie. Untersuchungen über die Formen der Vergesellschaftung* (Leipzig: Duncker & Humblot).

Simmel, G. (1908b), *Der Konflikt der modernen Kultur. Ein Vortrag* (Munich and Leipzig: Duncker & Humblot).

Simmel, G. (1917), *Grundfragen der Soziologie (Individuum und Gesellschaft)* (Berlin and Leipzig: Göschen).

Simmel, G. (1936), 'The metropolis and mental life', *Social Sciences II, Syllabus and Selected Readings*, trans. E. A. Shils, 5th edn (Chicago: University of Chicago Press), pp. 221–38.

Simmel, G. (1950), *The Sociology of George Simmel*, trans. and ed. K. H. Wolff (Glencoe, Ill.: The Free Press).

Simmel, G. (1955), *Conflict and the Web of Group Affiliations*, trans. K. H. Wolff and R. Bendix (Glencoe, Ill.: The Free Press).

Simmel, G. (1958), *Philosophie des Geldes*, 6th ed. (Berlin: Duncker & Humblot); first published 1907: rev. ed of (1900).

Simmel, G. (1968), *The Conflict in Modern Culture and Other Essays*, trans. K. P. Etzkorn (New York: Columbia University, Teachers' College Press).

Simmel, G. (1971), *On Individuality and Social Forms*, ed. D. N Levine (Chicago: University of Chicago Press).

Simmel, G. (1978), *The Philosophy of Money*, trans. T. Bottomore and D. Frisby (London: Routledge & Kegan Paul).

Skinner, B. F. (1975), *Beyond Freedom and Dignity* (New York: Bantam/ Vintage Books).

Sorokin, P. A (1928), *Contemporary Sociological Theories* (New York: Harper).

Sorokin, P. A. (1957), *Social and Cultural Dynamics* (Boston, Mass.: Porter Sargent).

Spencer, H. (1897), *The Principles of Sociology* (New York: Appleton-Century-Crofts).

Spencer, H. (1915), *Essays: Scientific, Political and Speculative* (New York: Appleton-Century-Crofts).

Spielberg, S. (1977), *Close Encounters of the Third Kind* (Columbia/ EMI).

Stokes, A. W. (ed.) (1974), *Territory* (Stroudsburg: Dowden, Hutchinson & Ross).

Strauss, L. (1963), 'Natural right and the distinction between facts and values', in *Philosophy of the Social Sciences: A Reader*, ed. M. Natanson (New York: Random House).

Sztompka, P. (1974), *System and Function: Toward a Theory of Society* (New York: Academic Press).

Tagliacozzo, G., Mooney, M., and Verene, D. P. (eds) (1976), 'Vico and contemporary thought', *Social Research*, vol. 43, nos 3 and 4.

Tagliacozzo, G., and Verene, D. P. (eds) (1976), *Giambattista Vico's Science of Humanity* (Baltimore, Md: Johns Hopkins University Press).

Tagliacozzo, G., and White, H. V. (eds) (1976), *Giambattista Vico: An*

International Symposium (Baltimore, Md: Johns Hopkins University Press).

TeSelle, S. (ed.) (1974), *The Rediscovery of Ethnicity* (New York: Harper/ Colophon).

Thomas, W. I. (1923), *The Unadjusted Girl* (Boston, Mass.: Little, Brown).

Thomas, W. I., and Znaniecki, F. (1918), *The Polish Peasant in Europe and America* (Boston, Mass.: Richard G. Badger); repr. New York: Dover, 1958.

Thrupp, S. (ed.) (1970), *Millennial Dreams in Action: Studies in Revolutionary Religious Movements* (New York: Schocken).

Tiryakian, E. A. (1962), *Sociologism and Existentialism* (Englewood Cliffs, NJ: Prentice-Hall).

Tiryakian, E. A. (1978a), 'Emile Durkheim', in *A History of Sociological Analysis*, ed. T. Bottomore and R. Nisbet (New York: Basic Books), pp. 187–236.

Tiryakian, E. A. (1978b), 'Durkheim and Husserl: a comparison of the spirit of positivism and the spirit of phenomenology', in *Phenomenology and The Social Sciences, A Dialogue*, ed. J. Bien (The Hague, Boston and London: Nijhoff).

Tiryakian, E. A. (1979), 'The United States as a religious phenomenon', in *Histoire du peuple chrétien*, ed. J. Delumeau (Toulouse: Editions Privats).

Toennies, F. (1926), *Fortschritt und soziale Entwicklung* (Karlsruhe: Braun).

Toennies, F. (1935) *Geist Der Neuzeit* (Leipzig: Buske).

Toennies, F. (1949), *Fundamental Conceptions of Sociology (Gemeinschaft und Gesellschaft)*, trans. C. P. Loomis (New York: American Book Company).

Toennies, F. (1961), *Die Sitte*, trans. A. F. Borenstein as *Custom: An Essay on Social Codes* (New York: The Free Press).

Toennies, F. (1963), *Community and Society*, trans. C. P. Loomis (New York: Harper/Torchbooks).

Toennies, F. (1965), *Einführung in die Soziologie* (Stuttgart: Enke).

Toennies, F. (1970, 1979), *Gemeinschaft und Gesellschaft* (Darmstadt: Wissenschaftliche Buchgesellschaft); 1st edn 1887.

Toennies, F. (1971), *Thomas Hobbes: Leben und Lehre*, new edn, with an introduction by K. H. Ilting (Stuttgart: Friedrich Fromann).

Torrance, J. (1974), 'Max Weber: methods and the man', *Archives européenes de sociologie*, vol. 15, pp. 131–2.

Trivers, R. L., and Hare, H. (1976), 'Haplodiploidy and the evolution of social insects', *Science*, vol. 191, pp. 249–63.

Turner, V. (1967), *The Forest of Symbols* (Ithaca, NY: Cornell University Press).

van den Berghe, P. L. (1974), 'Bringing beasts back in', *American Sociological Review*, vol. 39, pp. 777–88.

Vico, G. (1709), *De nostri temporis studiorum ratione* (Naples); English edn (1965), *On the Study Methods of Our Time* (Indianapolis: Bobbs-Merrill).

Vico, G. (1944), *The Autobiography of Giambattista Vico,* trans. M. H. Fisch and T. G. Bergin (Ithaca, NY: Cornell University Press).

Vico, G. (1948), *The New Science of Giambattista Vico,* trans. T. G. Bergin and M. H. Fisch (Ithaca, NY: Cornell University Press).

Waddington, C. H. (1957), *The Strategy of the Genes* (London: Allen & Unwin).

Wallisch-Prinz, B. (1977), 'A sociology of freedom. Georg Simmel's theory of modern society', dissertation, University of Bremen.

Watkins, J. W. N. (1965), *Hobbes's System of Ideas* (London: Hutchinson).

Weber, M(arianne) (1975), *Max Weber: A Biography* (New York: Wiley).

Weber, M(ax) (1930), *The Protestant Ethic and the Spirit of Capitalism,* trans. T. Parsons (London: Allen & Unwin).

Weber, M. (1947), *The Theory of Social and Economic Organization,* trans. A. M. Henderson and T. Parsons (New York: The Free Press).

Weber, M. (1948), 'Politics as a vocation', in *From Max Weber: Essays in Sociology,* ed. H. H. Gerth and C. W. Mills (New York: Oxford University Press).

Weber, M. (1961), *General Economic History,* trans. F. H. Knight (New York: Collier).

Weber, M. (1963), *The Sociology of Religion,* trans. E. Fischoff (Boston, Mass.: Beacon Press).

Weber, M. (1968), *Economy and Society,* 3 vols, ed. G. Roth and C. Wittich (New York: Bedminster Press).

Weingartner, R H. (1960), *Experience and Culture: The Philosophy of Georg Simmel* (Middletown, Conn.: Wesleyan University Press).

Weinstein, F. and Platt, G. (1973), *Psychoanalytic Sociology* (Baltimore, Md: Johns Hopkins University Press).

Werner, K. (1879), *Giambattista Vico als Philosoph und gelehrter Forscher* (Vienna: Faesy & Frick).

Whitehead, A. N. (1949), *The Aims of Education* (New York: Mentor).

Whyte, W. F. (1955), *Street Corner Society,* 2nd edn (Chicago: University of Chicago Press).

Wiley, N. (1979), 'The rise and fall of dominating theories in American sociology', in W. Snizek, E. R. Fuhrman, and M. K. Miller (eds), *Contemporary Issues in Theory and Research: A Metasociological Perspective* (Westport, Conn.: Greenwood Press).

Wilson, B. R. (1973), *Magic and the Millennium: A Sociological Study of Religious Movements of Protest Among Tribal and Third-World Peoples* (New York: Harper & Row).

Wilson, E. O. (1975), *Sociobiology: The New Synthesis* (Cambridge, Mass.: Harvard University Press).

Wirth, L. (1926), 'The sociology of Ferdinand Toennies', *American Journal of Sociology,* vol. 32, pp. 412–22.

Wirth, L. (1964), 'Urbanism as a way of life', in *On Cities and Social Life,* ed. A. J. Reiss, Jr (Chicago: University of Chicago Press), pp. 60–83.

Wrong, D. H. (1978), 'The end of the "Waiting for Newton" syndrome', *Contemporary Sociology*, vol. 7, pp. 734–7.

Wynne-Edwards, V. C. (1962), *Animal Dispersion in Relation to Social Behavior* (Edinburgh: Oliver & Boyd).

Yinger, J. M. (1977), 'Presidential address: countercultures and social change', *American Sociological Review*, vol. 42, pp. 833–53.

Zeitlin, I. M. (1973), *Rethinking Sociology: A Critique of Contemporary Theory* (Englewood Cliffs, NJ: Prentice-Hall).

Index